IS THERE A REALM BEYOND OURSELVES? ARE WE ALL RELATED IN SOME VAST COSMIC PURPOSE? IS THERE LIFE BEYOND DEATH?

The answers are in *The Psychic Quest*. Follow it and experience the mind-expanding realities of the paranormal senses by discovering . . .

- THE SPIRITUAL CONNECTION TO PSYCHIC PHENOMENA

- THE MEANING OF PSYCHIC READINGS, TELEPATHY, AND CLAIRVOYANCE

- THE STARTLING FACTS BEHIND NEAR-DEATH EXPERIENCES

- WHEN TO HEED THE WARNINGS OF PRECOGNITION

- HOW TO READ YOUR DREAMS

- THE PSYCHIC IMPORTANCE OF SYNCHRONICITY

- THE ORIGINS OF PSYCHIC HEALING POWER

- AND MORE

The Psychic Quest takes you on a journey through the endlessly fascinating, and increasingly fathomable mysteries of the mind.

THE PSYCHIC QUEST:

UNDERSTANDING YOUR PSYCHIC POTENTIAL

Douglas G. Richards, Ph.D.

A SIGNET VISIONS BOOK

SIGNET
Published by the Penguin Group
Penguin Putnam Inc., 375 Hudson Street,
New York, New York 10014, U.S.A.
Penguin Books Ltd, 27 Wrights Lane,
London W8 5TZ, England
Penguin Books Australia Ltd, Ringwood,
Victoria, Australia
Penguin Books Canada Ltd, 10 Alcorn Avenue,
Toronto, Ontario, Canada M4V 3B2
Penguin Books (N.Z.) Ltd, 182–190 Wairau Road,
Auckland 10, New Zealand

Penguin Books Ltd, Registered Offices:
Harmondsworth, Middlesex, England

First published by Signet, an imprint of Dutton Signet,
a member of Penguin Putnam Inc.

First Printing, March, 1998
10 9 8 7 6 5 4 3 2 1

Contents

Acknowledgments

I thank

- the late J. B. and Louisa Rhine, for starting me on my psychic quest at the Institute for Parapsychology more than twenty years ago

- James Windsor, whose vision for Atlantic University included a research program

- the late Arnold Bernhard, whose generosity made this research possible

- Henry Reed, David McMillin, Mark Thurston, and Christopher Fazel, who helped along the way with their advice on psychic phenomena

- Eileen Wiener, for her help with many facets of the research

- Lyndall Dickinson and Laurie Grohowski, whose comments helped improve my manuscript

- Sandra Martin, my agent

- and especially my wife, Karen, and son, Brian, for their love and support at all times, and for Karen's efforts in improving my manuscript

Introduction

"I ca'n't believe *that*!" said Alice.

"Ca'n't you?" the Queen said in a pitying tone. "Try again: draw a long breath and shut your eyes."

Alice laughed. "There's no use trying," she said: "one *ca'n't* believe impossible things."

"I daresay you haven't had much practice," said the Queen. "When I was your age, I always did it for half-an-hour a day. Why, sometimes I've believed as many as six impossible things before breakfast."

—Lewis Carroll, *Through the Looking-Glass*

Have you ever had an experience that simply does not fit with what we know of the "real" world? That you thought people would find "impossible" to believe? When people have an unusual experience, they often seek out someone who will take the experience seriously, someone who has studied psychic phenomena and may be able to help them understand what has happened. As a parapsychologist, I receive reports of all kinds of experiences. For example, a sixty-eight-year-old woman wrote to me:

I had a dream about difficulty with an airplane and also sitting in a restaurant booth with wooden seats with my office manager and a co-worker. I woke up and tried to understand the meaning of the dream. I knew the president of our company was going on vacation to South America with his wife and another couple the following week. I told the president not to go, but didn't tell him about the dream and only mentioned unrest in that area. The plane crashed and there were no survivors. At a memorial service later on I sat with the manager and co-worker on wooden seats exactly like the booth in my dream.

Or perhaps you've been having these experiences all your life and learned from an early age that it was wisest to keep them to yourself. A thirty-six-year-old woman told me of an experience she'd had in her teens, which she had kept to herself for years: "Soon after my grandmother died, she appeared at the foot of my bed, and I knew that she was telling me not to worry. I have never told anyone about this—I knew my parents wouldn't believe it."

"Supernatural," "paranormal," "occult." These terms all imply something rare, something unusual, something beyond understanding. Yet in response to a 1990 Gallup poll, *three quarters* of the people questioned reported such experiences. What many people consider out of the ordinary is in fact an integral part of our daily existence.

It is time to bring these experiences out of the realm of the occult—which means, literally, the unknown—and to help people see them as aspects of a normal psychological process, one that may give clues to our ultimate spiritual nature. This book is based on the experiences of hundreds of people, collected in questionnaires and interviews conducted over the past ten years as part of my research into the potential of human consciousness. It integrates people's stories of their experiences with the experimental results of parapsychology and with the insights into meaning from transpersonal psychology. An extension to the more traditional scope of psychology, transpersonal psychology acknowledges not only a physical and mental dimension to life, but a spiritual dimension as well, a dimension that is "trans" or beyond the individual person.

The Quest for Understanding

A woman called my office on the telephone, very agitated. "I hope you can help me," she said. "My son is three years old, and he seems to be psychic. He is able to read my thoughts and can predict when someone is coming to visit. What can I do?"

I assured her that psychic ability, both in children and in adults, is reported quite frequently. I suggested some reading material on the subject, with advice to keep a record of the experiences and encourage creativity in the child, while at the same time not focusing on or worrying about the "strangeness" of the experiences.

My advice was greeted with silence. Then she said tentatively, "You . . . you mean you believe me?" I was apparently the first person who had considered her story to be anything but "fantasy" or "crazy."

This is a typical yet unfortunate situation. Experiences that are a common part of the everyday life of millions of people are ridiculed and thought to be crazy. I have no way of knowing whether this particular experience was truly evidence of psychic ability. But no one even wanted to offer her guidance in considering the possibilities.

On the other hand, I also receive calls like the following:

I had a vision about the recent murders in . . . I'm sure I know the identity of the murderer. I traveled there and told the police what I had seen—even described the home where the murder had taken place.

They didn't appreciate my help. They told me it was police business and to stay away from the crime scene. I know I'm right, but trying to prove it has taken over my life. I think of nothing else, and it is even part of my dreams. My friends tell me to leave it alone and come home. What should I do?

Here we have a man who believes in his experience, despite the skepticism of others, yet his life is falling apart while he tries to act on his belief. He may or may not be able to prove his experience was psychic, but he certainly needs some balance in his life. There could well be alternative explanations for his experience, or alternative actions he could take to give meaning to it.

These people, like many others, are on a journey into the exciting yet frustrating world of psychic phenomena. Recognizing that such experiences could be real is only the first step. Most people want to understand the meaning of the experiences. I, too, began a personal search for understanding at an early age.

My Personal Quest

We all bring our beliefs and prior life experiences into our efforts to understand psychic experiences, and I am no exception. As a teenager I had occasional experiences I couldn't explain, primarily dreams that came true. Mine were not as strong or compelling as some you will read in this book, but they inspired me to seek answers. I read all I could on psychic phenomena and became puzzled by the conflicting information. There were scientists—parapsychologists—who studied psychic abilities and seemed to have strong proof. Dr. J. B. Rhine of Duke University was famous for his studies of extrasensory perception. Yet the popular media treated it as science fiction. Ordinary books on psychology didn't mention psychic phenomena at all.

When I was in college in the mid-1970s, I decided to go beyond the books I had read in the libraries and do some hands-on experiments for myself. I tried guessing cards and influencing the fall of dice, without much success. To really achieve understanding, I decided, I would have to go and see how parapsychologists did their experiments in the laboratory.

Having been impressed by J. B. Rhine's accounts of his experiments, I decided to write to him and ask for a summer job at his Institute for Parapsychology in North Carolina, formerly at Duke University. To my amazement, after a short exchange of correspondence, I was hired as a research assistant. I hadn't even been sure he was still alive! (He was indeed alive. He had moved the laboratory across the street from Duke when he retired in 1965. He and his wife, Louisa, also an active parapsychologist, both passed away in the early 1980s.)

I arrived in Durham, North Carolina, without a map of the city, armed only with a street address for the laboratory. After fifteen minutes of driving around, I arrived at the front door. Psychic perception or lucky coincidence? I have often felt that gentle promptings or intuitions are of help in my life, but this was certainly not scientific evidence yet.

My summer was filled with the typical experiences of any research assistant: assembling equipment, building computer circuit boards, and spending long hours in the library studying. But I also had the chance to help in actual experiments, watching a psychic guess cards sealed in black envelopes and exploring the abilities of people to predict random patterns on a computer screen.

Across town, at the Psychical Research Foundation, Dr. William Roll and his colleagues were doing experiments on phenomena that even J. B. Rhine thought would be too difficult to study. They studied people who claimed they had the ability to go out of their bodies, seeking proof of a spiritual existence after death. They even went to haunted houses, looking for the truth behind ghosts. I was one of the many ordinary people who served as subjects in their studies of distant perception, relaxing in a chair and trying to visualize pictures that were in another room.

This summer research experience convinced me that psychic phenomena were well worth further study. There aren't any graduate programs offering a degree in parapsychology (but see the appendix for some educational resources, including the program in transpersonal studies that I teach in at Atlantic University), so I continued my scientific studies at the nearby University of North Carolina, receiving my doctorate in animal behavior. I have done many things in my subsequent career, but I've always returned to the question of the higher capabilities of human consciousness.

It became clear to me that scientific study alone was not enough to open the doors to understanding psychic phenomena. Experiments easily demonstrated to my satisfaction that psychic abilities were genuine. Even the very weak ability to guess cards, when multiplied by hundreds of experiments, provided solid evidence. There was no question in my mind that we were dealing with something real. This real ability manifested in ways that were powerful and transformative to individuals. The problem was that experimental science had no way of recognizing or talking about inner experience.

Seeking to discover the meaning behind these phenomena, I was drawn to the work of those few people who apparently had spectacular psychic ability, particularly Edgar Cayce (1877–1945), who is America's best-documented psychic. He would lie down on a couch, enter a trance state, and contact a higher source of information. The process became known as a "reading." He gave more than 14,000 psychic readings, on subjects from health to spiritual growth. Not only did he seem to have an amazing psychic ability, but his explanation of the purpose and meaning of psychic phenomena rang true. People with psychic experiences were not odd or crazy. These abilities were a core element of human existence.

I began working with the Cayce readings on dreams and soon discovered the richness of my own dreams. Most weren't psychic, but a few seemed prophetic of actual future events; I discuss some of them later in the book.

I became excited by the possibilities raised by Cayce. There were psychologists exploring the potential of dreams and meditation for achieving higher awareness. There were medical doctors applying Cayce's material to discover new forms of healing. There were groups all over the country working with personal application of spiritual principles. Yet at the same time they were cautious, not accepting strange ideas simply because they came from a source who claimed psychic ability. The Cayce readings always emphasized the importance of testing principles in your own life rather than relying on authority. I corresponded with other researchers who were exploring Cayce's concepts and discussed ways of combining scientific study with spiritual ideals. Many years later, this pursuit led me to take a faculty position at Atlantic University.

Originally founded by Cayce in the 1930s, Atlantic University now offers an accredited master's degree. The university provided me an opportunity to study the meaning of psychic experiences for the transformation of people's lives. I continue to grow personally as well, as I learn more of the awesome range of human potential. I have come to realize that there is much more to psychic phenomena than occasional unusual experiences. They are potentially the beginning of a path that can lead to a higher level of wisdom, but there are many pitfalls and distractions along the way.

Sensitivity, Discernment, and Wisdom

Psychic experiences are a complex mixture of conscious needs and desires, unconscious processes, and little-understood phenomena often referred to as "paranormal." Most books about psychic phenomena deal primarily with sensitivity, the observation that some people are more sensitive to psychic phenomena than others. Some books sensationalize unusual experiences, others provide instructions for you to increase your own sensitivity to such experiences.

But sensitivity is a mixed blessing. Of the inquiries I receive, only a few people are eager to have lessons in becoming more sensitive to psychic phenomena. Others are *too* sensitive and want to make the phenomena go away. The majority want to learn how to integrate their psychic experiences into a balanced life. They want to go beyond simple psychic sensitivity and learn to *discern* the meaning and develop the *wisdom* to make the most productive use of such experiences.

Where can you go to learn more? Parapsychologists have accumulated a great deal of evidence that shows that such phenomena are *possible,* but they have no way to tell you if your *particular* experience is psychic, or if it is related to some other process of the unconscious mind. Psychotherapists, on the other hand, are often skilled in unraveling unconscious processes, but may have little knowledge of the possibilities beyond the unconscious mind. While a knowledge of the results of parapsychological research can prevent you from rejecting these experiences as impossible, the danger lies in uncritical acceptance. We know such experiences are common, but are they *all* psychic or are there other explanations? While skeptics are often too strong in their criticisms, they do have a point. For example, there is ample evidence for psychic ability in dreams—well-controlled experiments—yet clearly not all dreams involve extrasensory abilities. What about all the dreams that don't come true? Many simply reflect our own internal unconscious processes.

Having an experience validated by scientific research, or understanding that there may be an alternative explanation for the experience, is not enough. There is the need to develop the wisdom to apply these experiences in the process of growth and transformation.

From Validation to Understanding

When you venture into the realm of the psychic, you find yourself on a difficult path—there are few standards for evaluating these phenomena in regard to your own needs. People may contact parapsychology researchers as a last resort, seeking anyone willing to listen to their experiences.

When I began my research at Atlantic University, I offered visitors a computerized experiment to measure psychic ability, designed to resemble a video game. The originators of the experiment—all computer programmers and video game fans—had reasoned that the game would be more interesting to the participant than the traditional card-guessing tests. What I discovered was that many people came into the experiment having *already* had a psychic experience—perhaps a dream that came true—and were looking for validation of that experience. They wanted a test, like a math test, that would prove they were psychic. Unfortunately there is no such test. The successful results in parapsychology experiments usually come from the combined abilities of many people, each scoring a tiny percent above random chance. In fact, the best way to validate your psychic experiences is to do *personal* research—keep a dream diary or a journal of unusual events, and compare it to what actually happens.

I also found that, rather than wanting to be *tested,* many people were more interested in being *counseled* on how to understand and work with their psychic experiences. One of the questions most frequently asked of parapsychologists is, "Are you psychic?" The researchers are often amused, since this is equivalent to asking a marine biologist, "Are you a fish?" Parapsychologists *study* psychic phenomena, they don't necessarily exhibit them personally. Yet the question is not simply a confusion of the student with the object of the study. What people are really asking is, "Can I trust you to understand my experience? Have you had that experience yourself?" They are wary of "professionals" who make pronouncements in areas where they have no personal experience.

I was trained not as a counselor but as a researcher. Rather than trying to help people by using counseling or therapeutic techniques, I took a research approach. Instead of *telling* people what to do, I *asked* them what they had done and how they were coping with these unusual experiences. I received a variety of answers.

For some people, these experiences had become part of their everyday lives. They had found a community of people with similar experiences and were applying their insights to facilitate their own growth and that of others. They were leading fulfilling lives with an extra dimension.

Others were not coping as well. Their experiences were so foreign to their beliefs about the way the world works that they could not fit them into the daily pattern of their lives. The experiences appeared to be a trigger for whatever defense mechanisms they typically used in other crises—denial or obsession, for example.

And, finally, many people were simply baffled by their experiences, unable to find meaning in them. They were coping well with life in general but couldn't fit the experiences into their life or use them to learn and grow.

I was able to offer some help by suggesting that the people having difficulty with psychic experiences, or wanting to learn more, try some of the approaches used by those who had made them an integral part of their lives. I also realized that some people could benefit from professional counseling, not for the psychic experiences per se, but for their habitual ways of responding to any distressing situation.

I found that neither the research of parapsychologists nor the popular books sensationalizing psychic phenomena had much to offer to people who wanted to integrate these experiences into their lives. To learn more, I expanded my research to include detailed questionnaires and had more than 1,200 participants in these projects. This book is based on the results from those interviews and questionnaires.

To give some perspective on how common these experiences are, throughout the book I will refer to surveys that have asked people about their experiences. The Gallup organization is skilled in making sure that its surveys are representative of the entire American public, and one important survey was a Gallup poll of adult Americans in 1990. Another survey, with more extensive categories of experiences than the Gallup poll, was conducted in 1979 by parapsychologist John Palmer, who studied the town of Charlottesville, Virginia, as a typical American town. I also discuss the results of my own surveys of members of the Association for Research and Enlightenment (A.R.E.), the organization founded by Edgar Cayce. The A.R.E., drawing on the information in the Cayce readings, attracts a wide range of people who are interested in psychic phenomena and presents diverse perspectives on integrating these experiences with spirituality. I found A.R.E. members often willing to go beyond short survey answers and to share their experiences in detail.

My work is not exclusively parapsychology—it is a broad-spectrum inquiry into the nature of consciousness, in areas ranging from meditation to energy healing. Yet psychic experiences are often paramount among the concerns of people who contact me.

The focus of the research is on understanding the experiences people are having, not on "proving" the existence of psychic phenomena. From reading the experiences you will see that they are typically a mixture of the inner images of the mind with material from somewhere outside or beyond the person. To explore their meanings I draw on both parapsychology and studies of the unconscious mind by psychotherapists and transpersonal psychologists.

In compiling the experiences for this book, I have selected examples of the diversity of phenomena in each category. Although I have used the traditional classifications of parapsychology, there is considerable overlap among the different types of experiences. In each chapter I have also provided some examples of studies by parapsychologists that address the nature of the phenomena and alternative explanations. I then suggest approaches that people have found useful in coping with and growing from these experiences.

Now let's take a look at the key issues of the book: What exactly are psychic phenomena, and how can we approach them in our quest for understanding?

Parapsychology and Psychic Phenomena

Parapsychology is the study of psychic or *psi* phenomena (pronounced "sigh") from a psychological perspective. "Psi" was the term chosen by parapsychologists to refer to psychic phenomena because it is a fairly neutral term, being a letter of the Greek alphabet and denoting simply "unknown." It is not an acronym ("PSI" in capital letters, as in "inflate the tires on your car to 30 PSI"). The terms "psi" and "psychic phenomena" should be interchangeable, but matters are complicated by different opinions on which phenomena should be considered "psychic."

What Are Psychic Phenomena?

The term "psychic phenomena" is used to describe a variety of unusual occurrences. Essentially, we are referring to those mental phenomena that cannot be explained by any known or "normal" mechanisms. Since our concepts of known and normal continually change, so does the classification of certain phenomena as psychic. For example, hypnosis, which was a major topic of study for the original Society for Psychical Research in Britain in the 1880s, is now considered a completely normal area of psychology. Other phenomena, such as precognition of future events, remain unexplained and outside mainstream psychology. Perhaps in fifty years precognition—seeing into the future—will be as well accepted by the mainstream as hypnosis is now.

The *Journal of Parapsychology,* founded primarily by experimenters, uses the precise terminology of psychology, which can be a bit daunting for the average person having a psychic experience. It defines "psi" as a "general term to identify a person's extrasensorimotor communication with the environment." "Extrasensorimotor" means beyond the capabilities of our normal senses and muscles. Psi includes "extrasensory perception" (ESP), which means perceiving something, such as someone's thoughts or a distant location, without using ordinary senses such as vision. It also includes "psychokinesis" (PK), "mind over matter," without muscle movement. For an event to be considered psi, there needs to be evidence that no normal mechanism could have been responsible. A card-guessing test for ESP might be conducted by separating the "sender" and the "receiver" in different rooms to rule out sensory contact. A test for PK might involve attempting to mentally influence dice rolled by someone else.

But people's psychic experiences are often far more compelling than simple ESP or PK. Apparitions, contact with the spirits of the dead, seeing auras—all these were considered suitable for study by the early parapsychologists. People do not typically report experiences in their daily lives with the "target objects" favored by laboratory experimenters. Often they feel there is a spiritual meaning to the experiences.

From the broader perspective of spirituality, each religious tradition defines these phenomena, and how one should deal with them, in a somewhat different way. All religious traditions acknowledge their existence but differ on their sources and their importance. In the Judeo-Christian tradition, there are psychic experiences throughout the Bible—prophetic dreams and mystical visions. The Bible is greatly concerned with the sources of these experiences, whether they are from God or from lower forces. In the Buddhist and Hindu traditions, psychic experiences are acknowledged to accompany progress on the spiritual path but are typically seen as distractions, not as goals in themselves. Psi may not be an ability or power as much as it is evidence of our connection with a spiritual level of reality. But we must actively choose to pursue the highest path; distraction by the lower levels is always a temptation.

One of the major themes of this book is that psychic experiences are not paranormal, set apart from our everyday experiences by some sort of enchanted boundary. There is, instead, a continuum. The range begins with psychological processes acknowledged by most of modern psychology, and goes through the types of experiences studied by parapsychologists, to phenomena pointing toward a higher, spiritual source. There is a continuum from simple altered states of consciousness to experiences beyond anything our current Western worldview considers possible. There simply is no clear dividing line between the normal and the paranormal.

As we move away from our normal, waking consciousness, we come first to what have been called "altered states of consciousness." Dreams are an example of an altered state that each of us experiences every night. Hypnosis is another type of altered state, experienced by fewer people but still quite common. Meditation is a still different altered state, practiced as a spiritual exercise by many of the people in my research projects.

Psychic experiences go a step further, often occurring during altered states of consciousness. Thus a person might be dreaming (an ordinary altered state) and have a dream about a future event (a precognitive psychic experience). The experiences that people call psychic generally have a correspondence with a specific event in the physical world. That is, a dream of a future event that comes true is a psychic experience. Some experiences seem to point to realities beyond the physical, however, and have been termed mystical.

Mystical experiences are those experiences of a higher state of consciousness that have an ineffable, indescribable quality. They may have specific religious content—seeing God or Jesus—or they may be feelings of bliss, universal love, or oneness with nature. There is no way to "test" or "prove" that someone has had a mystical experience. According to mystics, these experiences validate themselves—the concept of proof is irrelevant at the level of the mystical.

Historically, we are in good company in our quest to understand the full range of experiences. Parapsychology as a science *began* with experiences. When the Society for Psychical Research was founded in Britain in 1882, the concern was with documenting psychic experiences. These first researchers interviewed witnesses and gathered sufficient information to demonstrate that a given unusual occurrence could not be explained by hallucination or faulty memory. Since most experiences were spontaneous—they happened without warning—there was no way that controls could be imposed in advance. Séances with mediums who claimed to contact the spirits of the dead were also a major focus of early parapsychologists. Here it was sometimes possible to implement fairly elaborate safeguards against cheating, but the phenomena themselves were baffling. Parapsychologists were divided as to whether the results were evidence for survival after death, ESP on the part of the medium (for example, reading the mind of the sitter at the séance), or both.

With the rise of modern psychology and experimental methods in the 1920s, many parapsychologists began to restrict their studies to those phenomena that could be controlled in the laboratory. Thus, parapsychology came to mean primarily the study of psi in the laboratory, rather than the study of psychic experiences. In this book I will use the results of experiments as supporting evidence for psychic phenomena, but, following the lead of the early psychical researchers, I will focus primarily on understanding experiences.

The Transpersonal Approach

While the parapsychologists were proving the reality of psi, other explorers were seeking a comprehensive understanding of the human psyche, integrating spiritual and psychological perspectives. Their goal was to identify humanity's highest potentials and discover paths for attaining them. These explorers created a new area of psychology, one that knows no limits in the quest for understanding.

Transpersonal psychology recognized that much of our human capability lies beyond our everyday conscious focus. It saw the importance of not only the "lower" unconscious mind, studied by Sigmund Freud and his followers, but also the "higher" unconscious mind, or link with a higher spiritual source. Abraham Maslow, one of the founders of this approach, speaks of "peak" experiences that point to the "farthest reaches of human nature." A psychic experience, one where you sense someone else's thoughts and realize a higher connectedness, or an out-of-body experience in which you contact a spiritual source can be among the most compelling types of peak experience.

"Transpersonal" means going through and beyond the focused state we think of as our ordinary conscious self. Freud, the originator of much of modern psychotherapy, drew the original distinction between the conscious and unconscious (or subconscious) mind. For him the unconscious mainly contained repressed sexual impulses from early childhood. Years of research since Freud's time have shown the unconscious mind to be far more complex than he suspected; calling it by such a simple term is like referring to the entire population of our country as the "un-president." I will go into much more detail about the unconscious later in the book, since it is our primary route to understanding psychic experiences. But for now we should recognize that at the very least there are two divisions: the lower unconscious and the higher unconscious. The lower unconscious is the one with which we are all familiar—the unconscious of Freud, where repressed memories of childhood are buried and where the roots of many of our psychological problems are lodged. The higher unconscious, on the other hand, is that which points to something beyond ourselves, to the spiritual.

The term "transpersonal" refers to this distinction between the lower and higher unconscious minds. We normally function (as when reading this book, for example) on the personal, rational level; the lower unconscious is termed "prerational" or "prepersonal," and the higher, spiritual level is termed "transrational" or "transpersonal." One of the greatest obstacles to understanding psychic experiences is that from our perspective in the middle, it is very easy to confuse the lower with the higher.

When unusual experiences occur that we have difficulty interpreting in a rational way, we generally interpret them in terms of two competing views of the nonrational. One view, that most typically associated with Western science, looks at all nonrational experiences as prerational or prepersonal. That is, a vision of an angel might be seen as a hallucination related to a memory from infancy of a godlike parent. It would be a relic of the past, not a stimulus to growth. This would be the view of Freudian psychology, where all experiences are explained in terms of regression to perceptions and experiences in early childhood. A psychic experience would simply be seen as pathological—as a hallucination or even as evidence of mental illness. There is no recognition of the possibility of higher sources at all. Equally problematic, however, is the opposite approach, in which all unusual experiences are automatically invested with spiritual significance. This is the problem with much of the popular

"New Age" thinking. Infantile impulses and neurotic responses are sometimes elevated to the realm of the spiritual, and the result is gibberish being mistaken for transcendent insight. Not everything strange is necessarily good!

The Transpersonal Approach of Edgar Cayce

While Cayce's amazing psychic gifts are well known, few people realize that he had a great personal struggle to understand his own abilities. Cayce had a very conventional religious upbringing in rural Kentucky. He had many psychic experiences early in life but, like many of us, generally kept them to himself. Not until he was twenty-three years old, in an experiment with hypnosis to cure himself of a throat problem, did he discover his ability to psychically diagnose disease. He found that when he was in a hypnotic trance, he could diagnose medical problems in people he had never met and could prescribe successful treatments. Soon he was famous, but he felt like a freak. People tried to exploit his abilities for personal gain, and at one time he decided to cease doing psychic readings altogether and return to his work as a photographer.

Cayce's real struggle was to integrate his unusual abilities with his deeply held spiritual convictions. For him, psychic ability was not just a curiosity to be used for profit. He wanted to help people recover from sickness and, even more, to discover their spiritual identity. Many of Cayce's readings dealt with health problems, but others were devoted entirely to the question of spiritual growth and the place of psychic phenomena. In one part of this book, we will look at people in a program called *A Search for God,* based on a series of readings that Cayce gave for a group of people who wanted to develop their psychic abilities. I joined one of these groups more than twenty years ago, as a personal experiment, and found it to be an inspiration for practical spirituality. One of my recent research projects has explored the experiences of people in the program, seeking an understanding of both the potentials and the pitfalls.

The focus of Edgar Cayce's work was on providing tools for spiritual transformation: attunement to transpersonal consciousness and testing by application in daily life. All religious traditions have a concept of the transpersonal, and all specify a path or paths for transformation to attain realization of the spiritual realm. The philosophical basis of the mystical side of all the world's religions has been called the "perennial philosophy," because, like a perennial plant, it appears again and again in the writings of the great mystics. It emphasizes that realization of the spiritual realm can be attained through *direct experience* and that direct experience is universal, regardless of the beliefs of a particular religion.

Nevertheless, the paths to spiritual realization are many. In both the Christian and the Eastern mystical traditions, some paths are virtually unintelligible to the uninitiated because transpersonal experience cannot adequately be communicated in words. For those of us raised in the Western Judeo-Christian tradition, Edgar Cayce—who was both a psychic and a mystic— can serve as a bridge between the personal and the transpersonal.

What, then, is the Cayce perspective? First, there exists a universal awareness, spiritual in nature, with the potential to express itself in the world but not limited to time and space. This is the ultimate level, or the ground of all being, or God. Our relationship to it seems paradoxical. We are part of the whole, yet we experience ourselves as unique individuals. One aim of spiritual growth is to reconcile this seeming contradiction. In psychic and spiritual experiences we make contact with some aspects of that universal awareness.

Cayce reverses the idea that psychic phenomena are products solely of physical and mental forces. Rather, each individual is fundamentally a soul and has within him/herself universal or superconscious awareness. Only a portion of the soul projects itself physically into the limited dimensions of time and space; psychic experiences are a reflection of the greater reality and can lead to greater awareness.

What are the consequences of this perspective for the way we will be looking at psychic experiences in this book? The most important is that it gives psychic experiences meaning. It tells us that they point to something greater than the physical world and our personal selves. It doesn't tell us what a particular psychic experience means, but it does give us hope that the search for meaning is worth pursuing. It also encourages us to go beyond the "is" to the "ought." The crucial question for most of us is not what *is* a psychic experience but what *ought* to be our response to it. As Harmon Bro, a well-known religious scholar, has emphasized, Cayce provided not just a description of the reality to which psychic experiences point but advice on what this means practically in life. Cayce maintained emphatically that he was not trying to start a cult, "ism or schism." His advice was to begin with your own religious beliefs or lack of beliefs, apply insights derived from your experiences (including psychic experiences), and compare your results with your spiritual *ideal*. The ideal is the spiritual principle by which you choose to guide your life.

The Path to Transformation: Reconciling Opposites

Another major theme of this book is that psychic experiences highlight the polar opposites found in all facets of life, which can be precipitating events for major life changes. The message of Cayce, and of the perennial philosophy, is of ultimate oneness, yet we often experience our selves as fragmented. Psychic experiences may simultaneously point to that oneness while intensifying the feeling of fragmentation. Thomas Greening, the editor of the *Journal of Humanistic Psychology*, has spoken of the following four dimensions of human existence: life versus death, separateness versus connectedness, free will versus determinism, and meaning versus absurdity. We perceive these as opposites, yet we need to reconcile them if we are to grow. We often drift through life, unconscious of these polarities most of the time. Yet our psychic experiences have "shock value"—they force these choices into our awareness. Far from being outside the psychology of ordinary events, psychic experiences often highlight the major dilemmas of existence. When confronted with polar opposites, we are tempted to choose one and reject the other. However, we have an alternative: to transcend these differences.

Life versus Death. We grow up with the belief that there is an absolute boundary between life and death, yet our psychic experiences tell us otherwise. A woman sees an apparition of her grandfather, dead for fifteen years. A man has a heart attack and while unconscious journeys out of his body to a spiritual realm and returns to tell about it. Is it possible to bridge the gap between life and death?

Separateness versus Connectedness. Is the skin the boundary of the self? Does the mind reside in the brain? Or are we all united in some way that transcends our apparent separateness? A woman is thinking of a friend she hasn't seen in years. Suddenly the friend calls on the phone. A man in a motorcycle accident on a lonely road calls out, and his sleeping wife miles away wakes. Do psychic experiences link us all together at a higher level?

Free Will versus Determinism. Free will and determinism appear to be incompatible worldviews. Is our every action predetermined, or do we have the freedom to choose our actions and create our reality? A man dreams of a train wreck in which he is killed and decides to travel on a different day. The train crashes, as he foresaw it would, but without him aboard. He saved himself, but could he have prevented the accident altogether?

Meaning versus Absurdity. Are psychic experiences pointers to a great universal plan, calling out for us to divine its secrets? Or is there more to life than searching for the meaning of life? A man dreams of a fish, ends up having fish for lunch, is asked to go on a fishing trip, and has a meeting with a man named Fish—meaningful coincidence or humorous random events? By drawing our attention to absurdity, our psychic experiences may balance our "serious" spiritual search with humor. We will meet the mythological figure of the Trickster, who seems to disrupt the cosmic order but confronts us with the need to seek meaning at a level beyond the rational.

Embarking on the Quest

In our search for meaning, we rely on a variety of methods—scientific, emotional, and intuitive. Science appeals to experiment and to collective experience. Its hallmark is that its methods and results are open for public examination, criticism, and refinement. It should not be confused with dogmatic "scientism," a belief that a materialistic view of the world and rational study are the *only* valid ways of acquiring understanding. Science, particularly the science of parapsychology, will be our companion in this book, guiding us by expanding our view of our personal experiences with the wisdom of collective experiences in the light of experimental results. This is the intellectual dimension of the quest.

But the intellectual must be balanced with the emotional and intuitive dimensions. Ultimately the book seeks to aid you in finding your own meaning in personal experiences and your own path to transformation. It begins with the results of research but ends with an inner journey to which research can only point the way.

This book is divided into four parts, each dealing with a group of related phenomena. Part One looks at the psychic "senses," psychic experiences that resemble our normal sensory experience but have an added dimension. These include telepathy (mind-to-mind communication), clairvoyance (direct perception of distant scenes or events), precognition (perception of the future), and synchronicity (meaningful coincidences). These can all occur in dreams as well as in the waking state.

Part Two looks at the other side of psychic phenomena—the influence of mind on the physical world. Psychokinesis, or mind over matter, refers to the ability to mentally influence physical objects or events. This may be a mechanism related to healing ability—the power to heal self or others through psychic energy.

Part Three looks at more complex psychic experiences—those apparently involving spirits of dead or living people or contact with some other level of reality. These include apparitions of the dead or living, hauntings (apparitions that appear repeatedly in a particular location), out-of-body and near-death experiences, communication with spirit guides, and trance channeling or mediumship (communication from another realm using a person as a channel).

Finally, Part Four addresses the transpersonal aspects of psychic ability in more detail, developing a model that includes psychic functioning as one aspect of the overall process of spiritual growth.

Throughout all the chapters, the emphasis is on helping you understand *your* psychic experiences, through discussion of the diversity of experiences I have seen in my research. It has been said that the best book for understanding dreams is the one you write yourself. The same holds true for psychic experiences. This research is only a beginning. It is your personal application of the material in this book that will lead to understanding.

PART ONE

The Psychic "Senses"

CHAPTER 1

Telepathy

When I was quite young I had psychic knowledge
of the death of a loved one without being told.
This profound and emotional experience helped
start me on my search.

> —A forty-five-year-old woman
> at an A.R.E. conference

We begin the spiritual search here. Are we alone
in our bodies, isolated from all others, with only
our meager senses as windows? Or is there a realm
beyond our personal selves, one where we are all connected and where there is evidence of a higher purpose to life and of a life beyond death?

For many people the answer is yes. They have had
experiences far beyond those that can be explained by
our traditional Western worldview. Telepathy—mind-
to-mind contact—is the experience that often starts
people on their quest. In a 1990 Gallup poll, 25 percent of those responding reported having felt that they
"were in touch with or getting a message from someone who was far away without using the traditional
five senses." In a survey I conducted of 520 members
of the Association for Research and Enlightenment,
more than 86 percent felt that they had had a telepathic experience. For some people these were once-
in-a-lifetime experiences, for others they recurred on
an almost daily basis. Some experiences occurred at

times of dire emergency, while others formed a part of everyday life.

In this chapter we will look at the variety of telepathic experiences that people have, learn what parapsychology can tell us about the reality of telepathy, and work with some principles that will help us to explore the meaning of these experiences.

Varieties of
Telepathic Experiences

The popular image of telepathy is "mind reading," picking up specific thoughts from people, even from total strangers. This idea can be frightening, that people may know your secret thoughts or that you may suddenly begin to receive thoughts from people and be unable to "turn it off." Yet this is not actually the form that most telepathic experiences take. Even the most talented "psychics" are not able to pick up conscious thoughts reliably. Most telepathic experiences have two major characteristics: They involve close family members, and they are related to emotional situations, especially crisis situations. We will see these factors of relationships and emotional situations many times throughout this book. They are common to many types of psychic experiences. Even when telepathic experiences occur with acquaintances or strangers, they are typically related to emotional issues, not conscious thoughts. Here are some examples of common telepathic experiences, from crises and emergencies to communication at the moment of death to telepathic connections in everyday life.

A Call for Help: Telepathy in Crisis

A call for help in time of danger or pain is one of the most basic responses we have. From a child crying for its mother to a man yelling as he gets into a traffic accident, we express ourselves forcefully in times of great stress. Is it any wonder that telepathic experiences occur in similar circumstances? If psychic ability exists, we might expect it to manifest in time of need. A forty-eight-year-old woman wrote:

> *A Warning of Danger.* Seventeen years ago, as I was laying beside the swimming pool, sunbathing by myself, I had an overwhelming feeling that my two oldest children were in danger. I knew they had gone to the store—so I knew in which direction I should go. My two youngest children were asleep inside the house. I would never have left them alone. I had a sprained ankle and could barely walk. The feeling of danger for my two oldest children was so great that I completely forgot everything else (including that I had on a very scant bikini bathing suit, which I would never have let anyone other than close family see me in). I ran hobbling on the bad ankle for five blocks that were not a straight path, to find both of my children lying in the street (a busy intersection) surrounded by crowds of people. They had been hit in the crosswalk by a drunk driver who didn't see the red light. Their injuries were modest compared to what they might have been, and they recovered nicely.

Let's look at the details of this experience. Like many spontaneous psychic experiences, this one happened when the woman least expected it. She was simply sunbathing, relaxed, with no reason to expect a sudden crisis. Yet the telepathic message was "overwhelming," enough to spur her to walk five blocks on a sprained ankle, leaving two young children home alone. A mother responded to her children in need. Yet this experience was not precognitive—a prediction of the future. She received the message at the time the event happened and was unable to prevent it. What, then, could be the meaning of such an experience?

People often expect psychic experiences to be a forewarning of an event, and they may be distressed when they know something happened or could happen and feel powerless to prevent it. We will be looking at precognition of future events in a later chapter. But a telepathic experience raises the same question: Could I have helped? If there was no way I could be of help, why did I have the experience?

Let's look at another example of telepathy in time of crisis, this time sent to us by a thirty-five-year-old woman:

> *A Motorcycle Accident.* In April, 1986 at approximately 12:30 A.M. I awoke from a sound sleep with a feeling that something had just happened to my husband (who was very late returning home after bowling). My immediate impression was that he'd had an accident on his motorcycle. Upon calling the county emergency control dispatcher, it was confirmed that a motorcycle accident had in fact occurred in the city at, as far as I can determine, the exact time I awoke. I called the city police to get the name of the motorcyclist in the accident. It was my husband.

The woman was stunned by this experience! Could she have prevented the accident? Our research program receives a great many telephone calls and letters reporting such experiences. The first task is often to provide reassurance: There is often nothing you can do to *prevent* the crisis event. Naturally the first impulse is to try and help in time of crisis, but when that is not possible, the experience may serve as a strong impetus to action *after* the event. At the least, it is evidence of a deep emotional connection with loved ones.

The woman whose children were hurt was not able

to prevent the accident, but she included follow-up comments with her report that spoke of the profound effect this experience had on her life. The accident opened her up to recognition of a deeper connectedness between herself and her children than she had previously been aware of. Since the accident she has had many other psychic experiences with one of her children (a son), and those experiences and others have become a major part of her life.

The woman with the motorcyclist husband did not provide any follow-up information on the aftermath of the experience, but we can surmise that both the accident and the telepathic connection had a significant effect on her approach to life. The accident alone, of course, could have led to a change in her husband's riding habits. But a telepathic experience like this might make the difference between "just another accident" and a major change in life direction—not only a heightened awareness of mortality but a possibility of a greater reality.

The Final Good-bye: Telepathy at the Time of Death

The ultimate crisis is death, and it is not surprising that many telepathic experiences occur at the moment of death. In the case of a sudden or violent death they may resemble the calls for help discussed above, but sometimes they are just a final contact at the time of passing on. Here is an experience that a thirty-one-year-old man sent to us, about an experience he had when he was eleven.

Grandfather Passes On. About twenty years ago my grandfather died. I was laying in bed just before falling asleep. The phone rang and I said the words "Grandpa is dead." I felt no sadness. I just knew with absolute certainty that he had died. Ten minutes later my mother walked in the room and told us Grandpa had died.

Someone might raise the objection that recollection can dim after twenty years. This is certainly possible. Perhaps the memory of the experience is not entirely accurate. Independent witnesses to telepathic experiences are hard to come by, but parapsychologists have gathered several collections of well-verified events. Ian Stevenson, a professor of psychiatry at the University of Virginia, gives the following example in his book *Telepathic Impressions*. A middle-aged woman, "Mrs. Rudkin," reported to him:

> In 1930 I was living in London, England. My mother, aged 75, had not been well and was living in Cleveland, Ohio. On January 9th I awoke in the morning knowing that my mother had died during the night and I so informed my family at the breakfast table. They wanted to know if I had heard from home. Then I said I had not, but I knew with certainty that she had died. Before we had finished our breakfast a cablegram was delivered telling us of her death. I do not know why I was so sure. I only know that when I woke up that morning I was convinced that my mother had died during the night.

Following the report of the case, Stevenson quotes testimony from the woman's son, who was present at the time and had a "vivid recollection" of the episode. He confirmed that although the grandmother was elderly and infirm, her condition had been the same for several months. He specifically remembered that his mother had said in the morning, "Mother died last night," and that he had asked, "How do you know that she died?" He knew that there had been no letter or telephone call that morning, and he confirmed that the cablegram arrived later that day.

These experiences not only open up a new worldview in which we are all connected by unseen links in life, but they force us to confront the reality of death. For many people such a contact is reassuring—evidence of the power of love, even at the time of death. For others it may cause some anxiety. Is there anything I can do to help? Is death final? As we will see later in the book, some psychic experiences, particularly apparitions, may be evidence of life after death. But even without direct evidence, the concept of an afterlife plays a key role in the religious beliefs of many people. Edgar Cayce echoes this view. He advised that we can definitely be of help to those who have passed on, through prayer. For example, in response to a woman who felt she was being contacted by a friend who had passed on, Cayce said, "As we help another does help come to us. Pray for that friend, that the way through the shadows may be easier for them. It becomes easier for you" (Reading 262–25; numbers following quotations from the Cayce readings refer to the case number in the files at the Association for Research and Enlightenment).

For the living, as we saw in the quotation that opened this chapter, these experiences may serve as the beginning of a lifelong spiritual search.

The World at Large: Telepathy in Daily Life

Telepathy is not all gloom and doom, crisis and death. These are the most striking telepathic experiences, the ones most likely to be reported in a research project, but many people claim they have had telepathic experiences in daily life that are related to the immediate concerns of the living.

The important elements in daily telepathic experiences are still personal involvement and emotional intensity. Even when there is not an immediate crisis, telepathic experiences often occur in emotionally charged situations. For this thirty-seven-year-old woman, telepathy intervened to bring two estranged people together:

Emotional Connections. Going home on a Sunday evening, I kept thinking about my estranged husband. Our divorce proceedings have been rather hostile and my constant preoccupation was with the proceedings and whether what we were doing was in our best interest. As I was driving along I had this feeling that I would pass him on the road going home and coming from the opposite direction. Sure enough, we met at one point, turned into a spot where we parked our cars and started talking. He, too, said that he knew we would see each other on the way home even though it was highly unlikely that we should meet one another on a Sunday at that time of the day, both going home in opposite directions.

From the report this woman sent us, it does not appear that the couple was reconciled, but telepathy created an opportunity.

Such experiences can be embarrassing, as I will illustrate with a personal experience of my own.

Telepathy at the Movies. When I was in graduate school I asked a woman I'll call "Sally," a fellow graduate student, out to see a movie. She said she would try to meet me but might not be able to join me. Despite my skepticism of this ambivalent response, I waited, and when she didn't arrive and the movie had already started, I decided to drive to a nearby town to see a different movie. When I arrived at the theater, that movie had also already started, and in the dark I fumbled my way down several rows and sat down. As my eyes adjusted to the dark, I found myself sitting next to Sally and her friend "Mike." I said, "Hi!" and continued to watch the movie. She was quite embarrassed, since she had been trying to keep her relationship with Mike a secret from everyone, as at the time Mike was married to someone else.

This experience could be considered unconscious telepathy, since I wasn't conscious of the information guiding me to that movie and that seat. It was apparently related to an emotional connection. But Sally certainly didn't want to see me there, and while I was amused at her discomfiture, I probably wouldn't have consciously chosen that situation either.

Sometimes, however, people report that telepathy has been quite helpful. In my collection I received several reports of telepathy as a useful ability in business. Here are two short examples from business executives, both men in their fifties. They did not provide many details, but these reports are typical of those that many successful businesspeople will share.

Who Is Going to Call? I am a financial consultant and the name and face of a client will appear in my consciousness right before I receive a call from this person. This happens quite frequently, with increasing accuracy as I grow older.

What Are They Going to Say? In business meetings I often "know" what is about to be said by group members—also a sense of directing answers to mental questions I have before I have a chance to ask.

Douglas Dean and his associates, in their book *Executive ESP,* discuss their study of the use of psychic ability by top corporate executives. Their PSI Communications Project at the Newark College of Engineering in New Jersey tested numerous executives for psychic ability and found that many scored well and admitted that they used "intuition" and "hunches" to guide them in business decisions. Dean's group found that telepathy was often unconscious (recall my example of the woman in the movie theater). Executives said that their knowledge was "intuitive."

For a sensitive measure of unconscious emotional reactions, Dean used a plethysmograph, a device that measures blood volume in the finger according to dilation and constriction of the blood vessels. When you go "white with fear" or "red with anger," your reaction can be measured by a plethysmograph, even when you are not consciously aware of your emotions. In addition to business executives, Dean and his colleagues studied husband-wife teams and found that there were clear unconscious reactions to familiar names as targets, sent telepathically.

Can telepathic ability be exercised at will? Can it be trained? When people recover from their initial shock that it can occur at all, these are often their questions. Can telepathy be incorporated into life in a productive way, or is it simply one of those inexplicable occurrences that must forever remain a mystery? This woman from new York State volunteered to explore her telepathic ability in a laboratory experiment:

The Telepathy Experiment. Several years ago I took part in an experiment at SUNY College, Purchase, NY. I was in a room with sensory deprivation and white sound in my ears and a mike near me. My friend was two miles away across the campus. She was verbalizing and sending messages about a picture selected randomly. At the same time I was talking about the picture I was receiving. Later they brought in a batch of pictures. I was able to pick out each time the right picture. We did it three times and each time I was not only correct with the picture but I accurately got the wording also.

This type of experiment, and others like it in laboratories around the country, have shown that telepathy is not merely spontaneous, something that "just happens." Many people have found that, occasionally, they can receive telepathic impressions at will. Whether it is in workshops for the general public or in experiments at universities, people are discovering abilities they never knew they had. Here is where the science of parapsychology can offer some help. It seeks not simply to document the existence of telepathy but to understand the factors that potentially lead to reliable control of these experiences.

Parapsychologists Study Telepathy

Telepathy has been a core concept in parapsychology since its early days. Before 1900, most parapsychology consisted of studies of mediums in séances and collections of the psychic experiences of ordinary people. The Society for Psychical Research in Britain, in 1886, published *Phantasms of the Living,* an extensive collection of well-documented psychic experiences, in which telepathy figured prominently. Apparent mind-to-mind contact at times of crisis and death was a common experience, as it is in my collection today.

Some of the best-documented cases of telepathy, including an example earlier in this chapter, are discussed in the book *Telepathic Impressions* by Ian Stevenson. Stevenson found that 69.4 percent of the cases reported in several major collections occurred between family members, 28.1 percent with acquaintances, and only 2.5 percent with strangers. To document the cases, witnesses were interviewed, who had been told of the telepathic experiences before there was any possibility of the event's being known by normal means. These types of well-documented cases are important evidence that telepathic experiences are not simply the product of an overactive imagination and that we should take a serious look even at the cases which are not as well documented.

With the turn of the century, parapsychologists began to conduct experiments not just to prove that such phenomena as telepathy exist but to understand how they work. One famous study was conducted by Upton Sinclair, the well-known novelist, with his wife as the subject. In his book *Mental Radio,* published in 1930, he describes successful experiments with telepathic transmission of drawings. Notably, the preface to the book was written by the physicist Albert Einstein, who said in part, "The results of the telepathic experiments carefully and plainly set forth in this book stand surely far beyond those which a nature investigator holds to be unthinkable. . . . His good faith and dependability are not to be doubted. . . . In no case should the psychologically interested circles pass over this book heedlessly."

Perhaps the most significant advance in the field began with the arrival of J. B. Rhine and his wife, Louisa, at Duke University in 1927. The Psychology Department at Duke was the first to establish a laboratory with parapsychology as its primary purpose. One of Rhine's early efforts was an attempt to devise a conclusive test for telepathy. He developed methods of shielding the sender from the receiver and statistical procedures for analyzing the results. Rhine and his followers documented the existence of extrasensory ability in numerous well-controlled experiments, many reported in the *Journal of Parapsychology* and the *Journal of the American Society for Psychical Research.*

But when they tried to prove *telepathy* as *mind-to-mind* exchange, it turned out to be difficult to exclude *clairvoyance* from the test. Clairvoyance is the perception of distant events *without* the need for a *sender.* In card guessing, an experiment might consist of a sender and a receiver, with the sender looking directly at a pack of cards one by one and the receiver writing down his guesses. For a control test, some early parapsychology experiments used a deck of cards without a sender and had the receiver simply write down the guesses. This was an attempt at clairvoyance—direct seeing or intuition of a distant event *without* the need for a sender. And it worked as well as the experiments *with* a sender did! Rhine coined the term "general extrasensory perception" (GESP) to refer to the situation where you might have either telepathy or clairvoyance contributing to the result.

When we talk about telepathic *experiences,* as in my example of the woman at the movies, clairvoyance is often a possibility. The only way to show *pure* telepathy is in a carefully constructed experiment with targets that exist only in the mind of the sender. The targets cannot be written down anywhere; if they were, clairvoyance would be a possibility. But it is very difficult to have proper controls and statistics if the targets are not written down. For this reason, most parapsychology experiments do not attempt to test for pure telepathy. Instead they allow for clairvoyance as a possibility, but use a "sender" to add emotional interest and motivation to the situation. In the next chapter, on clairvoyance, we will take a closer look at these types of experiments, which provide strong *objective* evidence of the existence of psychic ability.

How Can We Explain Telepathy?

Though telepathy is hard to demonstrate *experimentally, subjectively* the sense of direct mind-to-mind contact is often very strong. Let's say *you* have had an experience that seems to be telepathic. How can we explain it?

There are two general ways telepathy has been explained. One is the "mental radio" model, where the mind functions like a radio. While simple, it does not account for many of the features of actual experiences. The other type of explanation looks more deeply at the phenomena of consciousness, especially the unconscious mind.

Parapsychologists first conceived of telepathy as analogous to radio, with a sender and a receiver. In experiments, one can explore the roles of sender and receiver separately, studying the characteristics that produce good senders and receivers. One can also separate the sender and the receiver by greater and greater distances, to see if telepathy is limited by distance. By shielding the receiver from the sender in various ways, it also might be possible to discover the types of waves that carry the signal.

But experiments have not supported this simple physical model of telepathic communication. Telepathy appears to be largely independent of distance. Experiments with shielding various types of waves, separating the sender and receiver with devices ranging from electrically shielded rooms to submarines deep under the ocean, have not revealed any currently understood form of energy as the carrier of telepathic information.

Parapsychologists, looking beyond the physical, explored the unconscious mind. It seems that such characteristics as motivation and emotion are far more important than physical factors in determining the "power" of the sender and the "sensitivity" of the receiver.

Rex Stanford, a psychologist at St. John's University in New York, proposes that psi may be involved in all of our daily actions, but at an unconscious level. Everyone has an unconscious, psi-based scanning mechanism, which is continually scanning the environment for information related to personal needs. This occurs not only without conscious effort but without any realization that there is anything "psychic" going on at all.

Stanford looked for spontaneous cases where unconscious psi caused people to make a "mistake" leading to unintentionally favorable consequences. Here is an example of one of his cases, from a retired attorney in New York:

One Sunday afternoon I was headed for Greenwich Village intending to drop in on my good friends and artists, Mr. and Mrs. P. I took an express subway train to 14th Street, where I would change to a local train to 8th Street. However, upon leaving the express at 14th Street, I "absentmindedly" walked right out through the gate and half way up the stairs to the street before remembering that I had intended to take the local train. Not wishing to pay another fare, I decided to go on to the street and walk the additional six blocks south. I had proceeded along Seventh Avenue as far as 12th Street when I met Mr. and Mrs. P. walking northward, on their way to some appointment in the area. I was able to walk with them for a few blocks and receive credit for the call. Obviously I would have missed them had I traveled as planned.

In Edgar Cayce's terminology, the phenomenon Stanford is studying might simply be called intuition, knowing something without realizing how or why you know it, or even *that* you know it. People sometimes think of intuition as a cruder form of psychic ability. But it is not cruder, it is simply unconscious. To the extent that you are willing to work with your unconscious mind, you may be able to use intuition creatively in your life.

Psi and the Unconscious Mind

Let's explore the relationship between psi and the unconscious mind in more depth. Historically, the discovery of the unconscious by psychologists paralleled the rise of parapsychology. In fact, many of the early parapsychologists were as concerned with the basic structure of consciousness as they were with understanding psychic phenomena. Prominent among these was Frederic Myers, a British scholar in classical literature and a leading member of the Society for Psychical Research. Myers developed the concept of multiple levels of awareness. In this view the conscious self performed the actions of everyday life, but beneath this conscious level of awareness lay the unconscious subliminal self, with access not only to the unconscious contents of the mind of a single individual, but also, potentially, to the minds of other individuals.

Carl Jung, a Swiss psychiatrist whose work we will also discuss in more detail in later chapters, likewise had a great interest in psychic abilities and their relation to the unconscious mind. For Jung, communications from the unconscious mind are in the form of symbols. Many psychic experiences are symbolic as well. A dream of a train wreck might refer to an upcoming stock market crash, for example. Jung noted that for many psychic phenomena he observed, the concepts of sender and receiver did not fit the experiences very well. Often a meaningful event just seemed to occur to the right person at the right time. He called this effect "synchronicity," the occurrence of meaningful coincidences. Since these coincidences often involved symbolism, he saw them as a form of communication from the unconscious mind.

Edgar Cayce's model of the mind is multilevel as well, including not just an unconscious or subconscious level but a superconscious level as well. As we saw in the introduction, the theory of psychic ability given in the Cayce readings makes the basic assumption that there is a universal awareness, spiritual in nature, responsible not just for psychic experiences but for *all* experiences. This is quite a departure from the theories most often put forth by parapsychologists. It does not lend itself to being tested by objective experiments. As an explanation of *experience,* however, it may speak to our intuitive sense of what is occurring and lead us to take further steps along the spiritual path.

For Cayce, each individual is actually a soul, but only a portion of that soul projects itself into the limited dimensions of time and space. Psychic ability is one form of soul expression; the problem is to remove conditions within both the conscious and the unconscious minds that block this natural manifestation. Cayce identifies *attunement* as the way to lift this block in order to have balanced, helpful psychic experiences. Attunement, for Cayce, means making self one with God's purpose and removing selfish motives. The proper motivation is to grow in spiritual awareness and in service to others. This contrasts with Stanford's concept of psi, where *self's* needs are the primary motivating force.

Working with Your Telepathic Experiences

What can you do if you think you have had a telepathic experience? For many people, the realization that an experience was telepathic comes as a great shock, forcing a complete change in their view of how the world works. For others, the occasional telepathic experience is so much a part of everyday life that they may pay it no special attention. But sometimes even such "psychic veterans" may feel a need for greater understanding. Separating truly telepathic experiences from other possibilities can be quite a challenge.

We have seen that telepathic experiences occur most often between people who are emotionally close, who often have a lot of knowledge about each other. This makes it hard to tell whether or not an experience was telepathic. If you suddenly get a feeling that your husband is buying you flowers, and he arrives home with flowers, is that telepathy? Does he buy you flowers frequently? Did you have an argument that he might try to settle by bringing flowers? For many people, experiences of this type are just a confirmation of an intimate connection, without there being any need to prove or disprove the telepathic nature of the connection.

Some experiences between people who are close are more problematic, for they reveal things the people would prefer to keep hidden. Actress and dancer Ann Miller, in an article in A.R.E.'s *Venture Inward* magazine, describes an incident in which telepathy was disruptive rather than helpful. She said, "My parents were having difficulties in their marriage. One night my father came home late for dinner and told my mother he had had a business appointment. I said, 'That's not quite right, Dad.' He had actually been having a drink with a pretty blond woman, and I told them so. My mother and father looked at me as if I were a little monster and said, 'What do you mean by that?' I said, 'Dad, you're not telling mother the truth.' And from that day forward they knew I wasn't like other people." Blurting out this kind of telepathic information is likely to make you quite unpopular!

When apparent telepathic information concerning a relationship is disturbing, or might lead to an inappropriate action, it is wise to consider some alternative explanations. Telepathy is at best an imperfect channel of information. Two of the major alternatives are *wishful thinking* and *projection*. Wishful thinking is an expression of your inner desires, not necessarily external truth, and can be a powerful distorter of your perception of reality. A woman may have turned you down for a date ten times, yet you "know" telepathically that she really loves you. Perhaps she does, but you should at least consider the possibility that wishful thinking is what is at work here.

Another alternative to telepathy is known by the psychological term "projection." Projection is an important concept, and we will refer to it throughout the book. Projection occurs when you attribute an emotion or characteristic of your own to someone else.

It is typically unconscious and often goes along with denying the feeling in yourself. While it is easy to see projection in the behavior of other people, it is frequently very difficult to see it in ourselves.

As an example, you might feel that your coworkers are angry with you, and you become very upset. The reality may be that you feel that you can't express your own inner anger openly, so you project it on your coworkers and can now feel justified in being upset with them. If you believe in telepathy, you could quite easily feel that you had been telepathically receiving their anger, when, in fact, it originated entirely within yourself.

Discernment is the ability to discriminate truly telepathic information from wishful thinking and projection. Even for experienced psychics, it is often hard to separate telepathic information from projection. Your overall impressions may be a mixture of your internal states and the thoughts of others.

Edgar Cayce once gave a specific technique for developing telepathy and discernment. He first emphasized the spiritual aspect, saying that the basic principle is "the consciousness of His abiding presence. For, He is all power, all thought, the answer to every question. For, as these attune more and more to the awareness of His presence, the desire to know of those influences that may be revealed causes the awareness to become materially practical" (Reading 2533-7). That is, Cayce felt that telepathy is a consequence of higher spiritual awareness, not simply mind-to-mind contact. The desire for spiritual awareness can result in materially practical telepathy, but spiritual attunement must come first.

Then Cayce gave the technique, which involved developing a telepathic relationship between two people. He said, "First, begin between selves. Set a definite time, and each at that moment put down what the other is doing. Do this for twenty days. And ye will find ye have the key to telepathy" (Reading 2533–7).

Sometimes people assume that Cayce meant this as a procedure for increasing *sensitivity*. I think it more likely that he was speaking to someone who already had a fair amount of sensitivity and was instead giving that person instructions for developing *discernment*. The key is reality testing, comparing telepathic impressions with their source. After a focus on what the other person is thinking, the need is for a deep and honest discussion of the thoughts and feelings that arise. Only by conscious sharing will the attunement develop that may allow sharing at a deeper level. Otherwise, practice of this exercise will result simply in increasing projection and wishful thinking.

Where does telepathy lead us? For the single crisis experience, there is often nothing that you *can* do at the time. In that ease the experience primarily leads to awareness of connectedness at a higher level. The message of the experience may be that you need to reevaluate your view of relationships, the world, and your spiritual search.

For repeated experiences, an effort to develop discernment is a productive path to take. The Cayce twenty-day approach is one way to work with discernment. Any honest self-examination that helps you discriminate wishful thinking and projection from true knowledge of another person is helpful in your development, whether or not you can "prove" your source to be telepathic. This working with discernment is a first step in understanding the complexities of your own unconscious mind.

Telepathy is our first type of psychic experience, but it is only the beginning. The complexities of actual occurrences of psychic phenomena show that we must go beyond telepathy to include clairvoyance and other, more unusual forms of psychic ability. It is to clairvoyance that we now turn.

CHAPTER 2

Clairvoyance

"I see nobody on the road," said Alice.

"I only wish *I* had such eyes," the king remarked in a fretful tone. "To be able to see Nobody! And at that distance too! Why it's as much as *I* can do to see real people, by this light!"

—Lewis Carroll, *Through the Looking-Glass*

Clairvoyance—the ability to perceive events at a distance without the use of ordinary senses. The early parapsychologists thought that clairvoyance was even less likely than telepathy. Telepathy can at least be understood in terms of "mental radio." Clairvoyance fits no reasonable physical model. Yet many people report experiences in which there is apparently no "sender." Experiments have shown that even such tasks as psychic perception down through a sealed deck of cards is as easy (or as difficult) as telepathically receiving the symbols. Many psychic experiences could be either telepathy or clairvoyance—perhaps an event is being witnessed through the eyes of someone else. But often the scene is too immediate, too realistic to be anything but a clairvoyant perception of a distant scene.

The Gallup poll did not ask a question specifically on clairvoyance. John Palmer, however, in his survey of the townspeople of Charlottesville, Virginia, did ask a question on "waking ESP," which includes both telepathy and clairvoyance. He found that 38 percent of the people reported such an experience. In my survey of 520 A.R.E. members, 61 percent reported at least one clairvoyant experience in their lives. In this chapter we will explore the varieties of these clairvoyant experiences, look at the discoveries parapsychologists have made, and learn some approaches to working with clairvoyant perception.

Varieties of Clairvoyant Experiences

Clairvoyance can occur in a wide variety of circumstances, from emotional encounters with relatives to strictly controlled experiments. Like telepathic experiences, clairvoyant experiences are most common in conjunction with close relationships and emotional situations. A thirty-two-year-old woman sent us this account of a clairvoyant experience that may have saved a life:

A Foiled Robbery. I work for my in-laws at a small neighborhood store. One night not long after we closed, two men came banging on the doors wanting in. My mother-in-law told them we were closed and I walked on to the other side of the store. My daughter, then two years old, was playing near the front. I had walked a little way down the aisle when I had a very clear picture in my mind of the two men—one holding a pearl handled pistol—and my daughter looking out the front door. And I had the feeling they were going to shoot through the door. Where I was you could not see the door. I quickly ran and grabbed my daughter, all the time hollering for my husband. As I grabbed her up I saw the same gun. The man had somehow dropped it and was bent over picking it up. My mother-in-law had run to the door also and she too saw it. I had never before seen something so vividly as that.

The striking part of this experience is the visual image of the two men and the pearl-handled pistol. If it was telepathy, who was the sender? The point of view was not that of the would-be robbers. Yet otherwise this was similar to the reports of some of the telepathic experiences. There was a crisis, and in this case the psychic experience occurred at just the right time to prevent a crime.

Like telepathy, however, clairvoyance does not always provide the opportunity to save the situation. By the time the forty-seven-year-old man in the following episode responded to his strong feeling, it was too late to do anything about the incident.

The Thieves Escape. As I left work one day, the words "theft" and "robbery" would not leave my thoughts. I was supposed to pick up a friend, but when it came time to turn my car in the direction (where I was to pick up my friend) I took my hands off the wheel and decided to go in the direction that the wheel took—and it "took" the direction of my house. Well—you obviously guessed it—when I arrived at my house, the house had been broken into.

This example shows the broad sense of the term "clairvoyance" that most parapsychologists use. It is not restricted to visual images but can refer to any form of sensation, or simply a strong "feeling." The characteristic that makes it clairvoyance is that there does not appear to be a specific "sender." In this case there were two aspects to the clairvoyance. First there were the actual words "theft" and "robbery" persisting in the man's thoughts. Next was the impulse to follow the direction that his car "wanted" to take. The lesson from this story is that the unconscious mind can communicate with us through automatic responses; conscious resistance can hinder the flow of clairvoyance.

As with telepathy, clairvoyance is not restricted to crisis situations. At times it can be useful in the daily business of life. A sixty-two-year-old woman sent us this rather unusual example of clairvoyant assistance:

The Clairvoyant Student. In 1943 I was a freshman attending my second class in Speech I at the University of California at Berkeley. We had been assigned homework and I was concerned because I had not been able to buy the textbook—evidently neither had any of my classmates. During the deadly silence following the professor's first question, I decided to take a stab at answering it. He seemed encouraged and we spent the rest of the hour with little, if any, interference from my classmates, discussing basic principles of public speaking, of which I knew nothing. When I did read the textbook a day or two later, I was stunned to find out that I had been quoting whole sentences verbatim from the book, sometimes several sentences in a row. I don't think I had been reading the professor's mind as I didn't deviate from the book's material, while he cited examples and concepts from other sources. As I don't have a photographic memory, if I had read the material before class, I would have had to paraphrase it and I would have remembered some concepts, forgotten others, and, I hope, originated something. I didn't. I KNEW that I had answered all of his questions by quoting from a book I'd never seen. Of course, no one else knew it—far from being impressed, they thought I'd done my homework.

Here we have an example of the kind of clairvoyance that tends to confound the "mental radio" model of psychic ability. The source appeared to be a closed book. As we will see below, parapsychologists have obtained similar results in experiments with sealed decks of cards and other hidden targets. In the case of the woman with the book, it appears as if clairvoyance did not require any physical possibility of "seeing" the target. It worked as well with a closed book as in any other situation. She, like the man with the car in the previous story, was not even aware consciously that clairvoyance was occurring; it operated at an unconscious level, in response to a need.

Although a case like the one above, in which detailed intellectual information is received clairvoyantly, is rare, Edgar Cayce as a young man apparently had a similar ability. Never an especially good student, Cayce became frustrated while learning spelling, since his father was pressuring him not to fail. He fell asleep on his spelling book and, when he woke up, astounded his father by correctly spelling every word in the book. This was one of the first signs that Cayce had an unusual ability.

The above experiences, like many of the telepathic experiences in the previous chapter, were spontaneous. But clairvoyance is certainly not limited to spontaneous experiences. Intentional clairvoyance is also occasionally possible, like this woman's experiment in "guessing" the contents of an unknown box.

What's Inside the Box? A friend asked me to guess what was in a small box that he handed me. I said it's light as a feather. Then I guessed "a feather" with conviction. It was a feather. He was very surprised. I said "Oh, it must have been a coincidence." Then he handed me a larger wooden box, about 3½ × 6 × 2 inches deep and said "guess what's inside." I closed my eyes, cleared my mind and waited. I "saw" rounded shapes which I described with my hand. I waited more, said "they're wood," then "I see colors, lots of colors." (My rational mind got in the way and I said "they must be painted.") My friend got impatient and opened the box to reveal about five large opals shaped like the signs I had made with my hand. The box had wooden dowels in each corner and the tops of the dowels were rounded. I doubt I was reading his mind because it is doubtful he would think of the dowels, as they were part of the box. Whether I "saw" the object or read his mind, I was surprised, intrigued and convinced of psychic phenomena after that. That was my first psychic experience, at about age 43.

The woman's description in this case makes it clear that she thought this was most likely clairvoyance, not telepathy. Is clairvoyant ability common? As we did with telepathy, let's turn again to studies by parapsychologists to learn the answer.

Parapsychologists Study Clairvoyance

To study clairvoyance, parapsychologists began by excluding the "sender" in experiments. J. B. Rhine, to rule out the possibility of telepathy, used a technique called "Down Through," because it consisted of guessing down through a deck of cards, without a sender looking at each card. Only at the completion of the experiment were the guesses scored to determine the degree of success. One of the outstanding subjects to be tested using the Down Through technique was a psychic from Trinidad named Lalsingh (Sean) Harribance. In one experiment, guessing through fifty decks of cards, the scores he achieved would only be expected by chance less than once in a thousand times. When researchers measured his brain waves, they found that the higher-scoring runs had a significantly higher percent-time of alpha waves (a specific frequency range). Harribance said his procedure for psychic reading involved *meditation and relaxation*, techniques associated with alpha waves in other psychological experiments. Alpha waves are not necessarily associated with psychic experiences, but in this individual they were predictive of high-scoring runs.

Here was solid evidence that pure clairvoyance was possible under tightly controlled conditions. Nevertheless, card experiments in most cases produced disappointing results for parapsychologists. One of the strongest effects discovered by J. B. Rhine was the "decline effect." The best scores tend to come early in a test, at the beginning of a deck of cards, and the success rate often declines to chance levels later in the test. The decline effect was impressive evidence that *something* paranormal was happening, since it is hard to imagine why many subjects would independently fake declines over years of research. But it was discouraging for researchers who were looking for a reliable demonstration of clairvoyance. Not only did scores decline within sessions, but subjects who guessed cards over long experiments often had their overall ability fade as well.

Remote Viewing

By the 1970s parapsychologists were beginning to realize that card-guessing experiments had taken them far away from the basic experiences of clairvoyance, which were images of distant scenes or events. They recalled the drawing experiments done forty years earlier by people like Upton Sinclair, in which the interest of the subject could be sustained much longer than with cards. They speculated that reviving the technique of allowing the subject to make a "free-response" drawing of whatever came to mind, rather than being forced to choose a specific card, might yield better results. Other researchers had reported success studying dreams in this way (see chapter 4). Rather than "mental radio," the term coined by Sinclair, parapsychologists now realized that they were dealing with the possibility of both clairvoyance and telepathy.

But the basic method—motivating the subject by creating an interesting experiment—seemed more valid than ever.

The challenge to create a better experiment was taken up by physicists Russell Targ and Harold Puthoff at the Stanford Research Institute (now SRI International) in California. The theme of their work was that it is necessary to create the proper environment to encourage psychic activity and that laboratory card guessing was probably one of the worst environments. Their insight was to focus on those aspects of psychic functioning that people find natural to use in their daily lives. They arrived at two important truths: First, forcing a person to do a laboratory experiment designed for the convenience of the experimenters produces poor results. Second, and somewhat surprising, the more difficult and challenging the task, the more likely the results will be good. This runs counter to the concept of beginning with apparently simple, trivial tasks such as card guessing and working up to the hard ones involving complex targets.

Targ and Puthoff called their experiment "remote viewing," a term more acceptable to the scientists than "clairvoyance," but meaning the same thing. The targets were not cards; they were actual locations in the Stanford area, such as a tower or a restaurant. They were richly detailed segments of the real world. As a control, the experiments were run "double-blind"— that is, neither the experimenter nor the subject knew the target location until the end of the experiment. To encourage good results, Targ and Puthoff's experiments allowed for both telepathy and clairvoyance.

To conduct an experiment, a group of researchers called the "target team" traveled to a randomly selected target location, known only to them. Meanwhile, back at the lab, another experimenter was isolated in a room with the subject. After allowing sufficient time for the group to travel to the target, the subject in the room would begin to describe his impressions of the target into a tape recorder and make drawings of his mental images.

To determine how well the subject did, independent judges compared the description of the target and the drawings to the actual target site and ranked the transcripts in terms of which best described each of the target locations. Statistical procedures were used to determine whether the matches were significantly better than would be expected by chance.

The results, which were excellent and highly statistically significant, were published in a leading engineering journal, *Proceedings of the IEEE* (Institute of Electrical and Electronics Engineers). Overall, with subjects ranging from professional psychics to occasional visitors, there was less than one chance in twenty of the results being due to chance alone. But for some outstanding subjects the results were far stronger. For Hella Hammid, a photographer who had never tried clairvoyance before, her success at describing targets up to eight miles away would happen by chance less than twice in a *million* such experiments.

While numbers are impressive for engineers, the pictures and comments from the subjects provide more clues for an understanding of how clairvoyance works. Many of the pictures drawn by the subjects, for example, picked up only a few elements from the target location. These were not necessarily those focused on by the target team, which suggests clairvoyance rather than telepathy as an explanation for the results. Hella Hammid, who as a photographer was especially attuned to patterns, was able to draw and describe visual images that she could not identify with her intellect. For a pedestrian overpass over a highway, she described some kind of trough up in the air. For another target, a bicycle shed, she described the pattern of light and dark from the slatted sides of the structure, but not the bicycles. This type of result—

images not recognized by the intellect—is typical in remote viewing experiments. It is further evidence of the role of unconscious processes in psychic perception.

Could something other than clairvoyance account for these results? Targ and Puthoff were extremely careful with their controls. With their double-blind procedures, there was no opportunity for the subject to perceive ordinary sensory information or even just plain cheat. The targets were selected randomly, from any location in the Stanford area, so simple guessing was unlikely to explain the results. Yet there are some possibilities, far-fetched if you believe in clairvoyance but taken quite seriously by skeptics, that might occasionally cause spurious results. There might be information in the transcript that could provide a clue to the judge about when the experiment took place— rain, for example. This might narrow the range of possible targets.

In hindsight it is always possible to come up with far-fetched, skeptical explanations for any result, and researchers often spend time defending their original experiments against critics. But it is basic to the process of science that experiments by any one group are not sufficient proof; independent replication is necessary. Parapsychology has often had the problem that repeatable experiments are hard to come by. Not so with remote viewing. Several other laboratories have obtained results similar to those at SRI. These include experiments by Marilyn Schlitz, now at the Institute of Noetic Sciences in California, and Brenda Dunne and Robert Jahn, in the Engineering School at Princeton University. Although not all experimenters report as high a level of success as the group at SRI, remote viewing seems to be one of the most consistently repeatable procedures in parapsychology.

Is remote viewing of any practical use? Stephan

Schwartz, of the Mobius Society in Los Angeles (an organization that explores applications of psi), had the idea of combining a "perfect" demonstration of remote viewing with a practical aim: a psychic underwater treasure hunt. He assembled a group of remote viewers who had been successful in previous experiments and instructed them to psychically search for shipwrecks containing treasure in a selected area in the Bahamas. They made circles on maps to indicate the area of the wrecks and described the contents of the ships. Schwartz combined the maps and selected the most likely area to search, based on the greatest number of overlapping circles. He brought psychics along to search at the site itself, throwing buoys overboard to mark the location of a wreck. The good news from this experiment was that they quickly found a shipwreck. Many of the descriptions of the contents of the wreck given by the remote viewers closely matched the actual wreck. The bad news was that the wreck had no treasure—it was simply a merchant ship. Making a profit from clairvoyant ability in this way has proved to be elusive.

Edgar Cayce had similar experiences. He, too, helped with treasure hunts in Virginia Beach, Florida, and the Bahamas and with searching for oil in Texas, all with no luck. His sons, Hugh Lynn and Edgar Evans, describe the frustration of psychic treasure hunting in their book *The Outer Limits of Edgar Cayce's Power*. It appears that motivation is a key factor in practical application of psychic ability—and not simply the motivation that psychologists usually refer to, that of making the subject interested in the task. Cayce maintained that motivation at the spiritual level is important as well. People with a desire to serve often did quite well with the Cayce readings. Those with selfish motives often wasted a great deal of time searching for treasure, oil, or whatever, without success.

Although experimental demonstration of psi has not been my primary concern at Atlantic University, I have conducted a few remote-viewing experiments. These were not intended to be rigorous proof of clairvoyance, but rather to give attendees at A.R.E. conferences an opportunity to experience clairvoyance for themselves. Unlike the more formal experiments with a single subject, my experiments involved hundreds of participants, all trying to view the same target. While it was not possible to obtain statistically useful results from a situation like this, the drawings made by the participants told us some interesting things about the way psychic ability functions.

A bias was very evident in the types of drawings the people created. The targets were all locations in the city of Virginia Beach. Although I never chose the beach itself as the target, many people made beach drawings. Such a response can be considered a form of "psychic noise," in which rational expectations interfere with psychic perception. That is, many people, asked to come up with an image of a target in Virginia Beach, have images enter their minds based on what they expect to find when they come to visit. When you are experimenting with clairvoyance yourselves, it is worth keeping in mind that it is the unusual images, not the logical ones, that probably contain the psychic information.

Another discovery that I made, confirming the observations by Targ and Puthoff, was that people rarely perceived the entire target scene. Instead, they selectively described certain parts of it. They also symbolically distorted the images. A good example of this occurred when the target was the computer keyboard on which I was typing (as I am doing now). From my point of view, it was a keyboard with two hands moving on it. One of the responses in the experiment was a pair of hands playing a piano keyboard! Right image, wrong kind of keyboard. Perhaps the person doing the drawing was a musician, not a writer, and "translated" the image into one that made sense to her. In another experiment, one woman drew two arches. In written comments she said that she thought the target was the inside of a church and that these arches were the windows. Actually, the target was the golden arches sign in front of a well-known fast-food restaurant! Again, right image, wrong interpretation. Trying to combine the images with logical interpretation rarely works; this is information received at another level, and our attempts to rationalize it usually just inhibit it.

The Ganzfeld Experiments

One of the most reliable experimental clairvoyance techniques is known as the ganzfeld technique. "Ganzfeld" means "whole field" in German. The term refers to a procedure that limits input to the senses in an effort to induce an altered state of consciousness conducive to clairvoyant imagery. In a ganzfeld experiment, the subject lies in a recliner chair, with halves of Ping-Pong balls taped over his eyes and a light shining on the balls. This results in a uniform visual blur. He wears headphones with white noise (like the sound of ocean surf) to mask any outside noise. Under these conditions, many people tend to enter an altered state of consciousness, in which they see visions and hear sounds.

Meanwhile, a person in another room looks at a picture and attempts to "send" it to the subject. The subject gives a running commentary into a tape recorder about his/her thoughts, sounds, and visual images. Following the experiment, the subject judges which one of a group of pictures was the actual target picture. Sometimes an independent judge is used, who listens to the tape and chooses the picture that seems most relevant to the descriptions given by the subject.

Charles Honorton's Psychophysical Research Laboratories in Princeton, New Jersey, originated this popular technique. Like any experiment in parapsychology, ganzfeld experiments do not always produce evidence for psychic abilities. But Honorton has analyzed the results from many ganzfeld experiments and come up with a set of conditions that tend to make the experiment successful. These are important, because they are the opposite of the conditions used in many mainstream psychology experiments, and frequently in studies by parapsychologists. First, the experimenter should work with subjects *individually;* large-group tests are rarely successful. Second, the subject should devote time to individual targets; rushing through an experiment does not help, but *immediate feedback* on how they did on each target does help. Third, *more interesting targets* lead to better results; especially good were "dynamic" targets—short video segments as opposed to simple pictures. Fourth, subjects generally did better if they were allowed to have a *friend* as the sender. Finally, subjects selected because they did well in a preliminary experiment tended to do better than unselected subjects; in other words, some people just seem to have a *talent* for these experiments.

To summarize, a personal connection between the sender and receiver, dynamic, interesting targets, and natural ability help to make an experiment successful. These are the same features that we see repeatedly in spontaneous experiences—emotional connections and needs. It is amazing that experimenters for years paid little attention to these influences on success. They had neglected the human part of psychic functioning.

Working with Clairvoyant Abilities

Can we put together our knowledge from experiences and experiments to help a person work with clairvoyant ability? As with telepathy, there will be times where spontaneous clairvoyance is immediately helpful and times where it is very frustrating because there appears to be no opportunity to help someone in need. It is useful to think of these experiences as examples of connectedness. Taking some action is important if you want to grow personally, learn more about your psychic ability, and help others. But the options for action are quite varied. Sometimes an action will come naturally—it will feel "just right." But at other times, as with the telepathic experiences in the previous chapter, you may be unsure which action will be most productive.

Try thinking of clairvoyant experiences as an opportunity for self-examination, rather than as something that requires action related to someone else. Follow up on the experience by examining the outcome of the situation you visualized or sensed. Was your perception complete or did it focus only on key details? How do these details relate to your own personality or goals? Was there an element of projection—aspects of yourself attributed to someone else or something in the environment? You may need to step back from the individual experiences and look for patterns. The most useful way to interpret a particular experience may be as a stimulation to self-exploration.

In later chapters we will look more deeply into the meaning of psychic experiences for spiritual transformation. But here, let's just have a little fun with remote viewing as a tool for self-exploration. The best way to learn about clairvoyance is to try it yourself.

Whether or not you have ever had a spontaneous experience, anyone can experiment with remote viewing. Unlike ganzfeld, it requires no special equipment, simply a pencil and a piece of paper.

Instructions for Remote Viewing

This is a "home version" of the remote-viewing experiments performed in laboratories around the country. This is not a "test"—it won't "prove" whether or not you have clairvoyant ability. Instead it is an opportunity to explore the types of imagery that emerge from the unconscious when you deliberately set aside your sensory experiences and rational processes. Such personal exploration of the unconscious can be valuable even if you do not have any verifiable clairvoyant perception. It is also a very safe way to begin to explore your capabilities, since it requires no induction of an altered state of consciousness such as hypnosis or meditation. The images are allowed to come into consciousness naturally.

Work with a partner, who will be the "agent"—this is a person to focus on to guide you to the location; you can think of him or her as the "sender," but you don't have to. This technique allows for the possibility of clairvoyance or telepathy. You can try focusing on a distant location without a partner, but research has shown that the personal connection yields better results.

Make up a pool of several possible target locations. The agent can choose the target from the pool by some random method—rolling dice to select from a pool of twelve targets, for example. It will help the spontaneity of the situation if you as the receiver do not know what the possible targets in the pool are.

While your partner is traveling to the location, relax in a place with as few distractions as possible. Have a sheet of blank paper and a pencil and sketch whatever impressions come to you. Don't try to figure out what the target is intellectually—this interrupts the flow of impressions. Just write down, either in pictures or in words, whatever comes to mind. Then take a break, look around the room for a few minutes. After the break, refocus on your remote viewing and add any new impressions that you may have gotten. Don't erase what you have already written; your first impressions may not make immediate sense, but they may be correct perceptions of a portion of the target.

When your partner returns, discuss your impressions. In a formal experiment, you would be asked to choose which of the possible targets in the pool was the real one. This, however, is a learning situation. So visit the target site and look for similarities with your imagery. Repeat this procedure several times to learn the internal cues that may tell you whether or not an impression is clairvoyant.

How can you interpret your results from such experiments? Often people seek an "ESP Test," similar to a math test, which will pronounce them "psychic." But psychic ability doesn't work that way, any more than trying to play a trombone the first time you were handed one would be a fair test of your musical ability. As studies by parapsychologists have shown, the more meaningful the target, and the closer you are tied emotionally to the experiment, the more likely you are to succeed. Edgar Cayce added to that the importance of positive action and the importance of a desire to be of true service. These are qualities parapsychologists have generally not tapped in experiments. But they are certainly aspects you can experiment with yourself. Be creative in devising situations where clairvoyance might be beneficial. I would not recommend things involving money—emotional impact and genuine interest seem to be the important factors, not material gain.

When working with clairvoyance, you also need to

work on discernment of what is not clairvoyance. Most of the time, for most people, images come primarily from within—they are memories and fantasies. We should never underestimate the power of imagination. That is why testing in everyday experience is so important. Never *assume* an image is psychic. Attempt to apply your intuition constructively, maintaining an awareness of the problems of projection and wishful thinking. You may find that even if a particular image comes primarily from within, it can be a creative inspiration leading to a productive accomplishment. Not all insights need to be psychic.

Is this approach "scientific"? Yes, in the sense that it is derived from testing, both in the experience of psychics like Edgar Cayce and in the experiments of parapsychologists like Stephan Schwartz and Charles Honorton. But emotional connections and significant meaning are different for every individual and cannot be specified by science. They can only be arrived at through a process of personal introspection. In this chapter we have begun with a simple introspective exercise. Successive chapters will build on your increasing awareness of the unique processes and imagery of your unconscious mind.

CHAPTER 3
Precognition

Question: Is the prediction true that I will die suddenly, at the age of 80, in Tibet?
Answer: If you go to Tibet and live to be 80 you may die there! This depends on many, many, MANY circumstances. You will not die in Tibet unless you go there; and there's not the prospect now of going there.

—Edgar Cayce, Reading 2067–3

Most of us at some time want foreknowledge of events to come; some of us may dwell obsessively on the future. We have seen that telepathy and clairvoyance are common psychic experiences. Yet when people say someone is psychic, they are often speaking of what parapsychologists call *precognition*, the ability to sense or predict the future. To our Western worldview, precognition is even stranger to comprehend than telepathy or clairvoyance. Even telepathy and clairvoyance do not really violate any laws of physics. It is certainly conceivable that we could discover the energy that transmits these forms of psychic impressions. Precognition, however, clashes mightily with our traditional concepts of how the world works. The cause—a future event—comes *after* the effect—a precognitive experience. This reversal of cause and effect is disturbing philosophically. The Gallup poll did not even ask a question on precognition. Yet

77 percent of the 520 people in my research survey of
A.R.E. members reported precognitive experiences.

Precognition can also be disturbing when you experience it yourself. Although we say we would like to
know the future, we often fear future knowledge. Who
really wants to know the time of his or her death?
While knowledge of a positive future event can be
reassuring, we often want to know how to *prevent*
traumatic events such as deaths and disasters. Foreseeing an event without the ability to prevent it can lead
to a great deal of guilt and questioning. Is the future
fixed and determined, or can I alter it with my free
will? Here is an example, reported by a thirty-five-
year-old man who has found precognition to be a
mixed blessing:

A Last Good-bye. My wife and I were leaving her
parents' house. We said our good-byes and were about
to go out the door when my wife went to say good-
bye to her Afghan Hound. I looked at her [the dog]
and something clicked in my head when the dog's eyes
and mine met. I knew at that instant that I would not
see her dog alive again. So I went over to her [the
dog] and petted her, and I saw in her eyes the same
feeling I felt. I never petted her dog good-bye, except
that night. She died at about 11:00 P.M. that night. I
did not tell my wife about this, because I did not want
to get her upset in case I was wrong. But this time I
was right. There have been too many instances where
I have been right, especially when it includes disasters,
such as air crashes, train wrecks, and whatever. A few
times I have mentioned this to my wife, but mostly I
keep it to myself. I started to scare myself by the
accuracy of my predicting, and when my wife's dog
died, I decided to try and quit predicting. It has mostly
worked but I do still get occasional flashes of future
events. And it still scares me.

All too often people keep such experiences to themselves for fear of ridicule. Yet the pattern fits with what we have seen with other psychic experiences. As with the typical telepathic and clairvoyant experiences, this glimpse into the future occurred in connection with a close family situation, here in regard to a pet rather than a person, but one with strong emotional ties. Like many psychic experiences, it involved a transition from life to something beyond.

If this had been the man's only precognitive experience, he might have written it off to coincidence. Yet he has had numerous other experiences as well. Like this man, many people with precognitive experiences learn not to share them with other people. While knowing telepathically of a death at the time it happens may be distressing, knowing of a death *before* it happens may be even more frightening. Guilt and fear often go along with precognitive experiences—guilt that you were not able to prevent the event and even fear that you might have actually *caused* the event by your thoughts. Still, the life disruption caused by precognitive experiences can also be an opportunity for transformation.

In Judeo-Christian religious history, the ability to see the future has been the province of those with divine connections. Prophecy is seen as a gift of God. The biblical prophets were not speculating on the future or guessing about it; their claim was to information from divine revelation. On the other side, we have divination and augury, from astrology to the reading of sheep entrails. These practices for predicting the future were typically rejected by the Jewish and Christian faiths. Many other ancient cultures, however, have practiced these arts; the Greeks used the oracle at Delphi, and the Chinese practiced divination with the I Ching.

Regardless of the religious attitude toward the prediction of the future, our modern Western culture often considers it to be superstition, a relic of an unenlightened past. But despite the prevailing social attitude, precognitive experiences are common, everyday occurrences that can be harnessed for good and offer a window into the processes of our unconscious minds.

In this chapter we will explore the varieties of precognitive experiences and work with the question of free will and changing the future.

Varieties of Precognitive Experiences

Precognitive experiences, though they always relate to a future event, are as varied in form as telepathic and clairvoyant experiences. Sometimes there is just a "knowing" that something will happen. At other times there is a sensory impression, a "vision," of what is to come. With some experiences there is clearly an opportunity to take an action. With others it is not clear what action could be taken. Here are two examples in which the precognition involved a strong feeling, one much more problematic than the other.

> *Unexpected Visitors.* At the age of nine I told my mother she would have visitors, today, that she hadn't seen for a long time. They arrived from Ohio at noon. We were in Virginia.

> *A Drowning Foreseen.* When a close friend visited me I had a strong feeling I would never see him again, all through his visit. I did or said nothing as I couldn't believe my intuition. About three weeks after he left for his home I had a call saying he had drowned.

Here the experiences took the form of a strong feeling. In the first, a nine-year-old girl felt no inhibitions about announcing the arrival of visitors.

Children are often naive about psychic ability—it is as natural as any other form of knowledge—and the foreknowledge of visitors was not threatening. In the second experience, a seventy-year-old woman related this fear-provoking event connected to a death. It led to denial, as she could not believe her intuition. Following the drowning it likely led to some guilt feelings as well. Could she have prevented the drowning?

As do clairvoyance and telepathy, precognition brings uncertainty. Should we take action on our visions and intuitions, even if we often find them to be faulty? We all know people who are constantly "catastrophizing"—imagining terrible events (that usually don't come to pass) and becoming exhausted through worrying. Others just ignore possible precognitive hunches and visions, only to feel guilt and regret when they turn out to be true. In this chapter we explore ways to make these decisions, but first let's look some more at the types of experiences people report.

Some precognitive experiences are more sensory— they mimic the ordinary senses. Here is one, from a thirty-four-year-old woman, that involved a vision:

> *The Flat Tire.* While in a relaxed state of mind I had a "vision" of the right rear tire of our vehicle blowing out. Our tires were new. I dismissed the thought. It was the day my husband and I were returning from our honeymoon. Shortly after getting on the highway there was a loud bang and the van was a challenge to control. As my husband guided us to safety, he asked, "What was that?" I was able to tell him without looking back.

Had she taken action at the time of the vision, this precognitive experience could have been put to good, practical use. But, as is often the case, the woman was not sure enough at the time to take action and realized only in retrospect that her vision was precognitive.

The following experience, another sensory impression, was positive, a welcome contrast to the ones involving crisis or death. Here there was a vision of a birth.

> *A Birth Foreseen.* On July 10, 1988, my daughter gave birth to her first baby, a son. Over a year ago I was meditating, holding a crystal in front of a candle. After I had been meditating for about three minutes I saw a small face. The face grew larger and soon it was a little baby. I knew it was my daughter—that she was going to have a baby. When she was about two months along my daughter came to visit me to give me her good news. I did not tell her that I already knew. When my grandson was born I went to the hospital to see him and it was the very same perfect baby that I saw when I was meditating. Later I told my daughter that I knew that she was going to have a baby and that I saw the baby in my meditation a little over one month before she conceived.

In this report the experience was apparently not completely spontaneous. Crystal gazing has a long history as a technique to induce visions. Meditation, too, can awaken psychic abilities. But is this truly precognition? Daughters often have babies. As with the cases of telepathy that we looked at, wishful thinking could have played a role here. The vision in the crystal, however, was of the actual baby, not just any baby. Still, children often resemble their parents, so the woman may have had an unconscious image of the looks of her daughter's baby.

Is It Really Precognition?

How can you tell if an experience is precognition or not? The alternative is that you may be using knowledge that you *already* consciously or unconsciously possess to predict the future. Of course, we do this all the time. It is logical inference, the "normal" way of dealing with the future. Conscious planning is not often mistaken for precognition—we are generally aware when we are thinking about future probable events. But unconscious inference is different—we may not be aware of any rational thought process, but an intuition about the future may suddenly spring into consciousness. Here are a couple of examples in which unconscious inference is a more plausible explanation than precognition. First, a woman predicted damage from a hurricane.

A Dangerous Hurricane. I had a feeling of impending doom when I saw Hurricane Camille out in the Gulf on a weather report. Was very concerned about my grandmother's home in Ocean Springs, Mississippi and her. She was evacuated but her home and property, everything she owned, were destroyed in the storm by wind and water.

This could have contained an element of precognition, yet most of us, knowing a relative was in the path of a storm, might have a feeling of impending doom and *consciously* infer damage to the relative's home.

In the next example, a man felt that he was able to predict events on television.

A TV "Guide"? M*A*S*H is a favorite TV show of mine. Over the last few years a scene from a particular episode will flash into my mind without prompting and that night or the next night it will be the one broadcast. A few times while watching sports events I will get a strong impression that a certain play will occur and does almost immediately. This has happened maybe ten or fifteen times overall.

Now if a person had images from shows he had *never seen before* appearing on television the next night, we might want to consider precognition. But this man states that he is a fan of *M*A*S*H*. The reruns have been going on for years and are often shown in a sequence close to the original. There could easily be enough unconscious knowledge of the sequence of the shows to allow prediction. Similarly, with the plays in sporting events, part of the challenge of the game is to predict what the other team will do. Experts, especially those familiar with a given team, are often able to infer the strategy for the next play.

So how can you tell if your sense of the future is truly precognition or simply inference? There is no rule you can follow, nor any clear dividing line. The less likely that you could have known about the event beforehand, the more likely it is precognition. But just because a prediction is inference, either conscious or unconscious, does not make it any less valuable. We are educated to think rationally and to ignore our intuition. Yet intuition is paying attention to the messages from your unconscious. Important ones often have a powerful emotion attached. Whether that intuition is precognition or unconscious inference, it is a potentially valuable guide for our lives. Edgar Cayce actually considered intuition to be the highest form of psychic ability. In a reading given for a group seeking psychic and spiritual development, he said, "The *intuitive* forces . . . make for rather the safer, the saner, the more spiritual way. . . . Hence, *intuitive* force is the better, for in this there may come more the union of the spirit of truth with Creative Energy" (Reading 261–15).

Before we explore ways to work with precognition personally, let's take a look at what parapsychologists have learned about it.

Parapsychologists Study Precognition

Although precognition was traditionally the "skill" of psychics, initially parapsychologists were somewhat reluctant to study it. It conflicted too much with philosophical concepts of causality. But once they had accumulated some evidence that clairvoyance and telepathy were real phenomena, J. B. Rhine's group at Duke expanded its scope to look at precognition. The collections of spontaneous experiences at the Society for Psychical Research were full of apparent precognition. Having shown that clairvoyance and telepathy are apparently independent of *distance*, the Duke group began looking into the question of whether *time* is a limiting condition in the functioning of ESP.

They designed the precognition experiments to parallel the telepathy and clairvoyance experiments, using the same five-symbol, twenty-five-card deck. For initial tests they used the Down Through procedure, in which the subject wrote on the record sheet the order of the twenty-five card symbols down through the deck, without looking at the cards. The difference in a precognition test is that the cards were shuffled (by someone else) *after* the subject wrote down the guesses. Thus the subject needed to predict a *future* order of the cards. In the first published precognition article by J. B. Rhine, in 1938, he concluded that they had highly significant evidence of ESP.

For virtually every type of clairvoyance experiment they had devised, they were able to create a precognition version where the targets were selected *after* the subject wrote down his/her guesses. Overall, the precognitive effects were very small—slight deviations from chance—but over thousands of card guesses highly statistically significant.

Since the early days in Rhine's laboratory, parapsychologists have conducted hundreds of studies of precognition. Charles Honorton, who pioneered the ganzfeld experiments in the study of clairvoyance, and his associate Diane Ferrari, reviewed all the precognition experiments performed between 1935 (the early days of Rhine's lab) and 1987—a total of 309 studies by 62 investigators, involving more than 50,000 subjects! They were looking, first, for overall evidence that precognition exists and, second, for factors influencing its behavior. They studied what are known as "forced-choice" experiments, those in which the subject must make a choice among a limited number of alternatives—for example, guessing whether a coin will come up heads or tails. Overall, the precognitive effect is small but reliable. People do not score very high in forced-choice precognition studies, but they do score consistently above chance. When the results of all these studies are combined, in what is known as "meta-analysis," the result is extremely significant statistically.

Honorton and Ferrari looked carefully at a number of factors that might have produced spurious results, among them quality of controls, randomization of targets, and care in recording results. They found that the results were equally strong even with the tightest possible controls.

They also looked at factors relating to the experimental situation and the motivation of the subject. As with the ganzfeld experiments, they found that separate testing of individuals led to better results than group testing. Working with people selected for psychic ability led to better results than working with people off the street (known in parapsychology as "unselected subjects"). They also made two further discoveries that are very important for understanding precognition. First, they found that *feedback* to the subjects on their performance led to better results. This is not surprising, since this would also be the case in tests of ordinary sensory perception. People do better when they are able to learn whether they were correct. Reality testing—comparison with the actual future situation—is important in working with your precognitive experiences as well.

They also found that the time interval between the prediction and the future event is a significant factor. Longer time intervals resulted in less accurate precognition. This effect, however, did not hold for the subjects who had been preselected for psychic ability. Honorton and Ferrari concluded that the decline may have been attributable to lowered motivation over long time delays, rather than to an intrinsic inability of precognition to see into the far future.

Recall the remote-viewing experiments in the clairvoyance chapter, where subjects could report images or feelings and make drawings, rather than having to choose a specific target. The group at the Princeton Engineering Anomalies Research Laboratory (PEAR)—Robert Jahn, Brenda Dunne, and Roger Nelson—have extended the free-response remote-viewing experiments to include what they call "precognitive remote perception." The experimental situation is very similar to that in clairvoyant remote viewing, in which a person attempts to perceive a remote location. For clairvoyance, the person tries to describe the target location at the same time that the agent is actually visiting that location. For the precognitive version of this experiment, the person tries to describe the target before the agent visits it—in fact, before a target location has even been selected. Jahn and his colleagues used a variety of time delays, ranging from less than one hour to more than twenty-four hours. They also had distances in space ranging from less than twenty-five miles to more than one thousand miles. In their results, they found the precognitive procedure to work as well as the clairvoyant one, producing highly statistically significant results. Neither time nor distance had any apparent effect.

What does precognition actually perceive? Is it an event that *must* occur, implying a predetermined future? Or is it one of a number of dynamically shifting *possible* futures? The question of whether precognition predicts actual or possible futures bears on the long-standing philosophical issue of free will versus determinism. Parapsychologist Dean Radin, now at the University of Nevada, conducted a study suggesting that precognition consists of an awareness of the pool of possible or probable futures. In his experiment, the probabilities of particular targets' being selected from a pool were changed randomly in a computer. Using himself as subject, Radin was sometimes successful in predicting the correct target. But even more interesting, his *errors* suggested an awareness of the *probability* of a target being selected, even when he missed the actual target. This could be interpreted as awareness not just of the actual future but of the other possible futures as well. A single experiment like this is never conclusive in parapsychology, but it is an example of the kinds of studies parapsychologists are carrying out to study the free will issue. Meanwhile, since they are unlikely to have the definitive answer in the near future (a prediction of mine!), we will look at ways in which you can work with understanding your own possible precognitive experiences.

Working with Precognition and Free Will

Your strategy for working with a precognitive experience will depend on whether it is an occasional episode or a repetitive episode. An occasional episode may be a once-in-a-lifetime event. With repetitive episodes, on the other hand, there is an opportunity to work with the issue of free will versus determinism as it applies in your own life and transform the nature of your psychic process.

Occasional Episodes

Occasional episodes offer the possibility for immediate action and the opportunity for later confirmation and reflection. If, at some time after reading this book you have a strong sense of premonition, what should you do? I suggest that you act on your intuition, unless it conflicts with your ethical principles or ideals. If you have a strong sense that you shouldn't go somewhere because an accident will happen, don't go. And if you "just know" that you need to warn someone, warn that person. On the other hand, use some common sense. A woman once came to my office because she had a vision of a disaster on the Norfolk Naval Base. She then called the Navy with the same message— they thought she was a terrorist making a threat! Luckily she told them to call me, and I confirmed that it was just a psychic impression (and in this case, the event didn't occur). And don't spend your month's paycheck on the lottery because you just have a feeling that you will win. But if your intuitive feeling is strong about an event, and you have a chance to take positive action that will be of service to someone, seize the opportunity. If you are acting from a desire to be of true service, it is possible that you will be mildly embarrassed if the event doesn't come to pass, but you may be of significant help. You need not be concerned about whether your intuition is "psychic." Unconscious inference is probably more common, and at least as effective, as true precognition. Learn to trust your unconscious promptings.

Whatever action you choose to take following an experience you think is precognitive, follow it up by *reality testing*. Did the event actually happen the way you envisioned that it would? Was your precognition only partially true—perhaps displaced in time and space? For example, you might have had a precognitive glimpse of an auto accident, but it happened next month, not next week as you had envisioned. Or perhaps your strong feeling didn't manifest as an event at all—perhaps your intuition referred to some internal anxiety rather than to a future event. Don't be dismayed if you find you can't identify any unusual characteristics about the precognitive experience, except in hindsight. While some people find strong cues about an experience, others—myself included—recognize these experiences only after the fact.

Sometimes the feeling is not strong enough to spur you into action. Only afterward do you become aware that your experience was precognitive. If the event was not major, perhaps it simply aroused your curiosity about the occurrence of psychic phenomena. But for a major event—an accident, a death—the most common response is a feeling of guilt: "Why wasn't I able to prevent this terrible accident?"

A belief in free will can sometimes lead to feelings of guilt. When I receive phone calls about problem psychic experiences, one of the most frequent subjects is guilt over precognitive experiences. One form of guilt occurs when the person has a precognitive experience of some crisis, a death or an accident perhaps, and does not act on the experience for some reason.

Perhaps he or she has never had a precognitive experience before and puts it down to an overactive imagination. Perhaps he fears ridicule and tells no one. Perhaps he didn't want to scare anyone with dire warnings. Perhaps he simply didn't realize it was precognition. Whatever the reason, he feels guilty, responsible for not having warned someone. In general, this guilt is misplaced. People assume that the meaning of the precognitive experience was a warning, to be passed on to someone else. But as we have seen with telepathy and clairvoyance, often psychic experiences are primarily a sign of *connectedness,* and nothing *can* be done. Precognitive experiences may involve tuning in to the crisis of someone else, but that doesn't always mean that the *purpose* is a warning.

We often search for the meaning of such an experience, with the assumption that the meaning is on the surface, a call to action for the specific event. Instead, the meaning may be on another level. The action called for may be to pursue the study of your own consciousness, with the choice of an emotionally powerful event as simply a way for your unconscious mind to get your attention.

Repetitive Episodes

When the precognitive episodes are repetitive, the question of free will demands attention. All too often people become paralyzed with confusion or obsessed with guilt because they are not sure how to handle their precognitive experiences.

We will look first at the issue of free will, then at the question of guilt and the "shadow" side of the personality. After that we will explore some exercises for developing the will and transforming guilt into a growth opportunity.

Precognition and Free Will

Is the future already determined or do we have free will? We have seen from these experiences and experiments that the future, at least as seen by precognition, is by no means fixed. But if we do have the ability to change the future, how can we exercise that ability?

Edgar Cayce's answer was, Through the power of the will. He said that only 20 percent of the influence in our lives can be measured by exterior signs and forces such as heredity. The remaining 80 percent is under the influence of the will. With Cayce's popular reputation as a "prophet," people are surprised to find that he was often unwilling to predict the future, as in the quotation that opened this chapter. When he did venture a prediction, he noted that it could be changed by the human will. When asked, "Will I marry so-and-so?" he was apt to reply, "You might— why not ask *her* instead of me?" Or he responded as he did to this question by a businessman:

Question: Please discuss plan and operation to cover next two years to guide me.
Answer: We wouldn't cover two days! These will have to be worked out by self and not from here. For remember, what you do TODAY reflects in what may happen tomorrow and, to be sure, bears fruit in its regular season. (Reading 257–234)

Mark Thurston, in his book *The Paradox of Power*, identifies the will as that power which makes us non-machinelike. While computers may eventually simulate the human mind, the will, one of the fundamental ingredients of the soul, sets us apart from deterministic machines and stands opposite to those impulses coming through the senses. The will is "an active principle within the soul." It is the faculty that lets us choose one act over another.

But there are problems with believing that you must make an absolute choice between determinism and free will. A belief in determinism can produce a sense of powerlessness and depression, whereas a belief in free will can produce a sense of guilt if you were not able to take action to avert a crisis.

If the future is already determined, you might say, then precognition or even planning is of no use. But the approach of William James can lead us out of this trap. James, whose book *The Varieties of Religious Experience* was recommended in the Cayce readings, is often considered the father of American psychology. What is less well known is that he suffered from depression for much of his life and was discouraged by the predominant deterministic tendency in modern Western thought. He resolved his own personal crisis by performing an experiment. He began by *assuming* that free will *does* exist, not by looking for someone else to prove it. For him, the first act of free will was to assert its reality and to live his life on that basis. He wrote in his diary in 1870, "I will assume for the present—until next year—that it is no illusion. My first act of free will shall be to believe in free will." From this act he went on to become one of the most influential thinkers in what became the modern study of consciousness.

Guilt and the Shadow

When precognitive experiences are repetitive, another form of guilt may occur. When people have repeated precognitive experiences of disasters that come true, sometimes they will become convinced that they are somehow *causing* the disasters. If you have had precognition of the deaths of several relatives, it is easy to feel very guilty about possibly causing the death of someone by imagining it. Again, it is often helpful to think of these experiences as a sign of connectedness. You have a particular sensitivity to the pain of others—you are not the cause of it.

Why do some people tend to have these experiences repeatedly? It is helpful to look at one of the components of the unconscious, termed the "shadow" by Carl Jung, and explore the ways in which it communicates with the conscious mind. As we grow and mature, we exile qualities we feel are negative to the unconscious mind. Jung called these qualities the shadow. Far from vanishing, however, they manifest in often painful ways. The Cayce material emphasizes setting an ideal, a spiritual principle to guide your life. Paradoxically, the process of setting a spiritual ideal can magnify the shadow as well, not eliminate it.

We encounter the shadow most commonly in the form of projection on someone else. We saw in the telepathy chapter that projection occurs when you unconsciously take negative qualities that you disown for yourself and attribute them to someone else. But the problem you project as being in the other person is actually part of *you*. Whenever we see negative qualities in others (and negative future events as well) that bother us excessively, it is almost certainly a projection of our shadow side.

How does this relate to the problem of guilt about precognition? Contemplating that you are the *cause* of negative events is a step between unconscious projection on others and full conscious recognition of the shadow. Many people, often those who deny their psychic experiences as well, never recognize that they have a shadow. They continue to believe that it is always the "other people" who are evil. When we begin to look at ourselves more introspectively, however, one of the first components of our unconscious that we come across is our shadow. The notion that the evil that we see outside us could be pointing at ourselves carries shock value, particularly in people with strong moral convictions. It takes courage to accept responsibility for one's shadow self.

With repetitive precognition of negative events, those who are becoming sensitive to the existence of their shadow go too far and begin to contemplate the possibility that they are causing the events. They recognize the shadow, but their moral sense pushes them into accepting guilt for events they are not responsible for.

Another way to look at the situation is that these experiences are a way the unconscious has of communicating "notice me!" The message comes through in a very powerful way. Meeting the shadow represents the first stage in integrating the overall self. But overcompensating for the shadow by being paralyzed with guilt does not lead to transformation. What kind of positive action can be taken?

One approach is to stop dwelling on the guilt and focus instead on something else. Become grounded in service. Instead of worrying about what you could have done to prevent a disaster, or whether you caused a disaster, do something useful or loving for someone. Harmon Bro's advice for dealing with the shadow, in his book *Edgar Cayce on Religion and Psychic Experience,* is to learn how to "convert hostility to courage, violence to vigor, and aggression to boldness." The other approach, which can be used in conjunction with the first, is to try to communicate with your unconscious. Take the position that the actual precognition was simply a convenient vehicle to wake you up to an issue regarding yourself. Speak to your unconscious and ask it for information that will help resolve the problem. The next chapter, on psychic dreams, will go into more detail on communication with the unconscious.

Working with the Will and Precognition

How do we resolve the problem of free will versus determinism in precognition? It is helpful to look on precognitive experiences as a special case of our general approach to the way we deal with the future. Here are some exercises for working with the will, adapted from Mark Thurston's *The Paradox of Power* and other sources, which may be of help in dealing with precognitive experiences.

Reduce Precognitive Experiences. Sometimes people simply feel overwhelmed by precognitive experiences. They find themselves dwelling on these glimpses of the future, to the detriment of their lives in the present. A helpful exercise is "Staying in the Now," in which you use the capacity of your will not to deal with the future but to refocus your attention in the present. This is an exercise used in many spiritual traditions. It will help you to limit your precognitive experiences to those that you can productively work with.

Carefully observe your thought patterns. Do you constantly anticipate the future, dwelling on scenarios that may not even happen? Do you fill your thoughts with anxiety-driven visualizations about the future, such as a showdown with the boss or a car accident? You may be wasting mental energy and exhausting your will. Instead, when you find yourself dwelling on the crisis that might occur in the future, gently return your thoughts to the present, focusing on what you are doing now. This can be difficult; in some spiritual traditions years of meditation are spent learning to focus on the present moment. But even a small amount of attention to the present may help in reducing anxiety about the future. When your unconscious mind sees that you are not willing to be "dragged into the future," it will respond to your new attitude by providing the experiences that you need for growth.

Choose and Exercise Your Spiritual Ideal. If you do decide to work with your precognitive experiences, consciously choosing an ideal is an exercise that Edgar Cayce strongly recommended. A spiritual ideal is your concept of the highest values to which you aspire. A single word may express it—love, Christ, Buddha—or whatever you hold as the highest possible realization. To exercise this spiritual ideal, Cayce recommended the setting of mental and physical ideals. By "mental ideal" is meant the ideal mental attitude to hold regarding all persons and experiences—relationships to self, home, friends, and enemies. The physical ideal is the material expression of the spiritual and mental ideals. What are you actually going to *do*? As an example, you might have a precognitive experience that a friend was going to suffer a car accident. If your spiritual ideal is love, how can you show love? Mentally, it is certainly not by worrying—perhaps you can focus on thoughts that will avert the accident. As we will see in the chapter on psychokinesis, there is strong evidence that thoughts have the power to directly affect the material world. But you can also exercise your physical ideal and take direct action, perhaps by suggesting that the friend take extra care in driving that day.

Exercise Your Free Will Step by Step. You don't have to start right out by preventing an earthquake. Look for little ways to apply your precognitive intuitions in your daily life. Even if you don't have strong precognitive experiences, each day choose an intuition that you can apply. You may think of a friend you haven't seen for a while: Write a letter to that friend. Or you may sense that someone you know could use some help.

Give that person a call on the phone; don't force your interpretation, just offer to help with whatever is needed. Reflect on the results of this experiment. What cues seem to lead to productive insights?

Develop Patience. Patience is another important element of the process. Precognition may open your eyes to *patterns* of change (whereas telepathy and clairvoyance present a more static view of the world). Patience is not passivity or indifference to the pace of change but rather the willingness to endure unresolved tension in the service of later transformation. It is an extension of the "staying in the now" exercise, focusing not on the future but on being aware and alive *now*. To improve your precognitive glimpses, you must apply yourself to the best of your ability in the area in which you are now working. Don't expect precognition to make up for laziness.

Part of the process of growth is to experiment with your own abilities. You will probably make mistakes and not all apparently precognitive experiences will prove out, but these are learning opportunities. As with telepathy and clairvoyance, you will learn from the feedback of reality testing.

Explore the Higher Will. Consider also the possibility of a greater purpose in these experiences. That is, they may not only point to a specific situation but also offer a comment on the nature of reality and your purpose in life. This transcendent aspect of psychic experiences and the need to balance the personal will with the higher will, will be considered in detail in the final section of this book. The Cayce readings encourage us to use fully at a personal level all that we have at hand before expecting a higher power to intervene. But for now, do not overlook the possibility of a higher meaning to even the most mundane experience.

CHAPTER 4
Psychic Dreams

"He's dreaming now," said Tweedledee: "and what do you think he's dreaming about?"

Alice said "Nobody can guess that."

"Why, about *you*!" Tweedledee exclaimed, clapping his hands triumphantly. "And if he left off dreaming about you, where do you suppose you'd be?"

"Where I am now, of course," said Alice.

"Not you!" Tweedledee retorted contemptuously. "You'd be nowhere. Why, you're only a sort of thing in his dream. . . . You know very well you're not real."

"I *am* real!" said Alice.

—Lewis Carroll, *Through the Looking-Glass*

Can dream events be "real"? When people recall psychic experiences, dreams often stand out as the most convincing personal evidence of the reality of psychic phenomena. Waking psychic experiences must push their way into conscious awareness, past the thoughts and activities of daily life. Images that seem irrational are often suppressed and forgotten. Dreams, on the other hand, can compensate for the rational mind with a wealth of imagery that overcomes conscious inhibitions. Images that might normally be disregarded by the conscious mind often appear with great power in dreams. Many of us rarely remember our dreams, but some dreams are too compelling to disregard.

Volumes have been written on dream interpretation, focusing on techniques for puzzling out the meaning of the confusing symbols that appear in our nightly sojourns. But while these books offer a wealth of information on learning from the unconscious, they often neglect the psychic component. All of the types of psychic experiences we have seen in the book thus far—telepathy, clairvoyance, precognition—are found in dreams. Indeed, dreams are often the source of the most striking and memorable psychic experiences. In John Palmer's survey of the townspeople of Charlottesville, 36 percent had a dream containing some type of ESP. In my Atlantic University survey of 520 A.R.E. members, 62 percent reported having had psychic dreams. When we look at collections of cases from other parapsychology laboratories, we see a similar pattern. Robert Van de Castle, one of the foremost researchers on psychic dreams (as well as a successful subject in experimental studies of psychic dreaming), looked at all the case reports and collections from a large number of laboratories and concluded that somewhere between 33 and 69 percent of all case reports consisted of psychic dreams.

There is a difficulty that confronts us when we look at psychic dreams. Although dreams may be the most significant source of psychic experiences, *most* dreams are *not* psychic. They deal with other psychological and physical aspects of the dreamer. Edgar Cayce saw dreams as the most natural way to expand psychic awareness, but he cautioned against interpreting every dream as telepathic, clairvoyant, or precognitive, since this narrow focus would cause us to miss valuable insights from our dreams that do not fit into the category of "psychic."

Dreams are complex and worthy of lifelong study. They can be a key element in self-transformation.

Here, however, my focus is intentionally limited to dreams with an extrasensory component. This chapter will look at the various types of psychic dreams, explore the complexities of literal and symbolic interpretation, and offer suggestions on discerning the psychic elements in dreams and applying them in daily life.

Varieties of Psychic Dreams

First, let's look at some examples of the various types of psychic dreams sent in to my research project. Remember that these are only a very small percentage of the dreams a person may have. For some people they are a once-in-a-lifetime event. For others they may occur on a regular, but unpredictable, basis. Some of the dreams are clear, literal images of an actual event. Others are symbolic or contain both literal and symbolic elements. Still others mix more than one event. In the examples below I have categorized psychic dreams into three types: literal, displacement (meaning a confusion of two events), and symbolic. Here are two dreams to introduce you to the mixture of literal and symbolic information often seen in dreams.

One woman reported the following dream to us:

> *Fire in a Restaurant.* I dreamed of a fire in a restaurant with a large crystal chandelier in the main restaurant area. The restaurant was on the other side of a river that I had to cross to get there. Two days later I saw on the news a picture of the chandelier in a restaurant that had caught fire. The restaurant was in Kentucky on the Ohio River. I live in Ohio. I know this was the restaurant I had seen in my dream.

Her dream is an example of a clairvoyant dream that can be interpreted literally; the image of the crystal chandelier stands out, and the other details she reported, the restaurant and the river, correspond to the actual situation. But what could she have done with this dream? Could she have prevented the fire? Could she have warned someone not to go to the restaurant? There also may be a deeper symbolic meaning, since such symbols as fire, crystal, and rivers often appear in dreams that have no psychic component and refer to inner issues.

The correspondence between dream events and actual events can be less literal. Seventy years ago a young stockbroker told the following dream to Edgar Cayce and asked for an interpretation:

> *Don't Buy Radio.* Dreamed a man was trying to sell me a radio. Then someone put poison on the doorknob of my door and urged me to come and touch it. I was terribly frightened. He tried to force me to touch the poisoned knob. Struggling, I awakened in a cold sweat. (Reading 137–17)

Cayce interpreted this dream as precognitive, reflecting actual conditions that were to arise but with a symbolic message. He said, "The presentation of a sale attempting to be made of radio refers to the deal that will be offered the individual in radio stocks . . . The presentation of the poison being placed by someone on the door represents the condition . . . if the body were to accept or invest in . . . corporations or stocks, of that nature. Hence the warning . . .—next sixteen to twenty days: Do not invest in stocks, bonds, or any conditions pertaining to radio activity work."

Having Edgar Cayce to interpret dreams personally is a resource we no longer have available. Yet by diligently working with our own dreams, we can apply the principles he used, and the experiences of others, to achieve insight.

Literal Dreams

Although the approaches of such figures as Sigmund Freud and Carl Jung emphasize the symbolism in dreams, a surprising number of dreams seem to picture situations literally. Edgar Cayce frequently gave dreams literal interpretations. Literal dreams may contain complete information on the event, or they may be incomplete, containing significant images but not the entire story. Here is a dream from a thirty-six-year-old woman that fits the pattern of being literally related to a serious illness; of special interest is the single image that caused the dream to stand out.

The Purple Outfit. A very disturbing dream I had on a camping trip: Upon waking, I told my sister: "You and I were waiting in the intensive care waiting room. Both of us were very distraught, and to break up the misery, I complimented you on your purple outfit." She said she didn't own a purple outfit. I told her "someone in our family was dying of cancer. It was either Mother, or her husband." As close as our family is, I couldn't understand why we were the only ones in the waiting room. Where was everyone else? In my dream, that day was day one of over seven months of this illness. Exactly one year later, our healthy mother had surgery to remove an ovarian cyst, and was found riddled with cancer. After surgery, everyone in our family met in the intensive care waiting room; my sister and I were alone while the others went down to the cafeteria, and I happened to compliment her on her purple outfit she had worn. At that moment we both remembered my dream the weekend of our camping trip (the trip verifying the date).

This dream is typical of those with literal images. The purple outfit stood out and served as a cue for remembering the dream. The entire dream was essentially a true portrayal of a future event. As we saw in an earlier chapter on precognition, such experiences can be frustrating. People ask, "What could I have done to correctly interpret the dream at the time it happened and perhaps help to change the situation?"

Like other psychic experiences, however, psychic dreams do not always deal with crisis. They can relate to other events in daily life. Here is an example of one of my own dreams with an isolated literal image. My personal psychic experiences are relatively rare, but my dream images have occasionally been so literally true that they stand out.

> *Air Freight.* When I was living in Hawaii, one night I remembered only the following fragment of a dream, "An air freight company that guarantees delivery to the mainland in two days." There was little here to work with in standard approaches to dream interpretation, and I gave it a try without much success. Air freight and guaranteeing delivery did not seem to apply to anything happening in my life at the time. About a week later I went out on a blind date; I had never met the woman and knew nothing about her. Being ill at ease in such a social situation, as many of us are, the first thing I said to her was, "Where do you work?" She replied with, "I work for an air freight company that guarantees delivery to the mainland in two days." Naturally, I told her of my dream. I was eager to share this evidence of a psychic connection. Unfortunately, she had little interest in psychic phenomena, and that was our last date as well as our first. Thus, as well as learning a little about psychic phenomena, I gained first-hand experience in the personal difficulties that attempting to communicate psychic experiences can often bring!

There is a parallel here between this experience and the one I discussed in the telepathy chapter regarding a social relationship and an unexpected encounter at a movie theater. An emotional connection exists, but we need to be careful in what we assume to be the nature of the connection. In neither example do we seem to have a case of "soul mates." The fact that a psychic connection was triggered does not automatically invest the event with great significance. This is an aspect of the polarity of separateness versus connectedness. Our psychic experiences may show us a higher form of connectedness, but that does not guarantee that we can overcome separateness at the personal level. Now, fifteen years after the event, I would say that the primary importance of this dream was to call my attention to psychic ability, not to alert me to the actual content of the experience. It also inspired me to pay more attention to *all* my dreams, since I had no way of knowing in advance which of them would be psychic.

Here is another example of one of my own dreams that turned out to be literal precognition, although it had symbolic overtones as well.

Marching in a Parade. One night I dreamed that on a Sunday morning I skipped church and was marching back and forth in a parade while an army major yelled things at me. On awakening, I tried to make sense of the symbols in this dream. Perhaps I felt too "regimented" in church. Perhaps this symbolized some kind of punishment for not attending more to spiritual concerns. I puzzled over the dream, and wrote down tentative interpretations. A few weeks later a friend asked me to join a group in a spoof of a parade, the "Gross National Parade" in Washington, DC. That Sunday morning, I skipped church and ended up marching in the "Precision Briefcase Drill Team," dressed in a suit and carrying a briefcase, while an "army major" yelled commands such as, "left shoulder, briefcases!" The dream had contained an entirely literal image of the parade.

Here we have a situation where a literal psychic image from the future could also be interpreted symbolically. I suspect this is frequently the case. The unconscious mind, trying to convey a message to the dreamer, searches for a symbol to make the point. A significant future event may have great power as a symbol. Although symbolic and literal can be seen as polar opposites, both ways of interpreting a dream may simultaneously be relevant.

Displacement Dreams

Life would certainly be simple if all dreams could be interpreted literally, but the universe and the psyche do not seem to be organized that way. Psychic dreams can at times lead you astray by containing an element or image that is literally true but is displaced in the dream to a different setting. The following two dreams illustrate this phenomenon, in which pieces of real future events are mixed with other dream material.

Harold Passes On? I was in my teens, living in Hollywood, working as an actress at Universal Studios, while visiting my mother in San Francisco. One night she awakened me from a dream where I had been bitterly crying. I was watching an R.K.O. newsreel film, where I saw in bold headlines, "Harold R—, Well Known Hollywood Agent Passes On" with the funeral procession and all! At that time I was engaged to Harold, who was also my professional agent. I told my mother I wanted to telephone him as I knew something was wrong. She discouraged me in doing so with the logic that it was 3:00 AM and he would think I was childish. A couple of days later while returning on the South Pacific night train "The Lark" with my roommate and closest friend, I said, "I'm sure Harold won't be here. I know Steve (his best friend) will meet me." Sure enough at the station, no Harold. Instead Steve greeted me with the explanation. Harold was at the hospital with his *father,* who was not expected to live through the day—having had a heart attack the very night I dreamed Harold had passed on.

Here we see one of the problems with interpreting dreams literally. The theme of the dream was literally true, and the emotional connection made a psychic interpretation plausible. But the lead character was displaced, apparently as a result of the combined emotional connections of Harold, his father, and his fiancée.

In the following dream reported by a sixty-year-old woman, we have another example of displacement, this time with a more distant relationship.

> *The Robbery.* I dreamed that a man, probably in his late twenties, came to our door in early evening. He forced his way into the front door and had a gun. He walked into the kitchen, with my daughter and her girl friend. I came out of the bedroom, clipped down the hall, and ran out the door. At the end of the driveway, he shot me from the front door.
>
> The next day I related my dream to my daughter and husband. The following night, a young man, late twenties, forced his way into the home of a neighbor three houses from me, robbed her, and forced her down the hall to get all the money she had in the house. He had a knife, but she did not see a gun. He did not injure her body, just her mind.

Again, a literal interpretation would have been unnecessarily frightening. The woman herself was not robbed or shot. Nevertheless, some of the elements of this dream were substantially true—for someone else!

Symbolic Dreams

Although literal psychic dreams are often strong personal evidence of the reality of psychic phenomena, for most people they are infrequent. When they do occur, they may be recognized only after the fact. Most dreams are filled with symbolic content. Some may at first seem to make no sense at all; others have symbols with fairly obvious interpretations. Even with dreams that prove to have a literal psychic element, don't abandon your efforts to work with the symbols. There may be many levels of meaning for you in that dream.

Early in the Bible, the importance of symbolic dreams was acknowledged. The first dream interpreter in the Bible was Joseph, in the book of Genesis. As a young shepherd boy, he had symbolic dreams of future greatness; in one dream the sun, moon, and eleven stars bowed down to him, symbolizing his family and prompting a rebuke from his father: "Shall I and thy mother and thy brethren indeed come to bow down ourselves to thee of the earth?" (Gen. 37:5–10). Even in biblical times, psychic experiences had to be shared judiciously! Joseph was sold into slavery in Egypt by his jealous brothers, but there he became known for his great ability to interpret dreams. Pharaoh himself was disturbed by a recurring dream and received an interpretation from Joseph. Pharaoh dreamed that he saw seven fat cows come up out of the Nile River and browse on the reed grass. Then seven thin cows arose from the river and devoured the seven fat cows. In the second dream, Pharaoh saw seven plump good ears of grain growing on one stalk, followed by seven thin ears blighted by the east wind. These swallowed the plump ears. Joseph's interpretation was that the seven fat cows and the seven good ears symbolized seven years of plenty. The seven thin cows and the seven thin ears meant seven years of famine. By storing the surplus grain from the seven good years, Pharaoh was able to feed Egypt during the seven years of famine.

Not all symbolic dreams have consequences as major as this one, but warning dreams are a common occurrence. One woman sent us this example:

Black—The Color of Death? I had a dream that I was going to have to go in a black stadium to get my purse from a man in black clothes. I was afraid but felt I must do it. In the dream, my husband told me a police-man could get it and I felt relieved. Within two hours I heard my husband's brother had died at the time I had the dream.

Here, after the fact, the symbols appear relevant to the death of her husband's brother—repeated images of the color black and fear. Black is not the only color that might be symbolic of death. As we will see in the chapter on apparitions, white is a color also frequently associated with spirits. The following example illustrates another way in which a dream might symbolize a death, this time from a man whose hobby was mountain climbing.

Accident in the Mountains. In 1933 I belonged to a group that went hiking and mountain climbing in the Sierras. One day we received news that two of our group—a young married couple—had not returned from a climb. A searching party was organized and left for the mountains. The same night I had this dream: I was in a big building with two wide marble staircases leading down. I followed one down to another large level. There were people reclining on a white sheet or blanket. In the middle of them sat the young couple. All were shrouded in a brilliant white light. The young woman greeted me. I sat down and she handed me a white cup of tea. It had no warmth though it seemed to steam. We talked for a while. Then the woman said, "It is time to go. For you must go up, and we must go down!" So I said goodbye and went up. That was the end of the dream. A few days later we got the news that the young couple had been found dead at the foot of the mountain.

Here the dreamer had an advantage in interpreting the dream—it was not entirely spontaneous. He was "primed" to dream of the fate of the mountain climb-ers. This dream would be given less evidential weight by parapsychologists because it need not have been psychic. There was already a fairly good chance of a serious accident. Since dreams, psychic or otherwise, usually relate to an aspect of your life, you should use your knowledge of yourself and the situation to interpret the dream, even if it is hard to know where conscious knowledge, unconscious knowledge, and psychic information separate.

As with other psychic experiences, a skeptic may reasonably ask, "Aren't these very rare and possibly due to coincidence?" Let's now take a look at the evidence parapsychologists have gathered for the reality of psychic dreams. Dream research is some of the best-documented evidence for psychic phenomena. Yale University psychology professor Irwin Child, writing in the prestigious journal *American Psychologist,* said, "The experiments at the Maimonides Medical Center on the possibility of ESP in dreams clearly merit careful attention from psychologists who, for whatever reason, are interested in the question of ESP."

Parapsychologists Study Dreams

Inspired by spontaneous cases of the types we have just seen, parapsychologists have sought more consistent ways to study psychic phenomena in dreams. They have concentrated on two areas: experiences related to psychotherapy sessions and controlled experiments.

Psychic Dreams in the Psychotherapeutic Setting

Psychic dreams are very common during psychotherapy, because therapists often work with dreams in detail, and there is a much greater opportunity for psychic information to appear that would otherwise be forgotten or ignored. These dreams may on the surface deal with events that seem trivial or meaningless, but they point the way to issues that need to be opened up in therapy. Therapists are alert for the kinds of defenses that alter and distort material as it enters consciousness.

Elizabeth Mintz, in her book *The Psychic Thread,* describes the case of "Liana," a patient who was painfully obsessed with a former lover and had a series of precognitive dreams. One day, when she had been in therapy for several months, Liana brought in a terrifying dream about her lover. She dreamed that he was in a fire in which he had been seriously burned, except for his legs, which were protected by a pair of boots. Shortly afterward Liana discovered that he actually had been caught in a fire and badly burned, except for his legs, which were protected by a pair of boots.

She had another dream that came true, in which he was shot in the shoulder, and yet another in which he was injured in an automobile accident. Liana was afraid that she was the cause of these events. But her therapist pointed out to her that her former lover was a drug addict, living on the criminal fringe, and his self-destructiveness constantly led him into dangerous situations. Her dreams were certainly precognitive, apparently due to a connectedness fostered by an obsession, but she was not the *cause* of the events. In the course of therapy, Liana gradually recovered from her obsession, and there were no more precognitive dreams. The therapist's awareness that precognition was possible allowed her to address the more central concern of Liana's obsession instead of focusing on the precognitive dreams themselves as a problem.

Patients often form strong emotional ties to therapists, known as "transference," in which they transfer their feelings about key people in their lives (such as their father) to the therapist. That is, they begin to relate to the therapist as they would to their own father. Not surprisingly, this emotional connection may result in a telepathic connection between therapist and patient. Since some forms of therapy involve dream analysis, a therapist may find that his or her own thoughts are appearing in the patient's dreams. Patients appear to unconsciously use knowledge about the therapist obtained by extrasensory means in order to elicit a greater personal interest by the therapist.

Psychiatrist Jan Ehrenwald, in the book *Dream Telepathy,* gives the example of "Ruth," who dreamed of a visit to a strange apartment and described it in detail. It was an exact description of the new apartment into which Ehrenwald himself had moved a week earlier. What prompted this dream? In a description of an earlier dream, Ruth said, "You were annoyed with me because I don't try hard enough [in therapy]. I was afraid you would drop me and say I have to stop and that further coming would be a waste of time and money."

An example that psychiatrist Montague Ullman gives in *Dream Telepathy* is that at a time when he was discussing the telepathic dreams of his patients at regular meetings of the American Society for Psychical Research, his patients were particularly likely to offer him telepathic dreams. When these meetings ceased, the incidence of telepathic dreams decreased.

Ullman notes that the more open the therapist is to the possibility of telepathy, the more likely the patient is to report telepathic dreams. "The very special situation of the patient-doctor relationship provides a strong potential bond conducive to telepathy," if the following conditions are met: "*interest* on the part of the psychiatrist; *need* on the psychiatrist's part that dovetails with the patient's need; and *anxiety* on the psychiatrist's part that dovetails with the patient's anxieties."

Psychic Dreams in the Laboratory

The most extensive experimental program on dreams was that of the Dream Laboratory at Maimonides Medical Center in New York, documented in *Dream Telepathy*. Beginning in 1962 Ullman and Stanley Krippner conducted more than ten years of experiments in what they referred to as dream "telepathy," although the experiments allowed for clairvoyance as well.

They tried to set up a situation as close to the natural psychic dream situation as they could get. They paid attention to the interpersonal relationship between the sender and the receiver, finding that a close relationship facilitated success. The dream experiment also differed from the repetitive card-guessing experiments in that a great amount of effort, an entire night, was invested in perceiving a single target. They believed the target material to be an important ingredient in the success of the experiments, especially potent, vivid, emotionally impressive human-interest pictures.

Each experiment had a sender (called the *agent* by parapsychologists) and a receiver (called the *percipient* because he perceives the ESP target). The percipient slept in a soundproof room, with electrodes attached to monitor his sleep and detect when he was dreaming (dreams are identified by rapid eye movements [REM]). While the percipient was going to sleep, an envelope containing a target picture—an art reproduction—was selected randomly from a pool of pictures and given to the agent. The agent did not open the envelope until he was locked into his room for the night. The same target picture was used for the entire night. Distances between the rooms of percipient and agent ranged from thirty-two feet to several miles.

During the night the agent concentrated on sending the picture. In several experiments, in addition to the picture, there were multisensory items that would hopefully enhance the sending. For example, the agent might be bombarded by music from stereo speakers, chosen to match the mood suggested by the picture. In one experiment the target picture, "Downpour at Shono," portrayed a Japanese man with an umbrella trying to escape a driving rain. Along with the picture, the experimenters included a box with an umbrella and instructions to the agent to "take a shower!" There was even an experiment in which the entire audience at a series of concerts by the rock band the Grateful Dead sent pictures telepathically to a percipient sleeping at the Dream Lab.

Back at the Dream Lab, the researchers monitoring the sleep pattern would wake the percipient during each dream, and tape-record the description of the dream.

The next morning the experimenters showed the percipient a number of art prints (usually eight or twelve, depending on the study), one of which was a duplicate of the target picture the agent had attempted to transmit. The percipient then had to rank the pictures according to his estimate as to how closely they matched the content of his dreams. The experimenters also sent the complete typescripts of the dreams to three outside judges, along with the set of art prints for the judges to make independent rankings.

This experimental design ruled out any sensory contact between the agent and the percipient once the experiment was under way. Since they had randomly selected the envelope containing the target picture from hundreds of potential choices, it was extremely unlikely that it would consistently correspond with any stereotyped dream imagery that a percipient might possess. Thus any significant results can be explained only on the basis of psychic factors.

In *Dream Telepathy* the author summarizes the results of ten studies using subjects selected for their psychic ability, ranging from Malcolm Bessent, a well-known English psychic, to Robert Van de Castle, a professor at the University of Virginia. There were many striking matches of the targets to the percipient's descriptions. One target was Chagall's painting *Green Violinist,* which depicts a man playing a violin with a dog in the background. The subject dreamed of a dog barking in a field and later mused, "I wonder if the target could have to do with a tune or something to do with music?" In other cases, descriptions were partial and sometimes either focused on features of the target that were not especially prominent or symbolically modified them. Although not all sessions were successful, overall the results were very statistically significant.

To see whether the effect was restricted to specially selected "psychic" subjects, the researchers also conducted one-night pilot sessions with eighty unselected subjects and concluded: "Regardless of profession, walk of life, waking psychic ability or knowledge of having ever before experienced ESP, the great majority of subjects [56 out of 80] were able to report correspondences that were suggestively telepathic."

Henry Reed, a faculty member at Atlantic University, together with Robert Van de Castle, one of the star subjects from the dream telepathy experiments, developed a new twist on this experiment. They used *people* as targets, with the objective not simply of learning about psychic functioning but of actually helping the people with specific problems. Reed calls his project "Dream Helper." A person who feels in need of help volunteers to be the target, from among a group of people gathered for the experiment. The target person does not discuss his problem with the group, but he secretly writes it out on a piece of paper before going to bed. Next morning the dreamers gather and share their dreams of the night. Very rarely does a single dream actually name and solve the person's problem. Instead, the themes from a number of dreams are often relevant to different aspects of the problem. By discussing these dreams, the group can aid the person in arriving at considerable insight into the problem. Red terms this "transcendent psi," since it goes beyond simply studying psychic ability, and applies it to aid transformation.

Working with
Your Psychic Dreams

How can you work with your dreams to (a) determine if there is a psychic component and (b) practically apply the psychic dream? The preparation for working with psychic dreams is an extension of the preparation for working with any dream. I can't emphasize too much that the occasional psychic elements in a dream are only a small part of the richness of our dream life. Some good books on learning from your dreams include *Dreams: Your Magic Mirror,* by Elsie Sechrist, and *The Bedside Guide to Dreams,* by Stase Michaels.

The first step in exploring the psychic aspect of your dreams is to work with them on a regular basis, so that you are completely familiar with the language of your own unconscious mind. There is no substitute for understanding the personal language of your own dreams. Of primary importance is a dream diary or journal, in which you keep nightly records of your dreams. If you don't normally remember your dreams, the books listed above offer a variety of suggestions to enhance dream recall. One method is to drink a large glass of water at bedtime. Your body's natural need for elimination will wake you up for a visit to the bathroom, right about the time to catch the first dream of the night.

In working with your dreams, there are two aspects: interpretation and application. Many books on dreams focus on interpretation, but Edgar Cayce emphasized application. Interpretation involves not only exploring the meaning of a particular dream but also considering that dream in the life of the individual and deciding on a way to apply the message in the dream. Then use the dream material constructively in your life and the lives of others, and your ability to remember dreams and interpret them will increase.

Interpretation: Exploring Your Dream Symbols

In the limited space here I can't possibly give a complete lesson in the complexities of dream interpretation. The books listed above can help with that. But I would like to discuss symbols. Psychic experiences often have a symbolic component, not only in dreams but in synchronicity, apparitions, and other phenomena. We are not used to interpreting "real" events symbolically (although we will have to learn to do so in order to understand psychic experiences), but dreams are so naturally symbolic that they are a good place to start.

The temptation is to seek out a dream dictionary, one that will give specific meanings to symbols, universal for all dreamers. Some books attempt to do this. To a degree, you can learn something from lists of symbols; because of our shared culture, certain symbols do have relatively universal meanings. These include what Carl Jung called archetypal symbols, a part of the heritage of our collective unconscious. Water is an example of an archetypal symbol, often referring to the unconscious. Water symbols might include the sea, streams, lakes, and rivers. Ascent and descent symbols are common: a staircase, a mountain. Symbols of light—rays, halos, and auras—contrast with symbols of darkness—shadows.

Other symbols are uniquely personal, and jumping to conclusions based on other people's meanings may produce a very wrong conclusion indeed for you. For example, early in my own career I conducted research with dolphins, feeding them every day and cleaning the tank they lived in. For most people dolphins are a symbol of joy or freedom; for me they are usually a symbol denoting responsibility.

Symbols are by nature multidimensional, and the first and obvious meaning rarely exhausts the possibilities. One of the easiest ways to begin to explore the meanings of a symbol is to list all your associations with it. This is especially useful in relation to human symbols. People who appear in your dreams may represent themselves, but they may also symbolize one of their primary qualities as experienced in you. For example, a child may symbolize creativity, a grandparent wisdom. An acquaintance who tells obnoxious jokes may symbolize a part of your shadow, those qualities that you disown in yourself and project onto others.

In addition to exploring your associations to a symbol, it is possible to approach the symbol more directly and "ask" it for clarification and elaboration. That is, you can engage in a dialogue with the symbol. The dialogue can take place entirely in your imagination. A more evocative procedure for dialoguing, developed by Fritz Perls, the originator of Gestalt therapy, is called the "empty chair" technique.

Place two chairs opposite each other about five feet apart and sit in one of them. In your imagination, place the symbol in question or your entire dream in the opposite chair and talk to it. Say, "Tell me more about why you appeared in my dream." Then move to the other chair and take the part of the symbol, giving it a voice. Let the answer come naturally, saying the first thing that comes into your mind. As you continue the dialogue, you may find that the symbol evolves, giving you much more information than appeared on the surface in your dream.

Recognition and Application of Psychic Dreams

As you work with your dreams, over a period of time—and this can be months or years—note the results of your interpretations and applications. You will find that occasionally there appears to be evidence of ESP in some dreams. Note the characteristics of the dreams that go along with the psychic content. For example, for some people there may be unusual vividness, little dream action except for conversation, or a sense of urgency upon awakening. But your own experience may be different. Not all psychic dreams announce themselves with these characteristics. An apparently ordinary dream may contain psychic information. You won't discover it until you work with it and try to apply it. Follow your intuition when you attempt to apply dream information. Then test your intuition by experience—was this interpretation productive? Be open to the possibility of ESP in dreams, but do not try to force every dream to be psychic.

When you are evaluating a dream for ESP, be aware that psi can manifest in both the content (story) and the characters. Ask yourself, (a) could both the characters and the content of this dream be literal, and (b) could the characters be literal, but the content symbolic?

To explore the application of the dream, if it is in fact psychically derived, ask yourself some questions: If this dream were telepathic, what would it be telling me about the dream characters? If it were a warning dream, what would it be warning me of?

Then develop and follow through with a constructive application for the dream. Ask yourself, If it is influenced by ESP, how could I apply it constructively? Then carry out your application, always evaluating your results and modifying your approach when necessary.

We have seen that the unconscious seems to call on symbols from the future or from the mind of another person to make a special impact. Thus a dream of an obnoxious acquaintance passing through a door into a lighted room beyond might be a symbolic message that you need to work with transforming a part of yourself. But it could originate from an actual future event—two days later you meet the acquaintance and he walks through a door into a lighted room. Precognition, yes, but well worth exploring beyond the literal meaning.

Fire or flame is an important symbol of transformation that is sometimes pulled from a future event. It can be interpreted on multiple levels; it may refer to heat, protection or defense, purification and transmutation, or destruction and danger. Fire coming down from heaven may symbolize universal spirit.

For example, you might dream of a fire beginning on the stairs and consuming a warehouse, then read in the paper the following day that the fire actually occurred. But look at the symbols as well: The warehouse may symbolize yourself, the stairs going up may symbolize an ascent to a higher level of consciousness, and the consuming fire may reflect a powerful unconscious desire for transformation.

The most disturbing dreams are those relating to deaths and disasters. Occasionally these are precognitive, but more often they are not. Death is symbolic of transition and rebirth. It can also be a message that we are taking things too seriously, appearing in the dream for its shock value. When these traumatic events in dreams appear to be precognitive as well, they often seem to be calling attention to serious issues in the dreamer's own life. That is, the origin of the symbols may be in a real future event, but your unconscious has chosen them to convey a strong message about your current personal life.

When you go to take action on the dream, then, don't assume that the need is to warn *someone else* of a problem. If you are moved to do that, it might help. But don't stop with that. Explore yourself and the reasons why your unconscious might choose to seek such a symbol. The following example was sent to me by a woman who soon realized the true meaning of her dream of disaster:

> *The "Crash."* I keep a dream journal, and often look to my dreams for guidance. My marriage was floundering. On a trip away from home I dreamed I was the pilot of a jet and my husband was in the control tower. No matter what I did I could not please the control tower because they kept changing positions. The plane took off—it was having trouble getting off the ground. I had to make a crash landing. No one in the plane was badly hurt. I could have interpreted this dream literally, since I was about to take a return trip on a plane. But actually the plane was my marriage— it never really got off the ground. My husband and I soon separated.

Some people still find that their dreams do correspond to actual disasters, and they often have the question, How do I stop these dreams? since the dreams may be frightening and result in guilt feelings due to an inability to prevent the disasters. Here we appear to have an example of attunement gone awry. Again, you are unlikely to be *causing* the disasters. It may be that your unconscious is reaching out and finding real disasters as especially powerful symbols to call your attention to a "disaster" in your own life. My suggestion is that you carefully examine your life and see if you can attune your conscious focus to positive acts. Work with your attitudes and emotions and see if you can tune in to more productive psychic material.

When considering how to apply a dream, as with conscious precognition, it is helpful to think in terms of possible futures, rather than a fixed future. That is, dreams, whether psychic or the product of the personal unconscious, often project the course of the future. There may be warnings, giving us the opportunity to exercise our free will and change the course of events, and there may be dreams of encouragement, inspiring us to continue to take positive action so that we can manifest an event. With dreams of this type, it is often very hard to determine where precognition leaves off and free will begins. If the dream is a warning and the event does not actually happen because you exercise free will to change the future, is this precognition? It can't be proved that the event would have happened. The question is, Can you use this information to make a positive change in your life, regardless of the source of the information?

If you want to explore your dreams in depth, or need help understanding them, the Association for the Study of Dreams publishes a newsletter and serves as a source for networking on dreams. The address is given in the appendix.

CHAPTER 5

Synchronicity

As a psychiatrist and psychotherapist I have often come up against the phenomena [of extraordinary meaningful coincidences] in question and could convince myself how much these inner experiences meant to my patients. In most cases they were things which people do not talk about for fear of exposing themselves to thoughtless ridicule. I was amazed to see how many people have had experiences of this kind and how carefully the secret was guarded.

—Carl Jung, *Synchronicity*

Meaningful coincidences—what place do they occupy in the realm of psychic phenomena? Are they simple "coincidence," meaningless chance events? Are they a form of unconscious telepathy? Or are they evidence of an intelligence beyond our conscious awareness, an intelligence with a puzzling sense of humor?

Nearly all of us, even those who report no striking "psychic" episodes, have experienced unusual coincidences—events that may jolt us out of our rigid habit patterns. Ninety-three percent of the two hundred people on one of my Atlantic University surveys reported having had such an experience. To learn more about these experiences, I conducted a project in which participants were given exercises to increase awareness of synchronicity in their lives. Some of the stories you will see in this chapter resulted from that project. Others are stories from my own life. Unusual coincidences often appear when I least expect them, and I have found the contrast between meaning and absurdity nowhere so evident as in my own experiences.

The Swiss psychiatrist Carl Jung coined the term "synchronicity" to refer to meaningful coincidences, events related by what he referred to as an "acausal connecting principle." "Acausal" means "without a cause." Jung meant that, unlike telepathy, where there is a sender and a receiver, with synchronicity we are unable to determine the cause of the event. It may not even make sense to think in terms of cause and effect. For Jung, *meaning* is the link between the events. He defines synchronicity as "a coincidence in time of two or more causally unrelated events which have the same or similar meaning." Jung introduced the idea of synchronicity to strip off the magic and superstition that surround such impressive events.

Jung extended the work of Austrian biologist Paul Kammerer. Earlier in this century, Kammerer made a study of events that repeat themselves in time or space too frequently to be passed off as mere chance. He terms this phenomenon *seriality,* or the "law of the series," because he saw it as a meaningful series of repeated events, linked symbolically. Jung looked more deeply into the meanings of these events and their relationship to the unconscious mind. In his book, *Synchronicity,* he relates a synchronous event that convinced him that such episodes were worthy of attention. It concerned a young woman patient who was having a difficult time in therapy because of her extreme rational concept of reality.

Over a number of therapy sessions, Jung had made several attempts to show this woman a broader concept of human understanding than she could rationally accept, but he had no success. Finally, he simply had to hope that something unexpected and irrational would happen that would provoke a change in her attitude. One day in a session, Jung was listening to her tell him a dream in which someone had given her a golden scarab—an expensive piece of jewelry. While he was listening to her, Jung heard a tapping noise at the window. He turned around to see a large flying insect knocking against the window, trying to get into the dark room. This seemed strange to Jung, since insects don't normally try to get into *dark* rooms. He opened the window and caught the insect. It was a scarabaeid beetle, or "scarab," whose gold-green color strongly resembles a golden scarab piece of jewelry. Jung handed the beetle to his patient, saying "Here is your scarab." This event was a breakthrough in therapy. It cracked open her intellectual resistance to Jung's wider view of the human psyche, so that treatment could progress.

Jung notes that the scarab is a classic example of a rebirth symbol, from ancient Egyptian mythology. This was not just an unusual coincidence—it had a symbolic meaning as well—to both Jung and the patient.

In contrast to the cause-and-effect approach taken by many parapsychologists, Jung felt that most events we think of as psychic are examples of synchronicity. He used examples from Rhine's work with telepathy and clairvoyance to support his concept of a phenomenon beyond chance. But we have seen that Rhine's experiments were framed in terms of cause and effect, with a sender and a receiver. The more interesting examples of synchronicity are those in which it is not possible to determine the cause. Here we will use synchronicity in this narrower sense, as a term for meaningful coincidences, especially those where some form of external or unconscious intelligence, often with a sense of humor, seems to be directing the events.

Varieties of Synchronicity

Early investigators of synchronicity, Kammerer in particular, classified episodes in terms of how many coincidences occurred together, with the larger numbers seen as less likely to be due to chance. Thus a series of events in which a particular name or number appeared five times would have been considered more interesting than a series in which it appeared only twice. However, Jung focused more on the *meaning* of the experiences and their effect on transformation of consciousness. I will follow that approach here.

Here is an example of a humorous meaningful coincidence of my own:

> *One Big Ego.* My wife and I were driving one day, talking about psychology, and about the difficulties caused by people with "big egos" (using those specific words). We pulled up at a traffic light, and in front of us was a truck with the license plate 1 BIG EGO.

What did this experience mean to us? As people often do with experiences of synchronicity, our first reaction was to laugh. Then we paused to think: The message served to punctuate our discussion and ensure that we would remember it. Looking at a deeper level, I reflected that we had been talking in a very judgmental way about *other* people's big egos. What about our own? For me, it was also a lesson to be less judgmental.

Here is another personal example, again from a license plate:

> *I Polly.* My wife and I were again driving along, discussing her boss "Polly" in the job she had just left, and whether she would continue to do consulting work for the company. Our discussion focused on my wife's

ambivalence about continuing in her role as an editor, and the office politics involved. As we pulled up to a traffic light, the car in front of us had the license plate I POLLY (the Polly in question lived hundreds of miles away—it wasn't her car).

How could we categorize this case? If it was telepathy, who was the sender? Polly herself wasn't involved at all. There could be some precognition—an unconscious preview of the license plate might have nudged our conversation in the direction of Polly and the office. But we were often talking about issues related to the situation at work. Perhaps it was psychokinesis—somehow our energy "manifested" that car with the license plate—but this is not a persuasive explanation. You can see how frustrating it can be to put a name to an event like this. Synchronicity is an easy term to use for events that don't fall clearly into any of our psychic categories yet seem unusual enough to be worthy of note. The event was certainly meaningful to us—it called our attention to the lengthy discussions we had over problems with my wife's job, problems that were no longer relevant since she no longer had the job. The experience seemed to say to us, "You are creating conflict when the actual conflict is long over. You are even able to physically manifest this conflict in the form of the license plate. Isn't that a waste of time?"

Here is another example from my own experience—a situation many people report—an unexpected meeting.

Roger at the Movies. My sister visited me one summer during graduate school, and one day she mentioned to me that a boyfriend of hers in high school, "Roger," had gone to college at a school about an hour away. She hadn't seen him in years and didn't even know if he was still in school. We reminisced about Roger for a few minutes, and went about our daily activities. That night, we went out to the movies. We got in a line of about a hundred people (in a university with thousands of students) and who should get into line directly behind us: Roger! He was not a regular student at the university, but just there for a summer course.

Now, certainly coincidences do occur. You are bound to meet someone you know in an unexpected situation occasionally. Nevertheless, what made this incident memorable was not just running into an old friend but running into him shortly after the first conversation about him in several years, in a place where he was very unlikely to be. Perhaps our earlier conversation was even precognitive of the later event. Yet it is difficult to find much greater meaning in this event. Their relationship was long over—they were friendly for a few moments while standing in line and then never saw each other again. This is often a problem with such experiences. They are meaningful, but it is sometimes difficult to divine their greater significance, if any. The sense of humor behind such experiences is puzzling.

The Trickster Archetype

In the chapter on dreams I mentioned Jung's concept of archetypes—particular themes or motifs that emerge from the unconscious and are universally present. Such themes as the Hero, the Wise Old Man, or the Great Mother often appear in dreams. In episodes of synchronicity another archetype frequently comes into play—the Trickster or Prankster. The Trickster is a figure, known in the mythology of many cultures, whose role seems to be to confound our attempts to deal with the world as predictable and rational. The Trickster is a part of each of us, yet, as an archetype, has a universal reality. Allan Combs and Mark Holland, in their book *Synchronicity,* refer to "the Trickster, who steps godlike through cracks and flaws in the ordered world of ordinary reality, bringing good luck and bad, profit and loss." The Trickster is the mythic embodiment of the unexpected, the unexpected eruption into awareness of truths hidden away from the ego. When we have an inflated self-image, the Trickster can bring us back to earth and make us look foolish, just when we want to look our best.

The following experience of mine is an example of the power of the Trickster archetype:

Strangers on a Plane. I was traveling by airplane to a professional meeting (the Parapsychological Association) and noticed that the person seated next to me was reading a psychology journal. We struck up a conversation, and I found that he was a researcher doing work similar to some I had done a number of years ago (on animal cognition). I told him of my interest in parapsychology, and he expressed quite a bit of skepticism. Despite my carefully reasoned explanations, he remained unreceptive to the possibility of psychic phenomena. He was headed to a completely different meeting and was from a university over a thousand miles from mine in Virginia Beach. As we were leaving the plane I asked his name: when he told me I had a strong feeling I had heard it before. I brushed off the feeling, assuming that I had probably read one of his papers in a journal some years ago.

When I returned to my office, I went through the pile of mail that I had received the day I headed out on my trip. There, on top, was a grant proposal that the National Science Foundation had sent me to review. I had opened it, looked at the cover page, and put it aside before my trip. Now I took a closer look— the author of the grant proposal was the man I had met on the plane!

This is truly the Trickster at work! Funding from the National Science Foundation depends on positive evaluation of proposals by anonymous reviewers. Here this person had been trying to convince me of how little he thought my research area was worth, while, unknown to either of us, I would be reviewing his own proposal for research funding. Actually, being a fair-minded person, I gave it a high rating, since it was an excellent extension of some work I had previously done in mainstream psychology. Because reviewers are anonymous, I was never able to tell him of the incident. Who knows if it would have changed his attitude toward psychic phenomena?

What is the message of this experience? That greater unity of which we are all a part appears to have a strange sense of humor. There is certainly a moral lesson warning us about being judgmental and an opportunity to be fair-minded, but basically I just had to laugh. It was at the same time sobering to contemplate how many similar incidents may happen to us each day, in which we have no more awareness of the greater implications of our acts than that man on the plane did.

The Synchronicity
Home Study Project

Synchronicity is difficult to study in the laboratory, since by definition it is not open to controlled experiment. Parapsychologists have pointed out that many apparent instances of synchronicity fit into our concepts of telepathy and precognition, particularly if we grant that our unconscious needs can be powerful stimulators of psychic phenomena. Rather than try to *prove* that synchronicity is truly a different type of psychic experience, we decided to suggest exercises designed to draw people's attention to the coincidences of everyday life and to encourage them to contemplate the meaning of these events for their transformative process. Christopher Fazel, a staff member in the A.R.E.'s Educational Development Division, designed the project several years ago, and I continued with it after his departure.

Participants kept daily journals of meaningful coincidences and their reactions to them. We encouraged them to keep a playful attitude when looking for interpretations and to remain open to multiple interpretations. As one exercise, they were instructed to ask the question, What talent or side of myself can I develop more completely which will help me be more fulfilled in life? We asked them to try to interpret synchronous events in terms of their question. For another exercise we instructed them to take a "random walk," with no particular destination, and watch for signs apparently bearing on the question.

Numerous participants returned results, reporting various amounts of synchronicity. Some had meaningful events happening virtually every day, while others had only one event in the entire three-week experiment. Most participants reported considerably more awareness of synchronicity than they had noticed previously. More important, they made an effort to interpret these experiences, reflect on their larger meaning, and seek guidance from them. Below are some examples of the experiences and the type of guidance the people felt that they had received.

This forty-one-year-old woman from Chicago, concerned with her son's illness as well as her own issues in life, related the following story:

Take a Different Path. One morning driving my son for tests at a Chicago hospital, I found that our normal route had detours. After the tests I decided to take a different route to avoid construction only to find that the route I had chosen also had detours. Later that night I went to drive over to my mother's house only to fine *another detour*! I feel the Universe is trying to tell me to take a different path at this time of my life.

The project increased her openness to experience. She wrote:

I try to remember to ask the universe a question each morning and then look for a synchronistic answer. Because I believe that the Universe (God) is constantly trying to talk to us and gives us signs and indicators of guidance to make our life easier. We just have to learn to "see" and "listen" in a different way, on a different level. We are all searching and growing whether we're aware of it or not. But when we are aware of it—it seems to be more peaceful.

A fifty-five-year-old woman from Texas sent the following story, in which synchronicity inspired her to explore the meaning of an important symbol in her life.

The Bonsai Tree. While reading a book on enlightenment, I found myself thinking about bonsai [the Japanese art of cultivating miniature trees] and how I had wanted one for a long time. Later that day, I saw an ad for a Bonsai store which had newly opened not far from my home. Eighteen days later, my husband offered to buy one for me.

During the project she also had a dream about a yew tree and associated it with the Tree of Life. Later that day, she and her husband had dinner in a country restaurant with yew trees in it.

Tree symbolism was clearly important to this woman, but she could have explored the symbolism even more. A tree has roots in the physical, with branches reaching for the sky with a diversity of alternatives. It is an archetypal symbol of growth.

She concluded from the project, "A simple balanced life in harmony with the universe (like the Bonsai tree) will help me remember my early education (by nuns) in love and service to humanity. I am guided to cooperate with others and be open to being used for good."

Many synchronicity experiences heighten the feeling of connectedness, but here is one where the connections span generations, from a thirty-one-year-old woman in the army, stationed overseas, who returned on leave to visit relatives.

Retracing My Ancestor's Steps. I had to go to Atlanta, Georgia to visit my son. Normally I would never go there because my son doesn't live there. He was visiting his aunt (my ex-sister-in-law). While there I was in Gwinnet County and visited Stone Mountain. I then went to visit my mother in Arkansas. She has been researching genealogy, and had the family tree traced back to when our first ancestor came to America. This man arrived in Atlanta, lived in Gwinnet County, and even worked on Stone Mountain. Up until I went to Stone Mountain I had never even heard of it, much less thought of going there. I was totally shocked when I read the genealogy report because I had just been in all those places.

This experience is a new variation on the past-life memories often reported by people. Here she did not feel that *she* had been the ancestor in question, but nevertheless she had a deep sense of continuity with the past.

Synchronicity occasionally has immediate practical value. I once met a person "accidentally" in an elevator whose work I had read and admired, and we ended up collaborating on some research.

Here is an example of the practical application of synchronicity from a forty-four-year-old businessman from Missouri.

The Mission. I was working on a mission statement for the company and was concerned with the changes others were making. I went to a seminar and discovered, unknown to me previously, that one of the speakers specialized in mission statements. I asked him to meet with my boss. Normally he leaves immediately following his presentation, but as it turns out he was available the next morning. It was unusual for him to stay overnight as he did. When I believe in something, help will arrive in unexpected ways.

Openness to the unexpected characterizes the people in the project who felt that synchronicity had the most impact on their lives. Recall Douglas Dean's book *Executive ESP,* discussed in the telepathy chapter. Many successful business executives appear to have a well-developed intuitive sense. Synchronicity is hard to classify; a parapsychologist would probably not classify the experience of the businessman as psi. Yet again and again people report that these types of experiences have been significant events in their lives.

Here is a final example from a thirty-four-year-old French-Canadian woman, in which synchronicity reinforced her commitment to spiritual values.

Charity Calls. Last weekend someone with whom I went to college died of AIDS. Louise, a mutual friend, had told me that he didn't want flowers, but that money should be given to the St. Vincent de Paul [a Catholic charity]. At the funeral two ladies working for that charity organization said they were very surprised that someone chose their organization for donations. And one who had led this organization for years said that although they experienced problems and sometimes what seemed like a shortage of funds, somehow help always arrived on time, unexpectedly.

So I arrived at the church to make my donation, and said, "I came to give some money for the St. Vincent de Paul." Then the phone rang. The secretary answered. It was someone requesting help from the St. Vincent de Paul. She wrote their names and said that someone would contact them the next day. I thought, "What a coincidence." And wondered as I saw that help arrived as the need came. I pondered to myself that it was always like that. For me, too, at this moment, all that I needed was being provided to me by someone, somewhere.

There is no way to know if the perception of synchronicity results from projection of your personal unconscious mind, from a joint projection of the unconscious minds of several people, or from the intervention of some higher intelligence. But, as the above examples show, many people have added meaning to their lives through awareness of synchronicity.

The Probability of Synchronicity

We have seen that episodes of synchronicity are meaningful, but is there any way to show that they are anything more than "just coincidence"? Despite the common occurrence of meaningful coincidences, it is hard to do experimental research on them. By its nature, synchronicity is spontaneous. Jung said, "The experimental method of inquiry aims at establishing regular events which can be repeated. Consequently, unique or rare events are ruled out of account." As soon as you try to do an experiment, you are setting the stage for psi as we normally conceive of it—as clairvoyance or telepathy, for example.

The obvious skeptical point of view is that these are simply chance coincidences, that any meaning we assign to them is a projection of our own. A skeptic might argue that if we find them unusual at all, it is because we don't understand the laws of probability. A skeptic might say that, far from being meaningful, they are evidence of a *deficiency* in reasoning ability.

For example, you could be asked in a class, "What is the probability that two out of the fifty people in this room have the same birthday?" You might at first think this quite unlikely, but actually it has a very high probability that can easily be calculated mathematically. Most of us, however, do not use mathematics in our everyday life. Instead, we use what are referred to as "heuristics." These are simple, practical rules for making decisions—jumping to "reasonable" conclusions rather than carrying out calculations. Unfortunately, when applied to questions of probability, they often lead to wrong conclusions.

You can imagine the stereotype of the person in a large group who says, "Oh, your name is John. What synchronicity! My name is John, too!" A person who does not recognize the likelihood of meeting someone named John might also consider many other ordinary events to be synchronicity—thus attributing significance to chance occurrences. Many experiments have been done to show that not only average people but even graduate students in statistics do not employ sound statistical reasoning in everyday life. But the important question for our purpose here is, Do people who report many experiences of synchronicity do so because they are particularly bad at estimating the probabilities of events? Or are certain people more sensitive to or aware of unusual events, in a way unrelated to their statistical sophistication?

One way to answer this question is to ask about people's belief in psychic phenomena or about the number of psychic or synchronistic experiences they have had. Then give them a problem that requires them to estimate probabilities. Do people who believe in such experiences tend to mis-estimate the probabilities? The actual results of such studies have been mixed. Some experiments have shown that people who believe in psychic phenomena mis-estimate probabilities more often than skeptics do. Others have not shown this effect. The difficulty with most studies of this type is that they have been conducted by people who openly admit that their objective was to show that believers in psychic phenomena are illogical, irrational, uncritical, foolish people. Yet, even so, there are studies showing that people with a belief in psychic phenomena are of *greater* than normal intelligence. We do not yet understand the important factors in these studies.

For practical purposes, an experimental demonstration of the reality of synchronicity may be much less important than exploration of the meaning it evokes in people's lives.

Working with Synchronicity

As with all forms of psychic experiences, your most important tool for working with synchronicity is a personal journal. Many of us simply do not attend carefully to events as they unfold—we miss the daily influence of coincidence on our lives. By keeping a journal of events, we can watch patterns develop.

Keep an open and playful attitude when looking for interpretations, for there may be several meaningful levels of approach. For example, in one day you might note that (a) you dreamed of a turtle, (b) saw a turtle on the road, and (c) heard a friend say that you lived in a shell. Possible reactions to this might be recognition of a need to be more open in relationships and that steady persistence is more important than speed—two interpretations of the turtle motif.

You can expand your approach by asking a specific question for synchronicity to answer, in the same way that you might ask a question of your dreams. The one recommended for the synchronicity research project was, "What talent or side of myself can I develop more completely to help me be more fulfilled in life?"

What kinds of patterns characterize synchronicity? Like dreams, synchronicity mirrors processes that are deep in the psyche. However, it differs from dreams in that the processes are manifested in actual events in the material world. Recurring symbols and puns are two of the most common manifestations. Try interpreting ordinary events as symbolic, as if you were looking at a dream (this technique is also helpful in improving dream recall, as it shows your unconscious that you are serious about working with symbols).

Jung writes in *Synchronicity* about a "fish story" he recorded in his own journal. One morning he made a note of an inscription containing a figure that was half man and half fish. Later, at lunch, fish was served. Someone talked about the Swiss custom of an "April fish" joke (the equivalent of our "April fool"). Then, in the afternoon, someone showed him some pictures of fish. Finally, in the evening, Jung was shown a piece of embroidery with sea monsters and fish in it.

The fish symbolism did not end with that day. The next morning, a former patient told him of a dream the night before about a large fish. Jung, struck by this series of coincidences, was writing it down a few months later, when he decided to take a walk out of his house to a spot by the lake. He saw a large fish on the seawall, which had not been there earlier in the day. Again he was surprised, since there was no one around who could have placed the fish there.

Jung says that this run of events made a considerable impression on him, but admits that there is no way to "prove" whether or not it was "mere chance." In fact, he leans toward chance as an explanation for this particular series of events. But Jung noted that this was an especially meaningful symbol for him. Fishes frequently occur as symbols of unconscious contents. His working on the fish symbol was one of the primary factors that motivated him to write his book on synchronicity. Thus the action that you take based on your analysis of the meaning of a synchronistic event may be more productive than evaluating the probability of its chance occurrence.

Where can we find synchronicity? Try some activities that encourage the appearance of synchronicity. Take a random walk with no particular destination. Observe your surroundings carefully. We rarely do this; instead we are always in a hurry to get somewhere and may thus miss useful sources of guidance. A walk through a library or bookstore is often especially stimulating. Synchronicity can be apparent in any aspect of our lives, but from my experience (an observation confirmed by Holland and Combs in their book *Synchronicity*), traveling, by bus, plane, or other mode of transportation, is a strong catalyst. Perhaps breaking habit patterns opens the door to these types of experiences. Mark Thurston's book, *The Paradox of Power,* gives several ways to exercise the will by breaking habit patterns.

When you have an event that you think goes beyond coincidence, do not jump to conclusions about its meaning. Examine it from several angles. Be observant and alert rather than blindly submissive to "fate." You will find that there are two sides to synchronistic events. They can be a message from the higher self, from the transpersonal level, a form of higher guidance. They can alert us to new opportunities: a book, a friend, or a new career. But don't look at every unusual occurrence as a sign of higher guidance. Remember the Trickster—synchronicity can also express our shadow, aspects of ourselves that we have buried in the unconscious. Synchronicity can embarrass us, make us look foolish, expose that which we wish (consciously) to keep hidden. Psychotherapists sometimes find that, like an unconscious slip of the tongue, synchronicity can be of value in revealing concealed material.

Synchronicity refers to *meaningful* coincidences, yet often the surface appearance is the opposite, one of absurdity. These experiences can surprise us, but they are an opportunity for reflection and growth as well. The saving grace is that the Trickster has a sense of humor. Adopt a playful attitude, even toward strings of strange coincidences that do not appear to present an immediate positive opportunity. Your unconscious may be joking with you. Lighten up!

Synchronicity can also be an antidote for too intense or obsessive a search for meaning. We all know of people who see "omens" in every event—they have trouble with letting events unfold naturally. By adding simple humor to the situation, synchronicity may cause them to reconsider their habits, relax, and laugh a little. As the saying goes, "There must be more to life than searching for the meaning of life."

The best way to work with synchronicity is not to be obsessed by analysis, nor to surrender to "fate," but to see it as an opportunity for a humorous look at the unexpected. So, be alert to the unexpected and enjoy your greater awareness of the complexity underlying daily life.

PART TWO

The Influence
of the Mind

CHAPTER 6

Psychokinesis

It staggers my imagination to conceive all the implications that follow now that it has been shown that the mind, by some means, as unknown as the mind itself, has the ability directly to affect material operations in this world around it. Let us look clear-eyed and fearlessly at what this means.
—J. B. Rhine in Louisa Rhine, *Mind over Matter*

Psychokinesis (PK)—mind over matter—is perhaps the most puzzling of psychic phenomena. I once received a telephone call from a man who related the following story.

The Flying Shelf. One night five years ago I was sitting in my living room with four of my friends. I am a retired policeman and so are they—we're all no-nonsense people, trained to observe accurately. While we were talking, a shelf on the opposite wall flew across the room and hit me in the head. I had solidly mounted the shelf myself—it was securely screwed into the wall. There is no way I can imagine that it could have come loose by itself. Yet five of us saw it happen. Nothing like this has ever happened again to me.

This form of experience is very rare, yet it can be compelling evidence that our solid, physical world may be subject to the forces of the mind, or even mysterious forces beyond the mind.

Psychokinesis is direct mental influence, without the use of muscles, on some physical object or process. In surveys of psychic experiences, it tends to be one of the least common, and statistically is only weakly correlated with such phenomena as clairvoyance and precognition. In the 1990 Gallup poll, for example, only 7 percent of the general population in the United States reported an experience of PK. Only 15 percent of the 520 A.R.E members in my survey had an experience of PK, and only 3 percent reported having had such an experience more than once or twice. In the laboratory PK is paradoxical. On what is called the "micro" level—the ability for someone's thoughts to influence computer-based random event generators—we have some of the strongest scientific evidence for psychic phenomena. But on the "macro" level—the everyday world of large objects—parapsychologists have found it almost impossible to demonstrate the influence of mind on physical objects in any kind of controlled situation. In fact, some of the greatest controversies between parapsychologists and their critics have centered around apparent demonstrations of psychokinesis—such phenomena as levitation and spoon-bending. One of the strangest types of psychokinesis is what has become known as the "poltergeist" (German for "noisy ghost"). Objects flying across the room, doors mysteriously opening and closing—the traditional explanation was that poltergeists were mischievous spirits of the dead. However, careful investigation by parapsychologists has revealed that poltergeist phenomena are apparently unconscious PK from a living person, and not ghosts at all.

This chapter will look at the experiences people report, examine the evidence for PK from experimental studies, and offer some suggestions for dealing with poltergeists and working with other forms of psychokinesis.

Varieties of Psychokinesis

Reports of experiences of psychokinesis differ from those of receptive psychic experiences such as clairvoyance. With receptive experiences, you can always identify the experience as "yours." With reports of psychokinesis, more doubt is usually expressed about whether the event occurred as a result of your thoughts or some other factor. In many cases, the people feel that the event *could* be attributed to normal factors, but it stands out as unusual. For example, a woman in her fifties sent in this report:

The Psychic Mechanic. One day in 1986 my son's car wouldn't start. It wouldn't make the least little bit of sound as he attempted to "jump" it. When he was finished I asked him if I could try. When I put myself and the car in a "light" and pushed on the accelerator the car started right up. It happened two more times with this car—no one could start the car and I could start it right away. Last time I told them to take the car and sell it—and they did.

Another report came from a nurse, known for her ability to speed healing in patients:

Fixing the Phone. I have had the ability to fix phones. I had control over a mechanical device (cellular phone) that shouldn't work—and by wishing it would, it did.

Some people feel that they have an ability to mentally *fix* things, yet we are also all familiar with people for whom mechanical devices never seem to work, people who can sit down in front of a computer and the disk drive always seems to "crash." What is happening here? Is this simply chance? After all, technology is sometimes fragile, and things do break down and spontaneously fix themselves. Kicking the television is not psychokinesis, but sometimes it does work and saves calling a repairman (and sometimes it doesn't work and smoke comes out!).

Since I received few reports of simple psychokinesis in my research, I am now going to take a look at the research parapsychologists have done, before I return to more complex cases such as poltergeists. While people may not often report spontaneous PK, there is abundant laboratory evidence for its existence.

Parapsychologists Study Psychokinesis

Modern experimental research into psychokinesis began with a visitor to J. B. Rhine at Duke University one day early in 1934. He was a gambler and claimed a special ability—he had found that he could control the fall of dice with his willpower. As Louisa Rhine tells the story in her book *Mind over Matter,* within minutes the gambler and Rhine were hunched down in a corner of the office, the gambler throwing his dice on the floor. His actual success is not on record, but it was great enough to lead Rhine into lengthy research in this new major area of psychic ability.

For many years before Rhine began his work, the so-called "physical mediums" had been producing not just the voices of spirits but raps, knocks, levitating tables, and materializations of what were claimed to be paranormal objects. Many such phenomena were found to be fraud, but some of the manifestations remain unexplained to this day. D. D. Home, a British medium, was able to levitate himself to the ceiling in a fully lighted room and even out one window and in another, in the presence of experienced witnesses. Yet the problems with controlling the situation sufficiently to be sure there was no trickery frustrated parapsychologists, and the research into physical mediums was not conclusive. Rhine's greatest contribution was to bring the phenomenon into the laboratory.

Inspired by the gambler, Rhine began his work with dice, enlisting student volunteers to use the force of their wills to make specific faces come up more often than would be expected by chance. The results suggested a real effect, but Rhine was cautious. He was still trying to win acceptance for the idea of ESP; PK was an even more unlikely possibility. Although he began his experiments in 1934, it was not until 1943 that he published his first results.

Rhine was convinced of the reality of PK, but it was not the average score that provided the strongest evidence. As with Rhine's ESP results, it was a form of the *decline effect,* where people's scores on these tests get progressively worse. In 1942, the researchers at Rhine's laboratory examined all the data accumulated to that point and found strong evidence for declines in performance. Success was strongest in the first quarter of a session, then dropped during the rest of the session. This effect could not be the result of dice bias, and it was not even expected at the times the sessions had been run, years before. The decline was strong evidence for the presence of real PK.

Over the years researchers tried many variations on the PK procedures—they altered the size of the dice, the lengths of the sessions, and the attitudes and motivations of the subjects and experimenters. As with ESP, motivational factors often turned out to be more important than physical factors. And intense "willing" of the desired outcome was not the most productive strategy. Relaxed informality was often the key to success.

As with ESP card experiments, a major drawback of dice experiments is that they are not very exciting (unless you happen to be a gambler or love to throw dice).

Several researchers came up with clever ways to stimulate interest. Of these, perhaps the most creative are the devices of W. E. Cox, a businessman and engineer from North Carolina who worked with Rhine for many years.

Cox's devices used the concept of "placement PK"—that PK could influence the course of a particular object to come to rest in a specific location. Cox's "objects" were a departure from dice, however! One of his devices used a bathroom shower spray mounted above a small grid whose narrow slits were connected with two vertical glass tubes. The objective was for the subject to will the target tube to fill faster than the control. Of course, the control and target tubes were periodically switched to ensure that there was no bias. Although much of the water ended up on the floor, the experiment produced evidence of PK. Cox's other devices included complex arrangements of electromechanical timers and even a machine with hundreds of small steel balls cascading down a ramp. In each case he found significant PK effects.

Although using PK to aim the shower may have been more interesting than watching endless rolls of the dice, experimenters continued to search for a PK task that truly motivated the subject and might tap into the real reason for the existence of PK. Living organisms were an obvious choice. Successful experiments have been performed with people attempting to influence organisms ranging from the swimming of single-celled paramecia, to the growth of plants, to the activity of insects. Among the most promising experiments were those that viewed psychokinesis as a means of *healing* living creatures. I will say much more about this in the next chapter.

Micro PK: The Effect of the Mind on Very Small Phenomena

A great breakthrough in the scientific study of PK came with the invention of the random event generator (REG), sometimes called the random number generator (RNG). The principle of the random event generator is simple. It is a form of electronic coin toss. An electronic counter is alternating between 1 and 0 at a very rapid rate—millions of times a second. A push of a button stops the counter in either the 1 or the 0 state. Now, since it is unlikely that anyone could synchronize their button push to select a 1 or a 0 with the counter changing so fast, some people might be satisfied at this point. Helmut Schmidt, a physicist then working at Boeing Aircraft, went a step further. Instead of the button push stopping the counter directly, he inserted a radioactive source and a Geiger counter tube to detect the radiation. A radioactive particle triggering the Geiger tube at some time after the button push would be the event that was actually responsible for stopping the counter. Since the emission of radioactive particles is random according to the laws of physics, this guaranteed that the counter was stopped at a random time, and that the 1 or 0 selected was a truly random number.

Schmidt then did extensive randomness tests with his device and was able to statistically confirm randomness. The excitement for parapsychologists came when he found people who were able to affect the random generator, to make it significantly deviate from randomness using only the power of their minds.

Schmidt devised a variety of ways to make his random generator experiments interesting. He designed a machine with lights in a circle, where the object of the experiment was to use the power of the mind to move the lit bulb clockwise or counterclockwise around the circle, in response to numbers from the random generator. He tried experiments with colored lights and other variations. Reasoning that motivation was the key to success, Schmidt even tried PK experiments with animals. For his pet cat in the winter, he rigged a heat lamp, connected to the random generator such that generation of a 1 would turn the lamp on and 0 would turn the lamp off. He hypothesized that the desire by the cat to keep warm would lead to psychokinesis producing an excess of 1's, and that is exactly what he found. For later experiments he used subjects ranging from cockroaches to brine shrimp, all with successful results.

The success of Schmidt with his random event generators captured the interest not only of parapsychologists but of other scientists as well, because it provided evidence that an "intrinsically unpredictable" quantum process can be controlled through psychic ability. One of the most active centers for work with this new technology has been the Princeton Engineering Anomalies Research Laboratory (PEAR) at Princeton University, under the direction of Robert Jahn, former dean of the School of Engineering at Princeton. Jahn, with his colleagues Brenda Dunne and Roger Nelson, developed even more sophisticated random generators and collected the largest database with this type of equipment in the world. The work at PEAR is unique, in that from the very beginning the researchers have kept a consecutive record of every trial run with their equipment. This has allowed them to do statistical analyses with millions of trials, revealing some surprising effects.

PEAR's unique contribution is the discovery of patterns of PK performance, specific to individuals. Individuals have their own "signatures," which appear in the data records. In the PEAR experiments, the subjects are instructed to strive for "high aim" or "low aim." This means that in one condition they are trying to get more "hits" and in the other more "misses." The graphs of their data are wiggly lines, sometimes going a little bit up and sometimes a little bit down. Overall, however, in the high-aim condition the trend is significantly up, and in the low-aim condition the trend is significantly down. Each person working with the equipment produces an individually distinct pattern. The PEAR group has termed these patterns "operator signatures." (They call their subjects "operators." The term "psychics" is a little too unconventional for an engineering department.)

Macro PK: The Effect of the Mind on the Large Phenomena of Everyday Life

At this point you may be asking, "Haven't we gotten a long way from 'mind over matter'? Why can't psychokinesis be studied in everyday life? Why can't experiments be done with the people who claim they can bend spoons with their minds or levitate? Studies of micro PK are fine for scientists to debate over, but is there any research that can explain our *experiences*?"

Macro PK, the effect of the mind on large-scale phenomena, has been hard to study in the laboratory, but some of the best efforts have been made by a group at what was formerly Stanford Research Institute (now SRI International) in California. Physicists Russell Targ and Harold Puthoff brought psychic Ingo Swann to their lab. Swann, also an author and an artist, claimed a variety of abilities. He was not only the first subject in the remote-viewing experiments discussed in the clairvoyance chapter, he felt that he could physically influence the things that he was seeing at a distance.

The task that Targ and Puthoff posed to Swan was to influence a small magnetic probe (called a magnetometer) located in a vault below the floor of the building and shielded by several layers of different types of metal. Swann focused his attention on the interior of this magnetometer, and, after about five seconds, the frequency of the normal oscillation in the equipment doubled for about thirty seconds. This astonished the physicists, since the whole point of the device was its specific design so that it would *not* be disturbed by outside influences.

Swann has been tested by other researchers as well. Gertrude Schmeidler, of City College of New York, studied his ability to change the temperature of a distant object. In well-controlled experiments she sealed thermistors—electronic thermometers sensitive to very small temperature changes—into a Thermos bottle at five or twenty-five feet from Swann, with control thermistors to show temperature changes on his skin and elsewhere in the room. The experiment produced very strong results.

The SRI researchers tested another psychic for PK, Uri Geller, an Israeli magician famous for his "spoon-bending" ability. Because Geller has put himself in the limelight, building a career on his claims, he has made scientific research difficult. In an ongoing debate with such critics as magician James "The Amazing" Randi over whether his powers are real, it has been hard to do serious scientific study. The problem is that a talented magician can do amazing tricks, tricks that may fool other magicians and can certainly fool scientists who are unskilled in detecting trickery. Geller's claim was that he could bend metal, start broken watches, and perform other startling examples of PK. Unfortunately it was hard to get him to demonstrate those abilities under controlled conditions. Despite some apparently well-controlled, successful experiments at SRI and elsewhere, most parapsychologists have not accepted his demonstrations as reliable evidence of PK.

Nevertheless, some very unusual phenomena have occurred in connection with Geller that cannot simply be dismissed as magic tricks. One of his claims is that he can inspire other people to accomplish the same feats that he can, even over television! There have been numerous reports of spontaneous PK following Geller's television appearances. For example, Geller might say that your broken watch will start running again, and, sure enough, it does. Critics have dismissed these phenomena as resulting from simple suggestion. Perhaps if you picked up the watch the motion would have started it anyway. I was personally quite skeptical about this effect, but the following event was reported to me by a very reliable staff member in the Edgar Cayce Foundation:

Psychic Watch Repair. In 1989 Uri Geller appeared on television, and told the audience to gather up their broken watches. I went upstairs and brought down all the broken watches from my bureau. There were five. Three were fairly new digital battery types. One was a Gruen given to my mother by my father as a Christmas gift in 1927. The next was an old Picard pocket watch with clear plastic front and backcovers. The Gruen had simply worn out and the Picard had a clearly visible broken mainspring. A jeweler told my mother in 1965 the Gruen was simply too old and worn to repair and that it would be too expensive to make a new mainspring for the Picard.

I held the 5 watches in my hands and joined with Uri as he said "Work!" He said this several times. I opened my hands and saw through the clear Picard cases that it was running. The break in the mainspring was no longer visible. I held the Gruen to my ear to find it, too, was ticking. Both watches are still running today (2 years later) and keeping good time. The digital watches remained broken.

This staff member had shared the story with me at the time it happened. While I can't speak to the previous condition of the watches, they were certainly in good working order when I saw them. The staff member feels that it was not simply Geller, but that her motivation played a major role—the old watches had great sentimental value to her, unlike the new digital watches. Was this truly PK? We have no way of knowing, but it is typical of the kind of cases that have spurred parapsychologists to look for ways to screen large numbers of people for PK ability.

PK Parties—Can Anyone Do It?

The difficulty with obtaining macro PK in the laboratory inspired a number of parapsychologists to search for people with PK abilities in an informal setting. Jack Houck of Huntington Beach, California, organized what he called "PK parties," where he created a lighthearted, nonlaboratory group setting for eliciting PK. The idea was to create a "peak emotional event." The targets were metal utensils, e.g., spoons and forks. Bending instructions consist of a brief guided meditation followed by the group shouting, "Bend!" in unison. The participants are allowed to touch the utensil but are also encouraged to "release their effort" and place the utensils in their pockets to let the bending continue unaided. Cynthia Siegel of the Institute for Parapsychology surveyed 311 participants at Houck's PK parties and found that 73 percent of the participants claimed that they had produced PK. But the conditions are very uncontrolled, with much opportunity for people to unconsciously apply more force to the metal than they are aware of doing. Julian Isaacs, another PK researcher, estimated that the true incidence of PK metal bending at these parties is between 1 and 5 percent of the people.

In 1987 I attended a PK party at a conference at A.R.E. in order to observe firsthand what occurred. There were motivational sitting and walking meditations, all intended to build confidence in personal PK ability. I was taking careful notes on the process and thus missed the experience of being motivated. Instead, I took a spoon and bent it as hard as I could by force. I then walked around the room, comparing my spoon to those of the people who felt their spoons had bent paranormally. Most spoons were not as twisted as mine, and I could easily imagine that the people unconsciously bent them as they were rubbing them. But a few were so distorted that I found it hard to imagine that they had simply been bent by hand.

I invited three people who had unusual bends in their spoons up to my laboratory to take a computerized random generator test for PK. They all scored in the positive direction, though none significantly by themselves. Combining the data from all of them, however, yielded a marginally significant score. Had we found reliable PK? Not yet, but these are encouraging results for the idea of PK parties as a screening system for people with possible PK talent.

Sitter Groups: Another Way to Encourage PK

In the heyday of mediums, séances and "table tipping" were the means by which most people were exposed to the possibility of PK. Spectacular phenomena, such as table levitation and materialization of objects, often appeared to occur during séances. But for more then fifty years parapsychologists have generally avoided séances because of the problem of guarding against fraud. In the 1970s, however, British parapsychologist Kenneth Batcheldor revived the séance concept as a way not to communicate with spirits but simply to encourage PK among the people present. His "sitter groups" duplicated the informal atmosphere of the séance. Most important, they relieved any one individual of the responsibility of being the person who was causing the PK event. Batcheldor reasoned that fear, either conscious or unconscious, tended to inhibit PK and that most people had resistance to acknowledging their own PK ability. He coined two terms describing resistance to PK. The idea that people are frightened by their own apparent power to produce such phenomena he called "ownership resistance." The idea that people can be upset by witnessing these types of PK events he called "witness inhibition." Batcheldor groups obtained many unusual phenomena, from loud knocks to levitating tables, but controls weren't tight enough to satisfy some parapsychologists. Still, the idea of a sitter group as a PK-conducive situation is promising.

A Canadian group took Batcheldor's ideas a step further and added an "imaginary ghost" to their sitter group. In *Conjuring Up Philip*, Iris Owen describes how her group made up a story about an imaginary ghost they called Philip, giving him a fictitious background. They then held séances to attempt to communicate with him, and he answered with raps on the table. They were able to carry on lengthy conversations with him, with different raps standing for yes and no. Spontaneous poltergeist cases and experimental sitter groups both suggest that our capacity for projecting our inner consciousness on the physical world is greater than psychology has ever suspected.

Poltergeists

Does psychokinesis have a negative side? I occasionally receive calls and letters from people who are concerned that they might psychically hurt someone. For example, a man called me on the telephone with this problem:

Projected Anger. Sometimes I get really "ticked off" at someone, and I'm staring at them, and my glasses break. Sometimes something on the table breaks. Sometimes I am simply having intense thoughts and things just move. I have noticed that by sometimes just being angry with someone I cause things to happen. What can I do about this?

This man fits the pattern of a "poltergeist agent," though he appears to be more aware of what is happening than most such agents. Can this really happen? Can pure thought really have enough influence to move objects and break things? Could someone be hurt?

Poltergeist phenomena, by far the most disturbing examples of psychokinesis, are rather rare. Only 8 percent of the people in John Palmer's Charlottesville survey reported possible poltergeist experiences. Our current understanding of poltergeists is an example of the power of careful observation. What people had traditionally assumed to be ghosts revealed itself to be unconscious PK by a living human. Poltergeist phenomena give new meaning to the concept of "projection of the shadow." It appears that projection of unconscious negative emotions can indeed cause physical effects in the environment. Occasionally anger, hostility, or frustration can be expressed in the form of psychokinesis. With poltergeists, it is typically unconscious and uncontrolled. But although the furniture may move and objects fly through the air, poltergeists never seem to hurt anyone. The effect seems to be a kind of psychic "tantrum," as a child might have, not capable of effective direction. The stories in movies such as *Poltergeist* or *The Amityville Horror* are simply fiction.

Dr. William Roll, previously the director of the Psychical Research Foundation in North Carolina, has probably done the most to advance our knowledge of poltergeists. He coined a new term for poltergeists, *recurrent spontaneous psychokinesis* (RSPK), to make it clear that these phenomena are not the result of spirits. The term refers to the observations that (1) the psychokinesis is spontaneous—not intentional but unconscious, and (2) that it is recurrent—poltergeist cases are a series of events that typically occur over a period of days or weeks. Roll began his career as a parapsychologist in the laboratory, but he found it difficult to get results with the standard card and dice tests of the 1950s. His first encounter with what appeared to be genuine psychic phenomena came not in the laboratory but in a private home in Seaford, Long Island, in 1958.

The Seaford Poltergeist. The house of Mr. and Mrs. James Herrmann had been dubbed "the house of the flying objects" by the newspapers—plates, figurines and other household objects seemed to be taking on a life of their own. Roll and his colleague Gaither Pratt from the Duke Parapsychology Laboratory went to investigate the case. They found numerous incidents of mysteriously moving objects which traditionally would have been attributed to a poltergeist. Roll and Pratt worked hard to rule out natural explanations— some poltergeist cases have been stopped when a chimney cap was installed to exclude downdrafts. But no ordinary explanation could account for all the events. Many of them seemed to occur in the vicinity of Jimmy, a twelve-year-old boy, but it didn't seem possible that he was causing the events physically. Roll and Pratt couldn't prove what was happening, but they began to suspect unconscious psychokinesis by Jimmy.

There was still the question of whether the poltergeist phenomena might have been caused by normal means—someone simply throwing objects. In many cases it is hard to tell, and both normal and paranormal events may be occurring. But in a later case of Roll's, the researchers were able to make more-controlled observations.

The Miami Poltergeist. The case took place in a Miami wholesale warehouse, specializing in souvenir objects. Objects fell from the shelves or moved greater distances with loud impacts and frequent breakage; 224 separate incidents were recorded. Roll and his team spent a number of days at the site, during which they observed many disturbances and also interviewed witnesses to events that took place during their absence. Early in the case they observed that objects were most often disturbed in particular locations, and that the disturbances were connected with a nineteen-year-old shipping clerk named Julio. There was no evidence of fraud—in several instances objects were disturbed that the investigators had placed in selected target areas and had kept under careful surveillance.

Roll and his colleagues looked at Julio's personality profile on several psychological tests. Comments from testers included, "evidence of anger, rebellion, a feeling of not being part of the social environment," and "aggressive feelings and impulses which are disturbing and unacceptable to him. He prevents the direct expression of these feelings." Roll saw this as a classical example of a thread that runs through most poltergeist cases—tensions in interpersonal situations, often involving an adolescent.

Thus poltergeists are related to the unconscious mind, a way of expressing stress, frustration, or hostility. Most people would express these feelings physically, either externally by throwing something or internally by developing ulcers or high blood pressure. Poltergeist agents, however, respond unconsciously to stress by spontaneous psychokinesis. Adolescents, whose stress level is often high, are the most common poltergeist agents, but by no means exclusively. Adults, too, are sometimes apparently poltergeist agents. Recent research has also shown that neurological factors as well as psychological factors may be involved—occasionally epilepsy appears in the background of poltergeist agents. This does not mean that most or even many frustrated adolescents or epileptics exhibit spontaneous PK, but rather that they are common factors in those very rare people who do show evidence of psychokinesis.

There are still cases in which the typical poltergeist explanation does not seem to fit. The flying-shelf incident at the beginning of this chapter happened only once, whereas poltergeists are recurrent. We know nothing at all about single spontaneous events, except that they *might* be psychokinesis.

Dealing with Poltergeist Phenomena

If you think you have a poltergeist situation, begin by working through the possible explanations for the phenomenon, starting with normal explanations. Decide that there is an actual poltergeist only when no normal explanation seems to suffice. There are basically three alternatives when you have phenomena suggestive of poltergeist activity, which I list roughly in order of likelihood.

First are natural phenomena. These are such things as a house's settling noises or banging pipes. Such sounds can be very suggestive of a poltergeist, much more so than you might at first think. Here is an example from my own experience:

> *A Non-Poltergeist.* We have a house with heating wires in the ceiling. As the heat comes on, there are often raps and bangs, beginning on one side of the house and traveling across the ceiling. One night we had a new babysitter who became terrified, since the sounds sounded exactly like footsteps crossing the floor in the unoccupied upstairs room. We had become so used to it that we hadn't thought to tell her about the heating system.

True poltergeist phenomena are *very rare*. Don't jump to paranormal conclusions until you have carefully ruled out the natural possibilities.

Then there are normal, but intentional, phenomena. Poltergeist-like pranks are a common activity of children, especially if they receive attention for them. Even for adolescents or adults, the excitement caused by a "poltergeist" may be very rewarding to someone who seeks attention. It is very hard to separate pranks from actual poltergeists because both have a living agent around whom they center. In some of the cases studied by parapsychologists, there seem to be aspects of both PK and pranks, further complicating the situation. In both situations, the agent may be stressed, frustrated, or emotionally disturbed. Again, before concluding that you have a poltergeist, search very carefully for normal explanations. To illustrate with another personal example:

Holes in the Pajamas. My 3-year-old son came to us one morning, pointing at the new pajamas he was wearing, and said, "Mommy, they have holes!" Sure enough, the pajamas which had been intact the night before had odd-looking small, neat holes in them. Good material for a call to the ghostbusters, especially if we had taken the babysitter's story of the upstairs ghosts seriously! Instead, we asked him how the holes had gotten there, and he said, "I snipped them!" and produced a pair of baby fingernail clippers that he had found. Equally easy for many children, of course, especially if they suspected that they would be punished for cutting up new pajamas (or breaking the crystal bowl on the table, etc.), would be to blame it on "the ghost."

Finally, there are true poltergeist phenomena, i.e., phenomena that actually are psychokinesis. As we have seen, these are interpreted by most researchers as *unconscious* psychokinesis. Though some form of counseling may help in the situation, it would be a mistake to identify a particular individual as the scapegoat and say *he* (or she) needs counseling. The problem may well be one of relationships in the entire family or social situation. Sometimes a session or two of family counseling is enough to make the poltergeist go away.

It is important to remember that you don't need to *prove* a phenomenon is paranormal to deal with it successfully. The phenomena may be partially normal and partially paranormal, but they are likely to go away when the psychological dynamics of the situation are addressed. Identification of the persons and the stressful situations and working with a counselor sympathetic to the possibility of psychic experiences are likely to be of help in these situations. But again, make sure you have eliminated simple "normal" explanations before going to the trouble of seeking out a counselor—you may only have needed a plumber!

Is Psychokinesis a Sign of Spiritual Progress?

PK parties appear to be relatively harmless, if not very spiritually enlightening. In a discussion at the 1984 Parapsychological Association Convention, the participants identified a number of benefits to this approach. Most important was that the experiences of people at PK parties challenge the belief that PK ability is freakish and limited to a select few. Whether or not actual PK is responsible for the metal bending in a particular case, the experience is empowering; it gives a feeling of self-confidence. The experience also tends to reduce fear. At PK parties, people discover that PK feels natural and easy, not unlimited or uncontrollable. But the realization that there may be a potential greater than previously suspected heightens the need to pay attention to psychological and spiritual development.

In daily life, of course, we usually have no way of knowing if PK is the sole or partial cause of an event, or, if it is, whether we are the agents of the PK, or it comes from another source. Some of the experiences reported in my surveys seem to reflect wishful thinking. One woman wrote, "I am able to change traffic lights to green." A man told me, "When I walk by streetlights, I can turn them on and off." PK is certainly a possibility, but it is more likely that we are seeing normal events. Traffic lights eventually turn green without PK. Streetlights are controlled by light-sensing switches. Small changes in light at dusk or passing car headlights can easily cause an illusion of control. As we have seen, researchers have found PK to be weak, sporadic and difficult to control. In most cases a belief that you can exert reliable control over physical systems is probably not justified.

So far, we have looked at the possibility of psychokinetic abilities in "ordinary" people. The data are frustrating because we are faced with a sporadic phenomenon, which seems to vanish when subjected to close scrutiny. The transpersonal perspective suggests that one may need to reach a certain level of spiritual awareness to manifest such abilities consistently.

In the Western world, India has acquired a reputation for the seemingly miraculous feats of yogis, individuals with a long history of experience along the spiritual path. During recent years we have acquired some solid scientific evidence of the astonishing physiological abilities of yogis. Elmer and Alyce Green in *Beyond Biofeedback* discuss their research with Swami Rama, in which the Swami was able to warm and cool different parts of his hand simultaneously and even stop his heartbeat. Even more amazing, he was able to move a device consisting of balanced knitting needles and located across the room. The Greens controlled this experiment by requiring the Swami to wear a face mask to prevent his breath from moving the device.

One guru in India with a reputation for even more miraculous feats is Sathya Sai Baba, a man whose devotees are convinced he is an avatar (an incarnation of God). Parapsychologists Karlis Osis and Erlendur Haraldsson visited Sai Baba to try to document his claims of extraordinary psychic abilities. These abilities, if genuine, are so far beyond the PK studied in laboratories as to justly deserve the designation "miracles." Followers of Sai Baba, including many well-educated professionals, spoke of his ability to perform such feats as materializing precious jewels from thin air and full, hot meals from sand. Materialization, seen occasionally in studies of mediums, consists of an object appearing or disappearing in circumstances in which no physical cause of the event can be detected. Osis and Haraldsson, both experienced field investigators, were skeptical. A good rule of thumb for investigating claims of PK or materializations is "If it looks like a magic trick, it probably is!" Yet in extensive interviews with those who knew Sai Baba personally, both current and former followers, the researchers found no hint of fraud. In their own interactions with him, they had inexplicable experiences. For example, Sai Baba produced for Osis a large gold ring with his (Sai Baba's) picture imprinted on the stone. Later, while the ring was on Osis's finger, Sai Baba removed the stone with his picture on it without touching, bending, or breaking the ring.

Sai Baba, a spiritual leader, had no interest in science and would not participate in controlled experiments. When asked, "How do you do this?" Sai Baba replied, "Mental creation. I think, imagine, and then it is there." Sai Baba preferred to discuss his philosophy: "Spiritual love is central, miracles are small items. Love is giving and forgiving."

Osis and Haraldsson did not view their observations as conclusive proof but could find no reasonable explanation for what had occurred. They state: "In spite of a long-lasting and painstaking effort, we found no direct evidence of fraud."

In his book *Modern Miracles*, Haraldsson calls attention to the parallels between the feats claimed for Sai Baba and the miracles described in the Bible, such as raising the dead, materialization of food, and healing. Haraldsson notes that such feats are reported not only for Jesus but for later Christian saints as well. As with Sai Baba, the feats are not supposed to be important in themselves but are intended to point to the existence of a higher spiritual truth.

Working with Psychokinesis

Although we will look at the spiritual path in the final section of the book, most of us probably feel little likelihood that we will equal Sai Baba in the near future. Can it be dangerous to experiment with PK, perhaps creating a poltergeist? Are PK parties a useful way to work with this ability or does it have a more noble purpose?

The Cayce readings say: "The spirit is the life, the mind is the builder, and the physical is the result." Many people have found that focus on a spiritual ideal and exercising your personal will are excellent ways to improve your life. You may never know whether your positive results came from psychokinesis or your own physical efforts, and it is probably not important. A belief in the possibility of PK is not a substitute for taking physical action. We need to employ all the resources at our disposal to achieve success. The alternative—leaving everything to chance—is sure to produce poor results.

Bending spoons and controlling dice do not seem to be very spiritual objectives. When we look for an appropriately lofty purpose for using PK, healing immediately comes to mind. PK still appears to be the weakest and most sporadic of psychic abilities, and we know virtually nothing about how to control it in most situations. In its healing aspects, however, there is a long tradition and some interesting recent research. The next chapter will look at the healing applications of "mind over matter."

CHAPTER 7
Psychic Healing

Question: Is there likelihood of bad health in March?
Answer: If you are looking for it you can have it in February! If you want to skip March, skip it—you'll have it in June! If you want to skip June don't have it at all this year!

—Edgar Cayce, Reading 3564-1

The process goes by many names—psychic, mental, faith, spiritual, and paranormal healing. The healing tradition is backed by thousands of years of history. For many people it is still a practical alternative or adjunct to drugs, surgery, and the other tools of modern medicine. The views that our natural state is wellness, not disease, and that anyone can heal with the power of the mind are still alive and well, despite twentieth-century medicine.

Edgar Cayce pioneered the field of holistic medicine, the approach that the body, mind, and spirit are all part of the healing process. An editorial in a 1979 issue of the *Journal of the American Medical Association* said: "The roots of present-day holism probably go back 100 years to the birth of Edgar Cayce in Hopkinsville, Kentucky." Volumes have been written about Cayce's success at psychic diagnosis of disease at a distance, his seemingly miraculous cures, and his complete philosophy of health. But the letters I have received and the research of parapsychologists show that healing abilities are not limited to a few psychic "stars"; they are a regular part of the lives of many people.

Varieties of Healing Experiences

We will look at experiences and evidence in three areas: self-healing, healing of others, and psychic diagnosis.

Self-Healing

As the quote that begins this chapter implies, self-healing begins with the mind. In Edgar Cayce's day, disease was thought to be caused primarily by external influences—germs or injuries. The idea that the mind had the power to cause *and* to heal disease was not popular in mainstream medicine. However, the medical community's consciousness is slowly changing. Now we have "behavioral medicine" and "psychoneuroimmunology," areas in which modern medicine has begun to recognize the power of the mind. Healing through visualization is now one of many strategies employed in the treatment of cancer. The 1990 Gallup poll reported that 25 percent of the American people felt that they were able to "heal [their bodies] using the power of [their minds] without traditional medicine." One might think that this type of healing is now so well accepted that there is no need to write about it in a book on "psychic" experiences. Yet several of the people I surveyed cited "healing" as their most significant psychic experience. Here is an example, from a thirty-eight-year-old woman:

The Power of Thought. Through self-hypnosis and laying on of hands (on myself), I've been able to control migraine headaches I've suffered with for 19 years and increase my hormone level after a complete hysterectomy. I have also been able to induce out-of-body states when I needed them—the first time this happened was on the operating table during emergency surgery in which I almost died.

You can see here the connection between self-healing and psychic experiences. This woman had been working actively with self-hypnosis and was able to control her illnesses. On the operating table she was able to go out of her body, an experience we will look at in a later chapter. While the idea of self-hypnosis is an accepted part of behavioral medicine, out-of-body experiences are still on the other side of the "enchanted boundary"—that region considered to be beyond science—in the opinion of most medical practitioners.

Here is another example of a self-healing related to self-hypnosis, from a thirty-three-year-old woman:

Anesthesia. While in the emergency room with my sister, I lay on a table waiting to be checked. I was in great pain with what was later diagnosed as a kidney infection. Suddenly my entire body went into spasm and I cried with fear, having no idea what was wrong and thinking I didn't want to die. My sister reminded me that I had learned a self-hypnosis technique to control pain. Using this method, I placed my hand on my body over where the pain seemed to be centered. The convulsions, which had been happening continuously for several minutes, suddenly and immediately ceased. A doctor later told me that the convulsions were caused by the infection having reached my bloodstream, and I had almost died.

Here again we find that the mind has remarkable power over the body, power that we do not normally recognize in everyday life. Hypnosis, especially self-hypnosis, is one of the most common means used to communicate with the body's healing capacities.

What exactly is hypnosis? It is a state of enhanced and focused concentration that can lead not only to major alterations in perception, mood, and memory but also to significant physiological changes. Hypnosis is a well-known tool for anesthesia in dentistry, and it has proven very useful in controlling stress-related illnesses, today's major killers and cripplers. This capacity for self-healing addresses a significant medical need, since the acute infectious diseases, like pneumonia and tuberculosis, are no longer the threat that they once were. Now chronic, stress-related conditions predominate, like heart disease and cancer, and hypnosis can aid in their treatment.

Contrary to popular misconception, hypnosis is not primarily something that occurs during a hypnotic induction, where a "hypnotist" tells you that you are "getting sleepy." Rather than being a state of sleep, hypnosis is a state of alertness and receptivity to suggestion, and the state is self-induced. In other words, all hypnosis is self-hypnosis.

As with any ability, some people have more hypnotic ability than others. About 10 percent of the general population have very high hypnotic ability and may be able to accomplish great feats of self-healing. Another 10 percent have very low hypnotic ability and can be very resistant to learning self-healing techniques. The rest of us are somewhere in the middle and can, to some degree, enhance the capability of our bodies for self-healing. Even the people with low hypnotic ability are not left out. They can often be helped by biofeedback, in which an instrument measuring temperature or brain waves feeds back to them a measurement of their own internal state, which they are not normally able to perceive. With this feedback, they, too, may be able to gain more control of their physical health.

Self-hypnosis and biofeedback are now standard procedures in behavioral medicine clinics, yet they have their roots in the same sorts of questions that stimulated the early parapsychologists. The Society for Psychical Research in Britain originally included hypnosis in the paranormal phenomena they wanted to study. Researchers in the late 1800s realized that hypnosis was able to enhance human capabilities far beyond those manifested in the ordinary waking state—not only healing but psychic phenomena as well. Healers in numerous traditions, from Brazil to the Philippines, enter a trance state from which they heal themselves and others.

Since hypnosis and self-healing employing cooperation between the conscious and the unconscious minds has become so widely accepted, I turn now to the healing of other people, including "laying on of hands" and "remote healing." There is still a controversy over whether effects can be explained entirely by the power of suggestion—that is, as a form of suggested self-healing—or whether something paranormal is happening. Recent research demonstrates that the process does indeed go beyond self-hypnosis.

The Power to Heal Others

Many people feel that energy from their body is closely tied to the healing process. Through some form of "laying on of hands," the traditional Christian religious term, they send an energy into the patient to effect a healing. Often perceived as heat or vibrations, the nature of this energy has not been identified. As we will see later in this chapter, it has commonalities both with psychokinesis and with more conventionally understood energy. A thirty-year-old woman sent us this story:

Healing a Knee. I went to my cousin Penny's to clean and to help her care for her infant son. She had fallen down the steps earlier and the doctor had diagnosed her as having twisted the ligaments in her leg. As was often the case (at the time), my hands were radiating heat. For some reason I passed my hand over her foot. She said she felt something in her knee. I did it again and again. She felt it in her knee. I then moved my hand to her knee. I concentrated slightly while we talked and passed my hand six inches above her knee. After a half hour or so, she took a nap while I cleaned. About an hour or hour and a half later, while I was cleaning the bathroom, the phone rang. Before I could get off my knees, Penny had jumped up and run into the kitchen to answer it, When I did emerge she was walking around the kitchen. Her knee did not pain her nor was it swollen.

How can this event be explained? Did the heat from the woman's hands heal her cousin's knee? Was the energy really "heat," or was it some other form of healing energy? From a simple report of an experience, there is no way to tell. Certainly heat—from a massage, for example—can be of great benefit to injuries of this type. But, as we will see later, there is evidence for more than heat in cases of psychic healing.

For some, the experience of healing others becomes a vocation. A sixty-three-year-old man sent us this report:

A New Life's Work. While working with a psychic, I went into a trance-like state and my arms and hands felt as if they were on fire or plunged into boiling oil. This feeling lasted for several hours. There was a feeling of joy that I had never experienced before and I had the feeling that this was to be my life's work in the future. My wife and I are volunteer members on the Palliative Care Team at a large hospital in the city, we also do pastoral care work at this same hospital. We find both these activities very rewarding.

Here again the metaphor of heat plays a part. This man's hands felt like they were on fire. Yet the heat appears to have been more of a stimulus to become a healer, rather than part of healing technique. His story reflects the joy and rewards in this work.

Other people see themselves as catalysts in the healing process. They feel that the healing energy is not theirs but comes either from the person being healed (the healer stimulates self-healing in the patient) or directly from a higher spiritual source. One sixty-five-year-old woman had this to say:

The Catalyst. Experience in healing leads me to believe that I am a catalyst. I give people faith to open to accept miracles. I pretend to be the instrument and meditate on the affirmation that they are healed. When I say "pretend," it's as though I'm taking on a power that I have no right to, but the other person needs me.

Similarly, a forty-five-year-old man shared this example of a direct effect of prayer for healing:

God Heals a Tumor. I go deep inside myself and call on God when there is a legitimate need for healing. For example: a friend was dying from a tumor growing on his brain. The doctors came out and said it was only hours now. "Steve" was a drug addict and the tumor was caused from dirty needles. He was my friend and deep inside he was a good person. I was sitting in the waiting room with his wife and some other friends. I didn't want anyone to know what I was doing, but I closed my eyes and went deep inside myself. I asked God (as I write this it still stirs emotions and tears, not only because of Steve's illness, but because of the gentleness and kindness God shows to such unworthy souls) to save Steve because he was a friend and a good person with some terrible problems. Within hours the tumor started to shrink. After a few days Steve was well on his way to recovery. No one could explain why. It just happened. I never told anyone about this before because I feel that it's a personal thing between myself and my creator.

Here the effect was direct, but the man attributes it not to himself but to God. This is another way of looking at healing, not as an ability or a skill but as evidence of the power of God. To apply it one does not need to take a course in healing but rather to invoke faith.

Finally, healing can be done at a distance. It need not involve hands, or even the proximity of the healer and patient. In this case a twenty-eight-year-old woman participated in a healing group.

> *Healing at a Distance.* We have a group of five individuals using an amethyst crystal as a focus to help us do healing projections. Each of us picked one distant individual to be healed. We each visualized cleansing the individual with a net. Unknown people were described in detail by members of the group with each adding something different. The first individual healed called immediately after we were done healing him, to say he felt better and confirmed "unknown to us" symptoms that we perceived while healing. This occurred the second we completed the healing. For each of the other group members descriptions and health problems were fairly accurately described to the knowledge of the individual who chose them.

As the preceding example shows, prayer for healing need not be a solitary activity. In fact, one of Edgar Cayce's lasting legacies was the creation in 1931 of a healing prayer group called the Glad Helpers, which still meets weekly at A.R.E. headquarters in Virginia Beach.

We have found that people conceive of their healing experiences on different levels. For some, the healer himself "does it," either with heat or with some other form of "energy." For others, the person being healed plays a major role, and the healer is just a catalyst. And for still others, healing comes from God, and the healer is just an intermediary, facilitating the process through faith.

Different methods are required to study the healing process at these different levels. If the healing is being caused by a simple physical energy such as heat, for example, it should be fairly easy to measure using standard instruments. If the energy is more related to psychokinesis, parapsychologists should be able to design experiments to rule out ordinary energies. If the healer is just a catalyst, and the real healing come from the patient, through a mechanism similar to self-hypnosis, this can be studied by hypnosis researchers as a normal psychological process. Finally, if God is the primary agent, a study of the faith of the healer and patient may be appropriate, rather than a study of the energy involved.

Researchers Study Psychic Healing

Laying on of hands is an ancient healing practice, common in diverse religions. Because of the religious nature of the practice, modern medicine has had little use for it, despite claims of its effectiveness. Medicine has explained the effectiveness of laying on of hands in terms of the "placebo effect." (A placebo is a presumably inert or neutral substance, such as a sugar pill, that elicits a therapeutic response.) Only recently have scientists come to realize that much of the healing that results from drugs and medical procedures is due to the placebo effect, rather than to the drug or procedure.

Belief in the healing power of the procedure is important in placebo healing. Ian Wickramasekera, in his book *Clinical Behavioral Medicine,* discusses numerous studies in which the placebo was as effective in healing as the medical procedure was. For example, approximately 35 percent of the patients who were given a placebo had severe clinical pain reduced by at least one half its original intensity. Placebos have proven useful in a wide variety of conditions, including asthma, ulcers, diabetes, cancer, and multiple sclerosis. Even a surgical placebo effect is possible. Research cited in Wickramasekera's book has shown that in some cases, patients with "dummy surgery," in which a skin incision is made but nothing else is done, may do as well as those undergoing the full surgical procedure.

This effect complicates our attempts to understand psychic healing. If belief alone can heal, how can a controlled test of a therapy such as laying on of hands be performed? It is hard to do a study of healing without the patients' being aware that they are being healed. Most of the studies of healing by parapsychologists have involved "healing analogs." These are experiments similar to the human healing situation but allowing better control. It is quite difficult to establish the accurate diagnoses and controls required for medical research with human subjects, especially on the very limited budgets available to most parapsychologists. Instead, researchers have conducted studies with plants, animals, and people in nonclinical situations.

One of the first researchers to do controlled studies of psychic healing was Bernard Grad, a biologist at McGill University in Canada. His involvement began in 1957, when he first met Oskar Estebany, a Hungarian who claimed he could heal the sick by touching them with his hands. Grad invited Estebany to his laboratory, and they began a series of experiments on healing animals and plants that lasted seven years.

In one of the experiments, Grad tested Estebany's ability to affect plant growth, using plants to eliminate the possibility of a psychological effect of suggestion or placebo effect. Estebany watered barley seeds with water he had "treated" by holding a container of it in his hands. The control pots of seeds were watered by untreated water. Grad used salty water to inhibit the growth of the plants, reasoning that if the healing energy could overcome the effects of the salt, the plants would grow faster. The experiment worked—the differences in the heights of experimental and control plants after twelve days were impressive. Grad and his colleagues also did work involving the psychic healing of wounds in mice, with similar results.

The work using laboratory mice as "patients" was followed up by Graham and Anita Watkins, researchers at the Institute for Parapsychology in North Carolina. They tested twelve subjects (nine of them were professed "psychics" or were known to be exceptional performers in previous experiments) for their ability to cause mice to wake up more quickly than normal from ether anesthesia. Pairs of mice were simultaneously anesthetized. The psychic was told to attempt to awaken one mouse (looking through a one-way glass from an outside room) while not affecting the control. The results were highly significant—on the average the experimental mice required only 87 percent as long to awaken as the controls did.

One of the most active current researchers addressing the question of psychic healing is William Braud, now director of research at the Institute for Transpersonal Psychology in California. His healing analog studies, like the studies with plants and mice, do not use actual patients in clinical settings. Instead, Braud's experiments are conceived in terms of psychokinesis on biological targets. Braud has found that individuals are able to remotely influence a wide range of biological targets, including the spatial orientation of fish, the activity of small mammals, and the rate of hemolysis (breakdown) of human red blood cells in a test tube. The most extensive research in Braud's laboratory has focused on the remote mental influence of another person's electrodermal activity. These are the electrical responses of the skin that are measured by the polygraph or "lie detector." Electrodermal responses are a measure of the degree of activation of the subject's autonomic nervous system (the part of the nervous system that controls heart rate, digestion, and other "automatic" functions). Because autonomic nervous system responsiveness is very important in many stress-related diseases, this measurement is relevant to psychic healing. In carefully controlled studies, Braud has found that his subjects can either calm or activate the distant subject remotely, without physical or sensory contact, using some form of mental influence.

Can we measure the energy of psychic healing? One of the intriguing results of Grad's work was that the water held by Estebany appeared to hold a "charge" of psychic energy, which could be transmitted to the plants. Douglas Dean (recall his work described in the telepathy chapter and his book *Executive ESP*) followed up on Grad's work. He found that apparently there was a change in the molecular bonds in the water, which could be measured by an infrared spectrometer. The most recent work replicating this effect was done by Stephan Schwartz of the Mobius Society in Los Angeles, an organization specializing in practical applications of psychic ability. Schwartz set up actual healing situations. While the healers were working with the patients, they wore gloves with pockets in them holding vials of water. The idea was that the healing energy had to pass through the water on the way to the patient and that it might be possible to measure this energy in a spectrometer. They found a significant change in the infrared spectrum of the water. There was a complicating factor, however: Some of the control water samples that physically were in the room but were not held by the healer also showed the effect. This may or may not have been a genuine psychic effect—further work is needed. But the basic idea that the healing energy can be physically measured is exciting.

The concept of laying on of hands, in a nonreligious form, has even begun to enter mainstream medicine. In the 1970s, Dolores Krieger, a nurse and professor at New York University, explored a procedure she called "therapeutic touch," a form of laying on of hands that was not religiously based. The practitioner must possess the conscious intent to assist or heal the patient but need hold no specific religious beliefs. The process also does not require a declaration of faith on the part of the patient. Conceptually, this is similar to using psychokinesis for healing purposes. The technique has been taught to thousands of nurses and other health care professionals. In doing therapeutic touch, the practitioner first "centers" herself by shifting her awareness from an external to an internal focus, becoming relaxed and calm. She makes a mental intention to help and heal the patient. She then moves her hands over the patient's body in a prescribed manner in order to detect and correct areas of imbalance and disease. Krieger and others have done considerable research with therapeutic touch, showing that it can increase hemoglobin levels in the blood, increase relaxation, decrease anxiety, and decrease headache pain.

But what actually *is* it? Is it the psychological effect of suggestion on the patient—a valuable tool for healing but not considered "paranormal"—or is it something more? Separating the psychic effects of laying on of hands from the effect of suggestion in an actual human healing situation (as opposed to an experiment with animals or plants) has not been easy. After all, it is hard to imagine an experiment in which the patient is unaware that someone is trying to perform healing at close range. And measuring whether healing has occurred is also difficult. Yet Daniel Wirth, a researcher with Healing Sciences International in Orinda, California, recently completed an experiment that *was* able to separate the psychic effect of the procedure from the psychological effect of being in a healing situation.

Wirth recruited subjects for what he told them was an experiment to measure body energy fields. He told them that the energy of the body could best be measured by removing a surface layer of skin, which would allow the energy to flow freely from the body to an external monitoring instrument. He had a doctor make a small, uniform-size circular wound in each person's arm, using a skin biopsy instrument.

For the experiment, the subject was instructed to put his arm through a hole in a door, so that he would be unable to see the equipment on the other side. Actually there *was* no equipment on the other side. Instead, for half the subjects, there was a practitioner of noncontact therapeutic touch. The other half of the subjects were a control group who received no treatment.

Each person participated in several sessions, and the doctor measured how fast the wounds healed. Even the doctor was not told the purpose of the experiment until it was over. This is an example of what is called a double-blind experiment, where neither the subject nor the person making the measurement knows the true conditions of the experiment, so no bias can enter into the results.

The result: The wounds healed much faster in the subjects who received the healing treatments, to a highly significant degree. Of course, at the end the true purpose of the experiment was revealed to all participants. This experiment was the first ever to demonstrate in controlled conditions that a technique related to laying on of hands could produce measureable results without the person's being aware that he or she was the subject of a healing session. Apparently there is some unknown energy aiding the healing process.

Is this the same energy found in psychokinesis? Because we really don't know what psychokinesis is, this is a difficult question to answer. We should not jump to conclusions—there may be many unknown forms of energy.

Healing Prayer: A Level above the Psychic?

The studies of healing at a distance demonstrate that there is more to healing than simply physically measurable energy or the placebo effect. Yet they are still designed with the assumption that the healer does something directly to the patient. In many cases, however, as in some of the examples earlier in this chapter, the healer may state that he himself does nothing, and credit God with the result. Is healing prayer just a form of psychokinesis, or is there something more?

Such a question cannot be answered by the methods of parapsychology. It is hard to imagine an experiment that rules out psychokinesis but not God. But it is important to look at work where prayer to God, rather than direct healing, was the focus.

In 1988, cardiologist Randolph Byrd published a study in the well-respected *Southern Medical Journal* showing the efficacy of prayer in healing at a distance. His study was well controlled. Over ten months, 393 patients admitted to the coronary care unit were assigned to a prayer group or a control group. (They were informed of the purpose of the experiment, but neither the patients nor their physicians were aware of which patients were receiving prayer.) Prayer was provided by participating Christians outside the hospital. The prayer patients showed significantly superior recovery compared to the controls: They were five times less likely to require antibiotics and three times less likely to develop pulmonary edema.

Dr. Larry Dossey, a well-known practitioner of holistic medicine, has written the book *Healing Words,* discussing Byrd's study and many others that demonstrate the healing power of prayer. There are many challenges in doing scientific studies of prayer, but it is rapidly becoming an accepted area for research.

Edgar Cayce constantly emphasized the importance of prayer, even while recommending a variety of other medical treatments. A belief in the power of prayer does not require abandonment of modern medicine but rather can work with medicine to effect overall healing.

In the view of the Cayce readings, prayer is not just a technique, like a specific way of moving the hands. "Prayer is the *making* of one's conscious self more in attune with the spiritual forces that may manifest in a material world. . . . Prayer is the concerted effort of the physical consciousness to become attuned to the consciousness of the Creator, either collectively or individually" (Reading 281-13).

Attunement to the Creator is the highest transpersonal realization. But focusing on this level changes our concept of the healing process. It is no longer only our will or the will of the patient that we need to be concerned about, but God's will. There is a need, then, for guidance as to how to help, not merely instruction in techniques.

When Cayce was asked, "How do we know when to help an individual?" he replied, "Do with thy might what thy hands, hearts, minds, souls find to do, leaving the increase, the benefits in *His* hands, who is the Giver of all good and perfect gifts" (Reading 281-4).

Meredith Puryear, in her book *Healing through Meditation and Prayer,* discusses the Cayce readings on healing prayer and brings in her own experience in the Glad Helpers prayer healing group. As she explains it:

The criteria for knowing what help we can give are fourfold. We should (1) do what is at hand, (2) do what we are drawn to by our hearts, (3) do that which we choose with our minds to do, and (4) do that which is in keeping with the ideals and purposes of the soul, always leaving the increase or the results in His hands.

This reflects the full-spectrum approach characteristic of Cayce's work, according to which we work at all the levels we can and leave the ultimate to God.

She goes on to say, "We must always be willing to do whatever we can for others at the physical level, but I am fully convinced that our help will be more enlightened if we are praying for ourselves and any others that we seek to help. Too often we serve the ego desires of others, rather than their real needs."

I would add that we may also be serving the ego desires of ourselves when we attempt to heal others. We need to deal with all the levels. Before you set yourself up as a "psychic healer," make sure you have attended to the basic physical needs of the *patient* and are working toward higher attunement. Meredith Puryear says, "The first step in developing the ability to heal through touch is to become the kind of person that others want to be near, the kind to whom they are drawn. . . . Proclaiming 'I am a healer' is the surest way I know to make people apprehensive."

Psychic Diagnosis

Psychic diagnosis is clairvoyantly diagnosing disease. This, of course, was Edgar Cayce's great talent, an ability that brought in thousands of requests for psychic readings—68 percent of the Cayce readings were medical readings. I am often asked, "Is there anyone *now* who can do what Edgar Cayce did?" and "Could *I* learn to do psychic diagnosis?"

From what we know about psychic ability, it would not be surprising if people could successfully diagnose disease in relatives and close acquaintances. Emotionally charged situations bring out psychic ability. It is a major step, however, to begin diagnosing disease in complete strangers. We would expect Edgar Cayce's feat—diagnosing at a distance, with no personal contact at all—to be even more difficult.

Psychic diagnosis, while an extension of clairvoyant ability, requires some special cautions in application. A partially correct diagnosis could tell us a lot about psychic ability, but the *patient* might not be helped at all or might even get worse. While a person may show a very high level of psychic ability, from the practical point of view of a parapsychologist interested in "hits," the quality of the material may still not be adequate. From my own research, here are two examples of the problems that arise when attempting to apply psychic diagnosis.

The Paralyzed Leg. This was an experiment in psychic diagnosis at a distance. "Betty," a psychic claiming an ability to diagnose disease, was in a room on the third floor of a building. The patient, "Dave," whom she had never met, was in his office on the first floor. I gave Betty his name and location and asked her to diagnose his medical problem. She began the diagnosis by noting that across from his desk was a shelf of red books with gold lettering. She then went systematically through his body, mentioning several conditions, none serious. Since I knew Dave had a spinal injury, leaving one leg partially paralyzed and in frequent pain, I asked her to focus on the spine. She said there was an injury, causing problems with the nerves to the upper leg. Then she described several more medical problems, rather serious illnesses, unusual for a middle-aged man.

We had taped the session and we took the tape down to Dave for evaluation. We were all impressed by her description of the books in his office—it was precisely correct. He was also impressed by her initial diagnosis of his minor medical problems—he had awakened with a cold that morning. But when the tape came to the problem with his leg, he said the psychic was wrong. The recurring pain was in his lower leg, not his upper leg as I had believed. Betty was apparently reading *my* beliefs, rather than *his* condition. Then, as the tape related the more serious medical conditions, he said the diagnoses did not apply at all. But his secretary, an elderly woman, was astonished—Betty was describing *her* medical condition.

A parapsychologist would classify this example as a form of displacement—picking up details of the wrong target. Though it is a fascinating example of psi at work, it is discouraging for someone who needs an accurate diagnosis. If Dave had uncritically accepted the entire reading, he might have been treated for diseases that he would not have for twenty years, yet not have found relief for the pain in his leg.

Here is another example of a psychic diagnosis in which there is ample evidence for psi, but it would not have been of much help to the patients.

The Diabetic and the Arthritic. Another psychic, "Susan," did two diagnoses for me, again at a distance, with only the name and location of the patient. The first patient was "Michael," a man with severe diabetes who had gone blind a few years earlier. In reviewing his body systems, Susan picked up many of the complications of diabetes, including circulation problems and kidney and bladder deterioration. But when she got to his eyes, she said simply that they were "weak" and advised him to see an eye doctor.

We had similar results with the second patient, "Anne," who had rheumatoid arthritis so severe that she could barely get out of bed and walk on crutches. The psychic, Susan, specifically sensed arthritis and correctly identified the knees as the location of the worst symptoms. But she said it was a mild case and needed no treatment. In fact the woman was barely able to walk.

Again we see strong evidence of psychic ability. The diagnoses were accurate, but in both cases they minimized the severity of the diseases. If either of these patients had been counting on the psychic diagnoses for a "miracle cure," he or she would have been very disappointed.

Although the examples above reflect my own experiences with psychic diagnosis, some medical doctors have found psychics to be a useful adjunct to traditional medical practice. Dr. C. Norman Shealy, the founding president of the American Holistic Medical Association, has worked with many psychics in search of this elusive ability. Carolyn Myss, one of his best subjects, taps into the emotional roots underlying diseases. The two of them have written books on diagnosis and healing by mixing traditional and alternative medicine, including *The Creation of Health,* a discussion of their work together, and Myss's new book, *Anatomy of the Spirit,* which explains her healing system. I am sure that many more practitioners are quietly using their own intuitive abilities to aid in diagnosis and treatment of patients. I have personally received help from health-care providers who work with their intuitive impressions. Such abilities may not provide a complete diagnosis, but they may suggest new avenues to pursue in understanding baffling ailments.

Psychic diagnosis, then, is an area in urgent need of further study. It has high potential as one of the most practical applications of psychic ability, but it also has serious pitfalls. A well-meaning person can do harm with inaccurate attempts at psychic diagnosis. And a person desperate for any solution to his health problem can be taken in, either by an innocent but inaccurate psychic or by a deliberate fraud, and left worse off than before.

So You Want to Be a Healer?

We are all healers, certainly in our capacity to heal ourselves, if not in our skill in healing others. On any of the levels on which healing occurs, sincerity of purpose appears to be the key. If you are called to heal at the physical level, by all means go to medical school, or to massage therapy school. If you are drawn to the mental aspect, pursue training in clinical psychology and hypnosis. These types of training are regulated by professional associations, so it is relatively easy to find a legitimate program. If you are moved to approach healing from the psychic or spiritual level, however, it is harder to discern an authentic path. The diversity is huge, and there is undoubtedly value in many approaches. Most agree on some of the basic principles, though with difference of emphasis.

Some approach healing from the perspective that there are subtle energies and that a healer can learn to work with the human energy field. Barbara Ann Brennan, author of *Hands of Light* and *Light Emerging,* is a leader in this area. She has a degree in physics and is well grounded in the physical world, but she has also spent years in training in psychotherapy, massage therapy, and energy healing. She sees self-knowledge as the first step in learning to heal, not simply technical training. Her books include exercises in finding your fears and dealing with them, exercises to find and transform your negative beliefs, and spiritual exercises to discover divine will and develop love and faith.

Deepak Chopra, a holistically oriented medical doctor, approaches healing from a Hindu perspective in his books, including *Ageless Body, Timeless Mind.* He practices Ayurvedic ("science of life") medicine and is a follower of Maharishi Mahesh Yogi, the leader of the Transcendental Meditation movement. Naturally, he focuses on the importance of meditation in the healing process. In meditation there is an encounter with the self—both lower and higher—and this is crucial in both self-healing and healing others.

We have already seen the work of Dolores Krieger, the originator of therapeutic touch. Although therapeutic touch is not tied to any specific religious system, it is more than a technique. Like the others, Krieger emphasizes the need for self-knowledge, motivation, and sincerity of purpose. She has found that people trained in therapeutic touch often experience a change in lifestyle, becoming more psychically sensitive and having telepathic experiences.

Finally, some healers go beyond technique altogether, relying on faith. For example, in Lee's Summit, Missouri, there is a group called Silent Unity, part of the Unity school of Christianity. Twenty-four hours a day there are people continuously praying and switchboard operators ready to take the calls of people in need of prayer. Thousands of people feel that they have been helped and healed. From a very different side of Christianity, there is Oral Roberts, the well-known conservative Christian evangelist. Roberts, too, has many testimonials to the effectiveness of his healing prayer. At A.R.E., there are the Glad Helpers prayer group and the Prayer Services Department, which maintains a worldwide prayer list. The power of faith and prayer seems to cut across denominational boundaries and tap a universal source.

Edgar Cayce's advice to the Glad Helpers healing prayer group was, "Keep on. Pray oft. Live right. . . . Keep faithful, then, in thine service, in being a channel of blessings to many. Be not weary. Be not slothful.

Be not unmindful of that which is set before thee. Turn not back, but press on to the more glorious light that comes with the closer walk with Him day by day" (Readings 281-9 and 281-19).

PART THREE

The Realms
of the Psyche

CHAPTER 8

Apparitions and Hauntings

BERNARDO: How now, Horatio! you tremble and
   look pale:
Is not this something more than fantasy?
What think you on't?

HORATIO: Before my God, I might not this
   believe
Without the sensible and true avouch
Of mine own eyes.
         —Shakespeare, *Hamlet,* Act 1, Scene 1

                  Who ya gonna call?
                  —*Ghostbusters*

Whether it is the ghost of Hamlet's father fore-shadowing the future or the antics of movie ghosts from *Topper* to *Ghostbusters,* apparitions and hauntings have played a major role in human affairs throughout history. These experiences, often among the most disturbing of psychic phenomena, can result in confusion or fear. Yet they can also serve as evidence and reassurance of a higher reality and life after death. Though many may be unquestionably "paranormal," others may be the result of misunderstandings of "normal" events or symbolic of events within the psyche. Can we know if they are simply internal hallucinations or truly evidence of life after death? In this exploration we will use the same techniques that have proved valuable for probing dreams and synchronicities and extend them to far more unusual experiences.

Precisely defining an "apparition" is difficult. The usual sense of the term "apparition" refers to the appearance of that part of the human personality that apparently either survives death or can detach from the physical body of a living person. It is often applied to a visual image, but not necessarily that of a dead person—some of the most interesting cases are apparitions of people who are still alive. The term "apparition" can also be applied to voices or other sounds, to smells that seem to behave as though something intelligent is controlling them, or even to physical sensations. Thus, feeling a "presence" would also be considered an apparition. The apparition may appear to behave intelligently and seem to be trying to communicate a message, or it may not try to interact with you or even recognize that you're there. An apparition can occur anywhere. It may appear again, but often it appears only once.

The term "haunting," on the other hand, usually refers to an apparition *repeatedly* seen by one or more people in a specific *location*. Hauntings often seem to behave like "recordings," going through repetitive motions rather than exhibiting the characteristics of a complete personality.

The term "ghost" covers aspects of both apparitions and hauntings. When most people speak of a ghost, they are referring to an apparition that they connect with an intelligent force remaining after someone's death. A ghost may appear once or may repetitively haunt a location.

Another term frequently heard is "poltergeist." The word "poltergeist" means "noisy ghost" in German and is generally used when objects float or fly around the house, unusual sounds occur such as loud bangs and raps, or appliances turn themselves on and off.

The traditional explanation was that poltergeists were mischievous spirits of the dead. But, as I discussed in the psychokinesis chapter, many parapsychologists now feel that most poltergeists result from the unconscious psychokinesis of a living human being.

How common are apparitions, and what types are reported? On surveys asking for the number of times a person has had a given psychic experience, apparitions are about in the middle of the pack. In John Palmer's study of the townspeople of Charlottesville, Virginia, in 1979, 17 percent reported apparitions and 7 percent reported having actually lived in a haunted house. About twice as many people heard or felt an apparition as actually saw one. The 1990 Gallup poll found that 9 percent of Americans claimed to have seen a ghost, and 14 percent reported that they had been in a house they felt was haunted. In my survey of 520 A.R.E. members, 44 percent reported at least one apparition experience. As with the other psychic experiences we have looked at, A.R.E. members typically report experiences at about three times the rate of the general population; even so, apparitional experiences are clearly very common. When we look at submissions of detailed descriptions of experiences that people consider striking or puzzling, apparitions rank with dreams as the most common in many collections.

Varieties of Apparitions and Hauntings

One simple way to classify apparitions is into categories of "crisis/death," "postmortem," "symbolic," and "hauntings." Crisis apparitions are occurrences when a person in a crisis state, sometimes at the instant of death, appears to someone at a distance. The second category, postmortem apparitions, refers to visitation by someone who has already been deceased for some length of time. Both the crisis and the postmortem apparitions are almost always appearances of relatives or friends. More puzzling are what I call symbolic apparitions, in which it is hard to identify the source as a specific living or dead person. Symbolic interpretation, however, may reveal greater meaning than is obvious on the surface. Often very puzzling, these events are sometimes dismissed as "simply hallucinations," yet they are windows to our unconscious mind and our spiritual potential. Finally, there are repetitive hauntings, where a person may feel a need for help, including counseling or "ghostbusting." These categories can all overlap, creating some very complex situations to untangle.

Crisis/Death Apparitions

Crisis apparitions are the easiest to verify objectively, since it is often possible to show that a crisis did in fact occur at the exact time the apparition was reported. The 1886 book *Phantasms of the Living* rigorously documented the truth of many apparition stories. The meaning of these events is also often obvious, simply an appearance at a time of crisis, without complex symbolic overtones. Here is a typical example from my collection of reports.

> *Grandmother with a Candle.* The night my grandmother died I was six. I woke up in the middle of the night and she was shuffling in, carrying a candle, to rub my back (something she did often to me, as a favorite grandchild). She looked very real, and the candle surrounded her with an eerie glow. She also looked a little sad, and I knew that she was saying good-bye. There was another occurrence connected with her death. This one happened to my mother. Mom was downstairs in the laundry and thought she

heard a knock on the door. So she went upstairs and looked out. No one was there. She opened the door and felt a wind breeze by, and she said, "Come in, Mama." Just then the phone rang. It was the nursing home, saying Nani had just died.

This case, reported by a thirty-year-old woman, has all the elements of the traditional crisis/death apparition. The apparition, of a close relative, "looked very real," not at all "ghostlike." This is frequently the case with crisis apparitions—they are so like living, physical human beings as to be actually mistaken for them, until they vanish. The apparition wasn't simply visual, it physically touched her as well. Apparitions do not require special circumstances; they often occur while people are engaged in their ordinary occupations or while they are lying in bed. Although there was no verbal communication, the message was clear: The grandmother was saying good-bye. What is especially interesting about this case is that there was a second apparition connected with the grandmother's death, this time entirely physical—a knock on the door and a breeze, perceived by the mother. Yet the communication that it was the presence of the grandmother was clear in this case as well. We will look more at symbols later, but remember the candle with the eerie glow. Candles weren't normally carried in the 1960s when this event happened, so it seems out of place. We will see that lights of various types are often connected with apparitions. What might a candle symbolize? Perhaps reassurance that the grandmother has a light to guide her on her path to the next world.

Wars, with their frequent episodes of sudden death, are another source for these types of apparitions.

Brother Killed in the War. During World War II, I awakened one night and saw my brother standing in a sort of white light, framed in my doorway. He stayed there, quietly, for a few seconds. Then was gone. He had just been killed in North Africa.

We have few details in this report by a seventy-three-year-old woman, but the ones she does provide are characteristic of this type of apparition. Again we have a light associated with the apparition, and he was "framed in my doorway." The symbols of a door as a transition and a white light as a guide are often seen in apparitions. This time he made no attempt to communicate, yet even without overt communication, the experience had enough impact to be remembered more then fifty years later.

What could be the meaning of these types of apparitions? They do not appear to be warnings or calls for help, as we have seen in some of the telepathic and dream cases. Perhaps the intuition of the six-year-old girl on seeing her grandmother is the best one: "I knew that she was saying good-bye."

Apparitions occasionally occur with no obvious crisis. In almost all cases, though, like telepathic experiences, they occur among people who are emotionally very close. Here is a case in which both people were aware of the apparitions of each other, but there was no crisis.

Visiting in Alaska. I had an experience recently where I was aware of the presence of a woman who is a member of my church. She was standing next to my bed while I was sleeping. I said to her, "What are you doing here, I thought you were in Alaska?" She replied "I am." When she actually returned from her trip to Alaska she rushed up to me to tell me that I had appeared in her stateroom on the ship—she awakened her husband to tell him about it.

Although with most apparitions there appears to be no action that one can take to prevent the crisis, occasionally there is a case where the physical manifestation is a warning resembling the telepathic or precognitive cases we have seen in previous chapters. Here is an example:

> *Warned by a Touch.* I was alone, driving my car in a narrow residential street. I felt a tap on my shoulder, slammed on the brakes, and then a small child chased his ball in front of my car, which was stopped.

This experience again shows an interconnectedness of which we are rarely conscious. All these experiences can point to something greater than themselves and be signposts along the spiritual path.

How can crisis apparitions help us in our quest for understanding? Transformation often requires a crises, and these apparitions may be a way of calling our attention to the opportunity for self-transformation. A crisis apparition, where there is no possibility of physically changing the event, can often be frustrating or guilt-producing when it is taken as a warning or a call for help. But it can also be a sign of something higher during a time of crisis, a sign that can aid in transformation by providing a glimpse of what lies beyond.

Postmortem Apparitions: Communication with the Deceased

Postmortem apparitions often have a very different character from crisis apparitions. They tend to be more symbolic and less literal and are often interpreted as opportunities for communication, either to reassure the living or to reassure the dead. They, too, are quite common. A recent book by Bill and Judy Guggenheim, *Hello from Heaven,* contains more then three hundred accounts of apparent communications from deceased individuals. Here is a short example from my collection of the reassurance type of post-mortem apparition:

Reassured by Grandfather. I saw my grandfather at the foot of my bed telling me not to worry about him anymore (he died in 1949). I used to worry that he was in hell because he was not a Catholic church attendee.

Such an experience is much more difficult to study objectively than a crisis apparition. There is no possibility of verification—the grandfather can't confirm that he paid a visit on that day. Yet the psychological impact on the person may be even greater than that from a crisis apparition. The message is not simply that there is life after death; the message is that death is a positive transition. As in the example above, regardless of religious belief before death, in the vast majority of cases the apparitions are reassurances of a positive nature.

In this next story, the form of the apparition, an olive green fog, is unusual, but the fog is symbolic and the message is again one of reassurance.

The Olive Green Fog. I was having tea in a well-lit kitchen of a friend. The children were watching *Happy Days.* Ellen and I were looking at astrology charts and trying to send each other picture images. I stated— "We're not alone." Ellen jumped up and brought a chair to the table. The room filled with "an olive green fog." An apparition which materialized and stayed. I found myself withdrawing from the room. After about twenty minutes it dissolved. The next two days it happened again. Once in my home. Once outside my home in the yard at noon. All three times we were together. The second time I tried to fight it by reciting and focusing my mind (my daughter was sleeping in the other room). The third time my friend jumped into her car and drove to the cemetery. Her first husband died in Vietnam and was buried in dress greens. (I did not know this since I met her later.) She had never reconciled to his death although remarried and had two children.

This example exhibits another feature sometimes present in apparition cases: It was *collective*. Two people saw it, although the symbolism of the olive green color was meaningful for only one of them. This feature, seen in about one-third of the cases in the Society for Psychical Research's original *Census of Hallucinations* and reported for 22 percent of the cases in Palmer's survey, argues against the hallucinations being merely subjective.

In contrast to apparitions whereby the dead reassure the living, occasionally there are experiences in which a person feels a need to reassure the apparition. Here is one such case. A woman felt a physical apparition and responded to it by sending a message of love.

Reassuring Mother-in-law. My mother-in-law passed over in June and that afternoon I was in my family room with my mother and my dog kept sniffing in the air all over the room and I knew my mother-in-law's spirit was in the room. I wasn't scared and I told her in my mind she was dead. She lost her memory completely in 1980 and was in a nursing home for six years. I told her years earlier I would care for her, which I did. She died of pneumonia and cardiac arrest. Going to bed that night I couldn't breathe. Felt like I was suffocating. Also I felt pushed backward. I felt my mother-in-law's death and her anger because she was dead and pushing me because I wasn't taking care of her. I talked in my mind and told her it was OK and her son, Bob, had died four years earlier and he and God and all her loved ones dead, were waiting to greet her.

Although we have looked primarily at visual apparitions, they can occur in any of the senses. The previous example included a physical sensation. Smell is often especially evocative of emotional memories—we often remember smells from childhood and can recall long-forgotten experiences simply by experiencing a smell. Here are two cases in which the communication was entirely by smell but was nevertheless a profound experience of reassurance.

The Smell of Roses. I was living on a Vermont farm as helper and member of an extended family. The eighty-four-year-old mother was a life-long Catholic while her daughter had found other sources of inspiration. Mother had had very definite ideas as to proper procedure for her burial. She died September 19, 1960. Her daughter arranged her funeral services in the Catholic church, her encasement in a proper casket (bronze) and her burial in her home cemetery. All these affairs had been taken care of and the family returned to the farm. I opened the kitchen door to enter the house to hear and see the daughter say as she crossed the room "It's as if I can feel that Mother is here in the room." At this point both a friend of the family and I were also in the room and became aware of a magnificent aroma as though the essence of uncounted multitudes of roses had suddenly bloomed. We, all three, walked around the room looking for the source of the odor which gradually faded out. We checked with each other and found that each one had experienced the same thing. The daughter concluded that her mother was answering her inside questioning which was "I hope I have done everything that Mother wanted." It was a gift from Mother to all of us as a "thank you" for what we had done for her.

The Smell of Incense. Six weeks after the death of my 18-year-old son, I was preparing to go out to lunch with friends for the first time since his death. I was alone in the house. As I came out of the bathroom into my bedroom, I smelled church incense—very strong. I walked out of the bedroom and checked the rest of the house, trying to find the origin of the odor—could find nothing. As I walked back into the bedroom, in the doorway again, the heavy odor of church incense. I sat on the bed and felt my son's presence. I did not see or hear anything, only felt calm and overwhelmed by peace and love. Lasted about five minutes. I never burned incense. My sister in New York later told me she had given some to my son the previous summer because he liked the smell of it.

How are apparitions created? They can evoke all the senses but are not simply realistic visits by a deceased person. If they are out-of-body people or spirits, why do they wear clothes? Wouldn't a person leave his clothes behind as well as his body? And why would apparitions carry candles—do they need light to see? Sometimes apparitions behave like physical beings, exiting through a door or walking down stairs. At other times they walk through walls or disappear suddenly.

Many parapsychologists feel that apparitions are neither simply inner hallucinations nor simply spirits. Instead, they are complex constructions with contributions from the unconscious mind as well as the spirit from the "other side." G. N. M. Tyrrell, a well-known apparitions researcher, sees them as a creative process rather than a perceptual one. The creation may be a joint effort of multiple unconscious minds, both living and dead.

Symbolism and Apparitions

As they are in dreams, symbols are fundamental to the creative process in apparitions. One of our best sources on the symbolic process is a book by Carl Jung's longtime associate, Aniela Jaffé, titled *Apparitions and Precognition,* which does not look at the surface meaning of these reports but rather explores the depths of the symbolism.

Jaffé's book is based on a collection of 1,200 letters submitted to the Swiss magazine *Schweizerischer Beobachter* in 1954 and 1955, in response to a solicitation for reports of unusual experiences. As with our Atlantic University collection, it is not possible to determine how accurate the reports are; their value lies in revealing the action of unconscious factors that are inaccessible to planned experiments.

Phenomena of light are among the most common symbols, usually occurring in the cases of deceased relatives or beloved persons. The concept of a spiritual or immortal man consisting of light or shedding light can be found in many ancient traditions: Egyptian, Persian, Jewish, Christian. In the Christian tradition light is associated with the spiritual body or the inner man, "Christ in me." A mystical interpretation of an apparition, given by one of the people in Jaffé's collection, was, "It might be the Christ in the shape of an angel who had come to save me." In more esoteric traditions light relates to the luminous or astral body and the alchemical idea of separation of the flesh body and the spiritual body. The halo seen in paintings of saints is considered by Jaffé to be a very fundamental archetype. The ancient symbolism of light is almost invariably a sign of wisdom and knowledge. "Illumination" and "enlightenment" are common terms for this knowledge-transcending consciousness.

We have seen that lights—from candles or around figures—form a part of some crisis apparitions in which the focus is a specific person. But in this experience from our collection the entire experience concerns light.

The Strobing Light. A month ago I was awakened at 3:00 A.M. by a nuisance caller who called several times. I rose and went to the kitchen to take the phone off the hook. I was passing through a small foyer next to my bedroom when the whole area was filled with a strobing brilliant white light. It was so white that I was surprised that it didn't hurt my eyes. My first thought was that there was a police car outside, the outside door is just a few feet away. I looked out and there was nothing. I turned and saw that the light was inside in the foyer. I went to the door again, again there was nothing outside. The strobing was inside. I thought "perhaps I should be afraid of this, but I'm not." I went to the door again and saw a tiny fragment of the light rise away and out of sight over the trees—it was too bright and it moved too quickly to be a firefly.

How can we interpret such a strange experience? It is not an apparition of a recognizable person; it is not a coherent communication. The symbolism suggested by Jaffé can help. Perhaps it is an archetypal symbol related to spirituality. Here, especially without being able to work with the person's own interpretation, we reach the limits of psychology. But perhaps the bridge to the spiritual offered by Edgar Cayce has something to offer.

The Edgar Cayce readings are especially rich in light symbolism. Cayce made a general statement on seeing lights: They represent "the attuning of self to the high vibrations of love and life and joy,—and is but that which heals and keeps peace among men" (Reading 5749-10). In specific cases, however, he tempered this enthusiasm with warnings and guidance.

Lights around Edgar Cayce. Question: Please interpret the meaning of the lights which I saw about Mr. Cayce's head during the last reading on Fellowship. Answer: . . . a symbol of the awareness of, the closeness of, relationships of the entity and the subject [Cayce]. . . . An attunement of self to the presence of that being manifest. All are wading in rather deep water! But learn what you are doing! (Reading 262–23, in response to a question by person 993)

Here Cayce interprets the lights as spiritual symbols but gives a warning. This reading was given for the original Search for God group, many of whom experienced unusual phenomena to varying degrees. Cayce was pointing out the importance of understanding the *purpose* of the spiritual path, rather than focusing on interesting phenomena.

Some people seeking Cayce's advice found experiences of light to be disturbing. A seventy-six-year-old woman described the following experience to him:

> *The Vibrating Light.* A tiny light comes into my vision, vibrating *rapidly*. It gradually forms a near circle with very brilliant lights zigzagging, gradually disappearing in the upper corner. This lasts *fifteen* minutes. In a few minutes a headache comes, which lasts *six* hours, then ceases.

Cayce's explanation was that this occurred because of phenomena being sought by the body, "without sufficient stamina in the coordination between the psychic body and the material or physical body. . . . Hence we have a pathological or physical reaction from that which should be an experience that may be made helpful to the body" (Reading 774-3).

This experience is also rather typical of a migraine headache. Most of us would probably want some medication to make it go away. But Cayce counseled that rather than seek the elimination of the experience, it would be better to understand and comprehend it from the spiritual angle. He recommended meditation, with an affirmation that only experiences of the light of God would occur. Even an experience with a primarily physical cause may serve double duty by calling attention to the spiritual.

Lights in the Sky

Flying objects and lights in the sky are often thought of in our popular culture as extraterrestrial visitors. In Cayce's time, before World War II, the concept of

UFOs as extraterrestrial visitors did not exist, yet people reported very similar experiences.

The Flame-Colored Light. Question: Please explain the significance of the flame colored light that [308] and I saw last Wednesday as we were watching the sky.
Answer: In the experience of those who have put their trust in Him, there has ever been those significant indications of an answer that He is mindful. Then, as was indicated, let it be an assurance that He knows, He understands, He hears, He IS aware. (Reading 585-9)

The Floating Sphere. Question: One night some weeks ago I saw floating above my head in space an exceedingly bright sphere or planet. It seemed to be moving within itself as well as through space. Please interpret this to me.
Answer: . . . So, in the vision seen it is the world without and the world within—their movements as one coordinating with the other, the brightness of the orb itself as reflecting that which is the movement within self, that makes for the shedding abroad of the light, the understanding, the enlightenment that is obtained from within. . . . Well was it said by Him, "Ye do not light a light to put it under a bushel." (Reading 262-40, in response to a question by person 303)

Thus Cayce interprets these experiences not as visitors from another planet but as experiences that have symbolic spiritual significance. These are not "close encounters" involving contact with other beings—more on those in the chapter on spirit guides and channeling—but they are typical of many UFO-sighting reports. This is yet another example of how a "real" event can have symbolic meaning that points toward greater spiritual understanding.

Complex Symbolism in Apparitions

Although light symbolism is certainly the most common, more-complex symbols also appear in apparitions and in an infinite variety of forms, often specific to the individual. By applying the same techniques that allow us to interpret symbols in dreams, we can explore the meaning of these apparitions. When the symbolism does not tie in with a specific living or dead person, the boundary between apparition and hallucination blurs, but this makes them no less useful as gateways to the unconscious.

> *The Struggling Comedian.* Three years ago I was much troubled by a recent move to a new city. It was in July. One night, I "woke" up and saw a man standing at the foot of our bed. He was smiling. He looked like a comedian type that you would see on television. He walked to the door of our bedroom and tried to get out but was struggling to get the door open. After a while he stopped struggling and the door opened easily and he was gone. I felt this had implications for my emotional life at the time.

The woman having this experience did not recognize this apparition as a specific person, and there is no reason to think that a television comedian was having a crisis at the time. But let's look at the symbolism here. The woman was troubled by a recent move, yet the apparition was a "smiling comedian." This could represent an alternative attitude. His initial impulse was to *struggle* to get the door open. Doors often appear as symbols of transition, and the woman was indeed having difficulty with her recent move. Yet when he *stopped struggling,* the door opened easily and he was gone. Although the woman did not go into more detail, she appears to have understood the implications for her emotional life at the time: Stop struggling and the transition to this new place will be easier.

The Cayce readings offer another example of a purely symbolic apparition:

> *The Queen of Clubs.* Question: Regarding the playing of bridge, I beheld standing in front of me right in the

room, as real and living, the "Queen of Clubs." I became frightened and jumped for [my husband].
Answer: . . . emblematical . . . the mental forces of the entity become so real as to bring these in an active way and manner, in figures or statues, or beings, with an activity. . . . this represents to the mentality of the being—that is, of self—that upon which the mind dwells to the extent that it takes shape and form. (Reading 136-55)

In other words, Cayce is saying that the apparition is a symbolic [emblematical] hallucination related to the intense focus on the game. Although he did not interpret the symbolism of the image itself, what might a vision of the queen of clubs mean? It could have been any card, the ace of hearts, for example. I can think of at least two interpretations, although, of course, only the person having the image can decide whether an interpretation is correct. Both refer to an assertive personality: a "queen" who tends to "club" people while playing the game, or a "queen of clubs," meaning a leader in the bridge club. Thus the vision may have been symbolizing her own intensity toward the game.

Hauntings

While apparitions that appear only once can be profoundly moving and transforming experiences, it is the repetitive ones, of relatively long duration, that sometimes spur people to look for answers out of desperation. The popular image of a parapsychologist is that of a "ghostbuster," able to function as an exterminator of problem spirits. In reality, however, there are very few experienced field investigators who have worked with hauntings.

Since finding someone who can help you with such phenomena can be very difficult, in this section I will discuss some cases and offer some suggestions for dealing with hauntings. I have received very few cases of this type in my collection of psychic experiences, so the examples I will give here are from parapsychologists who have specialized in this area. One source is Dr. William Roll and his colleagues at the Psychical Research Foundation. Their mission is to conduct studies of the evidence for life after death, and they have done some of the most interesting studies of hauntings, poltergeists, and out-of-body experiences. Another source is the group in the graduate program in parapsychology at John F. Kennedy University in California. Although the program no longer exists, this group did much to systematize the investigation of hauntings. Their work is available in the annual volume *Research in Parapsychology,* and in the popular book *ESP, Hauntings, and Poltergeists,* by Loyd Auerbach, a faculty member in the program.

Hauntings often appear to be fragments of a personality, carrying out repetitive actions. As with the apparitions discussed above, there are commonly symbolic elements present in hauntings.

Here is an example of a haunting case investigated by Thelma Moss, a parapsychologist at the Neuropsychiatric Institute of the University of California at Los Angeles, and Gertrude Schmeidler, a psychology professor at City College of New York. At a "haunted house" in Los Angeles, four witnesses, independently of each other, claimed to have seen a ghost. The descriptions, of a disappearing man, were similar. He was a middle-aged man, dressed in dark clothes and a white shirt. He was reported to be apparently searching for something, in various locations including a guest room, the living room, and the pool area. To explore the haunting further, the investigators enlisted a group of six "sensitives," who claimed sensitivity to psychic phenomena, and a control group of eight people, who did not believe they could sense the presence of a ghost. The sensitives individually visited the house and filled out checklists about the ghost's appearance, personality, and activity, without having an opportunity to share information with each other. The control group simply filled out the checklist without being taken to the house.

The descriptions of three of the six sensitives showed a statistically significant correspondence to the original witnesses' descriptions, whereas only one of the members of the control group reached a marginal level of significance. No witness or sensitive, and only one control subject, showed a significant correspondence to the descriptions of a different "ghost" investigated previously in a different "haunted house." In other words, the evidence suggested that a specific ghost was observed by the witnesses and three of the sensitives, and it was not just a stereotyped general idea of a ghost.

On the other hand, three of the sensitives did not report a ghost, and many other people had also been in the house and not seen any evidence of a ghost. Other recent studies have had similar results. New York parapsychologists Michaeleen Maher and George Hansen found that some sensitives reported the presence of a ghost, but so did some skeptics. They also brought in "high-tech" equipment, including a random number generator (to test for PK) and infrared photography, and found puzzling anomalies. Yet there was no ghost clearly perceived by everyone.

Clearly there is an interaction between the psychology of the person and the appearance of a haunting. Even Edgar Cayce cautioned against taking every apparent instance of a haunting at face value. A woman said to him, "I dreamed there were ghosts in my mother's house." Cayce replied, "Rather that indication of those fears . . . regarding the physical health of individuals of this household. Ghosts, then, of the mind, see? Fear" (Reading 136-45).

These "ghosts of the mind" may not just be simple

hallucinations. They can include "projections" of consciousness by more than one individual. Loyd Auerbach gives an example of a case with features of a haunting, poltergeist, and ghosts of the mind that he investigated, showing how complicated this can be in practice.

The Black Knight. Loyd Auerbach and his colleagues at John F. Kennedy University in California received a call from a divorced woman with children, reporting a "presence" inhabiting their house. There had been multiple appearances over a six-year period, increasing in frequency and magnitude. The family consisted of the mother, two daughters in their twenties no longer living at home, and a sixteen-year-old twin daughter and son living at home. The son had been committed to an institution for mentally disturbed juvenile delinquents following incidents of truancy, burglary, and running away from home. He was a likely candidate for a poltergeist agent, but the case was not that simple!

The first report of a figure in black at the foot of the bed was made by one of the older daughters, before she moved out. She also felt that there was a weight on her chest. After that experience, she asked her mother to stay with her, and the mother had basically the same experience. The younger daughter saw the apparition too and offered more information.

According to both mother and younger daughter, the figure was male, dressed completely in black, and wore some sort of helmet. There was a swirling effect around the body that suggested a cape, and the figure also wore black boots and carried a black broadsword. Both mother and daughter got the feeling of evil from the figure, and the daughter felt that he was quite ancient, stuck in time in their house, and waiting for an opponent to do battle with.

As things progressed, physical disturbances in the house began to manifest—problems with an alarm clock, unusual noises, and a window opening and closing in the son's room (he had already been placed in the youth home). The younger daughter felt that these were due to a second "prankster" entity.

The mother tried to connect the occurrences with her son's abnormal behavior. At first she thought it was pranks being played by the son—he had an obsession with such things as boots, capes, masks, and toy swords. But the apparition *continued to appear* while the son was with his father thousands of miles away. The mother then felt that the figure might have been the *cause* of her son's problems.

What is really going on here? As there is more than one witness, there is certainly the possibility of something paranormal. Yet as Auerbach points out, since it is very unlikely that a black knight had ever inhabited a house in Northern California, an explanation of this apparition as the spirit of someone who had died is not very reasonable. The physical disturbances could be termed a poltergeist, yet they occurred when the disturbed adolescent was *not* present, the opposite of the typical poltergeist case.

As they pursued the case more deeply, Auerbach and his colleagues found that it was more complex than it had first appeared. In lengthy discussions with the mother and the daughter, they found that the primary person experiencing the phenomena was the mother. The mother admitted to great concern about her son and said that she had seen the figure once with its helmet visor up and the face was not unlike that of her son. With repeated questioning, she became less clear about the details and was more tied up with her perception of the figure as "evil" than she was in looking at the situation objectively.

Auerbach's conclusion was that the mother had "created" the figure out of an idealized combination of the odds and ends that the son used to collect obsessively as a child. In the Jungian terminology I have used previously, the ghost was a projection of the mother's shadow. The mother herself was probably the poltergeist agent, rather than the son. Auerbach and his colleagues referred the mother to a family counselor who was open to the possibility of psychic phenomena. The situation was resolved through the mother's dealing with her feelings regarding both her son and the "presence." According to Auerbach, the black knight never returned.

How much was paranormal? How much was purely psychological? There is no way to know. But clearly the approach of simply "busting" or "exorcising" the ghost ignores the complexities found in this case and others. Auerbach describes a number of cases in which the apparitions were at least partially traceable to family dynamics—for example, as substitutes for absent fathers.

In my own experience, I had a case that I was not able to investigate but that fits this concept. I received phone calls from a mother, her twelve-year-old son, and the grandmother. All claimed to have seen an apparition, although the descriptions varied from a white presence to a black, shadowy presence. There were also physical phenomena, some rather extreme, such as locking the doors of the house and flushing the toilets. Since the house was only a few years old, the mother and grandmother were looking at the possibility that it was built over an Indian burial ground. I thought that unlikely and questioned the boy about the circumstances under which the ghost appeared. He said, "My mom sometimes gets mad at my dad and kicks him out of bed, and when he's sleeping in the other room, the ghost comes in and sits on my mom's bed." I realized that the first thing to do here was look at the family dynamics, not search for the ghosts of Indians.

How to Explore the Meaning of an Apparition or Haunting

For most people, an apparition is a rare event. Advice from other people who have had similar experiences is hard to come by. Instead, we have fictional horror stories fueling our imaginations with "facts" that simply aren't true. But apparitions can be frightening. As we have seen, many are associated with the dead or dying, so a fear of death may come into play, in addition to hopes for a life after death. How should you respond to an apparition?

First, it is important to realize, as this chapter has documented, that while apparitions are fairly rare, they are a normal feature of human experience. In order to explore the meaning of an apparition, one must first get past the fear of the unknown. For some people this is no problem—they are surprised and confused, but their worldview is not seriously disturbed. For others, the aftermath of the experience may be very painful. Parapsychologist Sharon Solfvin, from John F. Kennedy University in California, has coined the term "post-psi distress syndrome," an analogy to the posttraumatic stress disorder seen in war veterans and other victims of trauma. The features include being unable to let go of the experience, reliving it over and over, sometimes with uncontrollable flashback memories. Then, because the experience may call the entire meaning of life into question, some people may withdraw into themselves, afraid that no one will be able to understand their experience.

Solfvin advised counselors to approach these experiences on several levels, as this book does. On the cognitive, intellectual level, it is helpful to learn as much as possible about the experiences by reading the accounts of others. On the psychological level, the meaning can be explored in terms of communication and symbols, including dream-type and mythical interpretations. And on the spiritual level, the experience can be approached in terms of its ability to enhance the life and understanding of human experience for the individual. Now, let's look at two elements of an approach to apparitions: communication and working with symbols.

All apparitions are a form of attempted communication, either from an external reality or from another level of yourself. Something needs to be communicated, and the "normal" lines of communication are not working. There may be overlap—a spirit may be trying to call your attention to something important that you know unconsciously. There is no need to *prove* that the apparition is the spirit of a deceased person in order to deal with the experience productively. The unconscious mind, as well as spirits, may respond positively to sincere attempts to communicate.

The first step, then, is to try to communicate. This can be as simple as asking the apparition what it wants. Often people report an immediate sense of certainty about the meaning of the apparition—a deceased grandmother offering reassurance of a life beyond, for example. Many of us, however, do not have the presence of mind to speak to an apparition when it suddenly appears, or we attempt to do so and do not receive an immediate answer. If you no longer have the apparition present, you can try a version of the "empty chair" technique that we explored in the dream chapter. Address the apparition as if it were there and ask what its purpose is. Listen to your own consciousness, which may have an intuitive sense of the mission of the apparition.

What should you say? Most usefully, you can help the apparition to fulfill whatever unfinished business it has and assist it to peacefully make the transition that it began with death. Make the situation positive—be willing to help. Perhaps the apparition's mission is simply to reassure you that there is life beyond. If so, thank it and wish it well. If the apparition seems to want your help, you can visualize a positive outcome. For example, you could mentally assist the apparition toward a peaceful white light.

Dealing with more-complex cases may require some work with symbols. Often the symbols relate to your own *fears and needs.* Interpret the symbology as you would a dream. For each element of the manifestation, look for associations that symbolize underlying issues. As we saw in the example of "the Struggling Comedian," perhaps the difficulty the apparition has in making the transition calls attention to a transition with which you are having difficulty. The basic communication from the apparition, then, can be enriched by considering all the possible symbols.

In his book *Reunions,* Raymond Moody, who is well known for his work with near-death experiences, explores a technique for inducing apparitions at will. He studied mirror gazing, a practice going back to the ancient Greeks in which one stares into a mirror in a darkened room until an apparition appears. Moody called his version of this traditional practice the "psychomanteum."

Moody and other researchers, like William Roll, have had success in inducing apparitions with this method. The key seems to be a sincere desire for communication with a deceased loved one. The process is lengthy. Moody may spend an entire day with a participant discussing desires and expectations, leading up to the actual experience. Just trying it "for fun," on the spur of the moment, is unlikely to produce results. For people willing to put in the effort, however, the results have been impressive. Fifty percent of Moody's participants had a "visionary encounter," including not only apparitions but complex conversations with the deceased person. People found the process to be profoundly healing.

In working with apparitions, some spiritual sources emphasize that it is important to have a purpose aligned with your highest ideals, not simply a selfish desire to communicate with the dead. Edgar Cayce indicated that it was appropriate to try to aid the deceased in their transition. One woman asked him, "From time to time I have had come into my room a friend who has passed on. Is this contact harmful or beneficial?" Cayce replied, "In this, there are always those seeking that we may help, that may help us; for as we help another does help come to us. Pray for that friend, that the way through the shadows may be easier for them. It becomes easier for you" (Reading 262-25).

But for many people wishing to communicate with deceased relatives, Cayce admonished that it could hinder the development of the deceased person and distract the living person from his or her own spiritual development. A woman who was constantly dwelling on the idea of communicating with her husband who had passed over asked, "Does he [my deceased husband] know of my prayers?" Cayce replied, "Do you wish him to? Do you wish to call him back to those disturbing forces, or do you wish the self to be poured out for him that he may be happy? Which is it you desire,—to satisfy self that you are communicating, or that you are holding him in such as way as to retard? . . . Leave him in the hands of Him who is the resurrection!" (Reading 1786-2).

Further Advice for Working with Persistent Hauntings

Although some people may want to work with Moody's mirror-gazing process to contact a deceased relative, I have found that more commonly people want persistent spirits to go away. They are looking for a ghostbuster, and ghostbusters are in short supply. Here are some suggestions for dealing with persistent hauntings.

Repetitive hauntings are uniquely related to personal psychology and possibly family dynamics. No single explanation or advice can fit all cases. The first important point to remember when dealing with hauntings or with poltergeists is that, contrary to what you might see on television or read in the newspapers, these phenomena are *not* normally physically dangerous. Researchers agree that the phenomena themselves rarely appear to hurt anyone—the danger is in being so afraid of the experience that you panic and run into something, inflicting an injury on yourself. Nevertheless, they may be annoying or frightening, and if you are having the experience, you may feel an urgency to do something about it.

Before attributing the phenomenon to a psychic source, look for normal explanations. Discovering that the noises in the attic are caused by the heating system can lay to rest a lot of worry about ghosts.

If you are reasonably convinced that no normal explanation will suffice for the phenomena, you can begin to explore the possible paranormal causes. Remember that most research has shown such phenomena to be complex interactions between the people involved in the experience (both their conscious and their unconscious minds) and the possible external phenomenon (spirits). The key elements in working with simple apparitions—communication and symbolism—are just as important for understanding persistent or strong phenomena. Here, however, because the phenomenon persists, you have more opportunity to work with it.

Attempting to communicate with the ghost or poltergeist is a good first step. Ask it why it is there, what it wants, and what you can do to help it accomplish its purpose. This may be a hard step to take if the phenomenon is frightening, but humor is a good way to overcome fear. One family I know has a ghost they dubbed "Casper," after the friendly ghost in the cartoon. It was hard to see him as frightening with that attitude.

The ghost may respond with noises, or you may simply have an intuition of successful communication. Try to work cooperatively with the ghost to arrive at a resolution of its reasons for appearing and assist it in making the transition to a higher realm. Keep in mind the spirit of helping—you are helping the ghost on its way, helping it return to its own path. "Attacking" or "exorcising" the ghost usually generates more negativity in you and may make the problem worse. Think of yourself as helping with the therapy of a confused, lost soul. Whether this soul is the spirit of a deceased person or an unacknowledged part of yourself, a positive approach is likely to be the most productive.

What if, as Roll and others have found with poltergeists, it is not the spirit of a deceased person but the unconscious action of a living person? An attempt to communicate is still the most useful way to begin. The manifestations may be the result of a frustrated attempt to communicate, often not consciously acknowledged. Your attempts to communicate with the "spirit" may succeed at the unconscious level in the person who is causing the phenomena.

While direct communication may help resolve the problem, often a look at the symbolism in the manifestations and its connection with other individuals and relationships in the family (or group) will also be productive. Although the spirit may be "real," its manifestation at that particular time and place may be a result of the needs and fears of those present. Do the incidents point to someone's need to communicate or gain attention? Is there someone absent (a husband, father, child, perhaps) for whom the ghost is a replacement?

Try to interpret the symbols as you would in a dream. Keep a journal of the events. What do the incidents represent? Who or what might the apparition represent? What are the patterns of occurrence of the phenomena? If there is fear, is it a fear of the paranormal in general, or might it be a fear of the symbolic content of the experience?

You may find that devoting this level of attention to the phenomenon will make it go away of its own accord. If you are still experiencing difficulties, you could contact someone for help, a counselor, parapsychologist, or psychic. Before you do that, however, you should be aware that there are very few people with any experience in this area. Most parapsychologists have little experience with apparitions or ghosts—they are not "field investigators." Most professional counselors have little experience with psychic phenomena in *any* form. As a result, they may know less about the possibilities than you now do. Psychics may be sensitive to the psychic possibilities but have little knowledge of the psychological dynamics involved. In addition, anyone trying to help may have a strong vested interest in a particular explanation— whether it is a ghost to be "busted" or a family relationship problem. They may be more interested in the phenomenon than in helping *you*. A haunting investigator without sensitive counseling skills may disrupt your life more than the haunting did in the first place!

Where Do These Experiences Lead Us?

Do apparitions and hauntings "prove" the survival of bodily death? Finding conclusive evidence was one of the goals of the early parapsychologists. But it has been very difficult to produce satisfactory proof of life after death. Some parapsychologists, such as J. B. Rhine, decided that the question could not be resolved at all and directed their work toward laboratory investigation of the psychic abilities of living persons.

Although apparitions can be interpreted as survival of some part of the personality of a deceased person, with our knowledge of telepathy, clairvoyance, and the richness of the unconscious mind, other interpretations may be equally or more plausible. A common objection to apparitions as proof of survival is what has been called the "super-ESP" hypothesis. The idea is that it is never possible to completely rule out very strong telepathic or clairvoyant ability, combined with internally generated hallucinations, to create an apparition.

It is hard to prove survival after death as an alternative to super ESP. Since we can't arbitrarily define what it is that is supposed to survive, we do not know quite what to do to prove it is there. Does the whole personality need to survive, or only some fragments, or perhaps the "essence" of the personality—the higher self or soul?

The apparitions and hauntings discussed in this chapter do not appear to be complete personalities. They are fleeting, often with a single purpose or no apparent purpose, and rarely engage in lengthy communication. The evidence of Tyrrell, Roll, and others has shown, and our cases confirm, that the unconscious mind plays a key role in constructing the apparition.

Perhaps the personality as we generally think of it does not survive death, any more than the personality you had as a two-year-old child survives into adulthood. The transpersonal perspective suggests that at every stage transition our self as we know it dies and is reborn at a higher, more integrated level. The personality during life is seen as only a small part of the totality of the individual, what Edgar Cayce referred to as the "individuality." Looking for the personality to survive death untransformed could be a fundamentally wrong approach.

Apparitions, then, point to the richness of our unconscious minds, both individually and collectively, but in themselves tell us little about the possible nature of life after death. Nevertheless, they are an *element* of evidence that points to the possibility of the continuity of some aspect of the self following death. The virtue of the studies of parapsychologists has been to remove two major obstacles to understanding these experiences. The first obstacle was the concept that they are nothing more than hallucinations, without meaning. Both the correspondences to actual crises, in some cases, and the richness of the symbolism, in other cases, argue for the importance of apparitions as a meaningful feature of human experience. The second obstacle removed is the concept that all of these phenomena are caused by external forces or spirits. The new view, that apparitions result from an *interaction* between an unconscious psychological component and a possible external spiritual component, leads us into a deeper investigation of the processes involved. These experiences can be seen as an opportunity to grow, to better understand our needs and fears, to communicate with our unconscious, and to help others make the transition that begins with death.

While this chapter explored apparent visitations from the spirit world to our world, the next chapter will look at out-of-body and near-death experiences as possible opportunities to visit the world beyond death.

CHAPTER 9

Out-of-Body Experiences and Near-Death Experiences

> Because I could not stop for Death,
> He kindly stopped for me.
> —Emily Dickinson, "The Chariot"

We have seen that apparitions may be evidence of life after death, possible glimpses of the inhabitants of another plane of reality. But they can also be interpreted in other ways. Are they the projection of one's own unconscious, or are they visitors from the "other side"? In terms of their value for self-transformation, apparitions can be disappointing. While they may inspire us to exploration of the spiritual realm, they are unsatisfying because they are so transient. Apparitions may be frightening or they may be inspiring, but by themselves they rarely lead to major transformations of consciousness.

But if it is hard to interpret the visits of "spirits" to our world, could we possibly journey to theirs, learn a higher truth, and return to tell about it? Can our consciousness actually leave our physical bodies and travel at will? The experience of traveling out of the body, also known as astral travel or soul travel, was considered in occult tradition to be the province of only the most advanced psychics or spiritual masters. Yet modern research has shown that it is another common psychic experience. Numerous surveys over the past twenty years have shown that, on the average, about 15 percent of the general population have had at least one out-of-body experience (OBE), defined as an experience in which a person seems to perceive the world from a location outside his or her physical body. For example, John Palmer's survey of the people of Charlottesville found that 14 percent had had an OBE. *Twenty-five* percent of the students at the University of Virginia had had such an experience. In my surveys of A.R.E. members, the majority—over 65 percent— have had at least one OBE. These OBEs are distinctly different from dreams; they feel "real," and vision is often clear and not the least bit "dreamy."

Yet, like other psychic experiences, OBEs can be confusing and even frightening to people who have not had advanced spiritual training, or who have been filled with misinformation from the popular press. Even the majority of people who have these experiences (and who generally find them to be interesting and even pleasant) want to know how to integrate them with the rest of their life.

Another phenomenon related to the out-of-body experience is the near-death experience (NDE). These experiences occur when a person is clinically dead (that is, no heartbeat) or very near death. People returning from the brink of death often report a profound spiritual experience, including out-of-body travel, and a glimpse of life after death. Once considered a rarity, the NDE "came out of the closet" with the publication of Raymond Moody's book *Life after Life* in 1975. Now there are hundreds of published reports of NDEs, and they seem to be increasing in frequency as modern medicine finds better ways of bringing people back to life.

In this chapter I talk about both OBEs and NDEs, but they are not the same thing. Many NDEs include an OBE in which you view your own body, but there is much more to near-death experiences. They may include moving through a "tunnel," reviewing one's life, and meeting with spirit guides and deceased relatives. In contrast, in only a minority of out-of-body experiences is the person near death. Most OBEs happen to people who are perfectly healthy. Nevertheless, I include OBEs and NDEs together in this chapter because, for many people in my survey, there was a fair degree of overlap. This is a typical example, from a forty-three-year-old woman:

> *A Trip to Heaven.* At the birth of my daughter I had an out-of-body experience. I was bleeding to death and then went through darkness to St. Peter, where I argued with him about being let into heaven. I was told to return to earth to raise my daughter. I remember being very upset with this for I was ready to leave this body.

Here we see a classic near-death experience, including an out-of-body experience. The precipitating event is a crisis during childbirth, leading almost to death. The woman felt that she had left her body, traveled through darkness (often a tunnel is mentioned), and met a religious figure. In the ensuing discussion a decision was made to return to earth to fulfill a responsibility.

Varieties of Out-of-Body and Near-Death Experiences

The classic out-of-body experience and near-death experience are now well known from books by Raymond Moody and others. Yet the popular image of NDEs and OBEs often misses the diversity of types of experiences and the profound spiritual impact these experiences may have. Some people may find that an experience they regard as the most moving experience of their lives is trivialized, when other people simply do not grasp its transformative power. Here we will look at a range of experiences and people's responses to them.

Out-of-Body Experiences

Out-of-body experiences may occur either as a response to a crisis or, spontaneously, in ordinary circumstances. OBEs most often occur when a person is in a calm and relaxed state. One survey, by a group of psychologists and psychiatrists in Kansas, Glen Gabbard, Stuart Twemlow, and Fowler Jones, found that 79 percent do occur when a person is calm. The others are reported from a variety of crisis states, including childbirth, anesthesia, or severe pain.

Calm states, such as meditation and relaxation, practiced by many of the respondents to my surveys, are a common precursor to an OBE. Here is a typical example, reported by a woman in her sixties:

> *On the Porch.* About two years ago I had an out-of-the-body experience. I had been meditating in my bedroom with my eyes closed and had become very still. Then I was conscious of being out on the sunporch straightening some books. It was a very real experience—I was actually there, looking around, all my surroundings clear and vivid. When I opened my eyes it was with a real shock that I discovered I was in my bedroom.

The question most frequently raised by OBEs is, "Did I really travel out of my body, or was it just imagination?" This is a "veridical" experience. That is, at least subjectively, she traveled to an actual location. In many OBEs, the *subjective* experience is of travel to a physical location, but, as with the above experience, there may be no way to verify that the event actually occurred. In others, such as "Visiting in Alaska" in the apparitions chapter, there are witnesses. An apparition is seen that corresponds to the person who claims to be out of body. Later in this chapter we will look at attempts by parapsychologists to determine whether a person is *actually* out of body.

Not all OBEs are simple travel to a recognizable location. Some involve apparent travel to locations with no counterpart in this world. Here is an example of such an experience, from a forty-two-year-old woman, also triggered by meditation and relaxation:

> *A Meditation OBE.* In meditation, or sometimes just before falling asleep, I feel numbness, floating, hear a bell sound. As the sound becomes louder and the tone higher, I begin to vibrate all over. Then a white light flashes and I feel I am being "sucked" out of my body—out of the top of the head. If I become frightened, it stops. If not, I pass through a long, blue tunnel and begin traveling at a high rate of speed. I go different places, sometimes a blue dimension or a white room. Most of the time I get scared and "slam" back in my body before going very far—this literally hurts. I need to overcome the fear.

Here the OBE, though not initiated by a crisis, was more disturbing than the previous one. The feelings of numbness, floating, and vibration are common in meditation, and in some people are preliminaries to an OBE. The feeling of going out through the top of the head is also fairly typical; other people report rolling out of their bodies or simply finding themselves out. The sensation varies.

Then this woman says something very important. "If I become frightened, it stops." The majority of people with OBEs report them as pleasant, not frightening. But, as I have emphasized before in this book, psychic experiences are also an opportunity for you to exercise your *will*. If an experience is frightening, try to transform it. For this woman, fear stopped the experience.

Next, we see that this woman's experience is not veridical. Her journey is not to a location in the world as we know it, but through a long, blue tunnel, sometimes to a "blue dimension." Is she really traveling out of her body, or is this just "imagination" or "hallucination?" Certainly for the person having the experience, it is "real"—there is an out-of-body "feeling" to it, different from a dream or hallucination. Yet putting a label on this type of experience does little to explain it. In this woman's case, fear prevented her from exploring the experience—fear that she wants to overcome. As one possibility, she could explore the symbolism of the other dimensions she visits by asking for clarification as if it were a dream.

Other out-of-body experiences grade into near-death experiences. That is, they occur in a crisis situation when death is a very real possibility. Some are simple—the person views his or her own body and then reenters it. Others are complex, involving travel and meetings with other beings.

Childbirth is a frequent source of these experiences. Here is one where the woman saw the efforts being made by the medical team. Many people have reported verifiable details from such experiences, even though to the doctors they appeared to be unconscious.

A Childbirth OBE. When my first son was born, it was an emergency caesarean and I had an out-of-body experience on the operating table. The nurse told the doctor I was having a very bad time. I was looking down from above and felt surprised that the nurse was so alarmed. I felt I was being pulled away farther and farther from my body and had to really fight to stay near my body. I repeated "God will provide" 1,000 times over and tried to focus on life. I had been put under, couldn't open my eyes or talk, yet saw faintly what was going on.

Childbirth appears to be a special situation. I received reports of several OBE/NDEs in connection with childbirth. This makes sense for several reasons. First, the out-of-body experience may be a natural mechanism for avoidance of pain that can come into play during childbirth. Second, childbirth incidents may be a common opportunity for approaching death and recovering, since the apparatus for resuscitation is conveniently available when there are complications in delivery, and mothers rarely die in childbirth these days. Third, and more related to the spiritual dimension, is that birth itself is an interaction between the before-life realm and our living realm. It may also be a very spiritual (as well as painful) experience for the mother. This may open the door to experiences linking the realms.

Here is another example, from a woman who was twenty-three at the time of the birth:

Another OBE during Childbirth. I was in a hospital delivery room giving birth to my second child. There were complications which made the delivery procedure extremely painful. The next thing I remembered was floating near the ceiling telling an unknown entity that I was glad to be out of there (my body) because it was too painful to endure. I could see myself, the doctors, nurses, etc., below. When the doctor told the nurse that I was about to deliver, I tried to tell him that I wasn't ready (that I wasn't in my body). Suddenly I found myself sitting up on the delivery table as the baby was pushed from the birth channel. The doctor was saying to me, "What did you say?" I replied, "Never mind," and we both pushed it out of our minds. I had never heard of out-of-body experiences at that time of my life, but later realized that is what happened to me.

This case is hard to classify, since there was nothing in the report to suggest nearness of death but only intense pain. Yet the experience included not only an out-of-body experience but a conversation with an "unknown entity," often reported in near-death experiences as a religious figure or a being of light.

Near-Death Experiences

Near-death experiences are distinct from OBEs, in that by definition they occur during a crisis, one leading almost to death. There is sometimes some semantic quibbling about whether a person who has had an NDE has "actually" died. It is all a matter of definition. If death is defined as the cessation of heartbeat, then many people who had have NDEs have died and been brought back to life. If death is defined as the cessation of brain activity, then cases of revival with an ability to communicate are extremely rare (though the person may be kept "alive" on a respirator indefinitely). Finally, if death refers to actual decay of the body, it is hard indeed to find someone who has survived this condition except in horror movies.

There is a great deal of diversity in near-death experiences, which I can only touch on with a few examples in this chapter. The most striking feature of many NDEs is that they are often transformative experiences. While the reaction to an out-of-body experience may be "That was interesting" or "That was strange," the reaction to a near-death experience is frequently "That experience has profoundly changed my life." Pleasant and inspiring experiences are the norm, although negative experiences are occasionally reported, especially in the case of attempted suicide.

Here is an NDE reported by a forty-four-year-old woman, with some of the features seen in the reports collected by Raymond Moody and others:

A Drowning NDE. I was out of my body when I had been knocked unconscious as I went into a swimming pool. The experience was very euphoric and I did not realize at the time that I had an out of body experience. I would describe it to people as "I almost drowned." When they commented on how horrible it must have been I hastily said, "No, it was the most wonderful experience I had ever had." I described my life spinning incredibly fast past my eyes. Seeing my dad realize I was not coming up and going in for me. It was not until I read *Life After Life* that I realized that I had the out of body experience and had been observing from above my body.

Although many near-death experiences do not have all the following characteristics, this list, compiled from several people's surveys of experiences, is typical of the variety of experiences reported:

- a particular kind of out-of-body experience: finding oneself outside of the physical body but still in the immediate vicinity, watching one's own body and sometimes seeing the resuscitation effort
- traveling rapidly through a long tunnel
- meeting with deceased relatives and friends, who come to help in the transition
- meeting with a "being of light," who helps by presenting a panorama of life events
- approaching a border and being given a choice: go on to the next world or return to life. Sometimes there is no choice; you are told you *must* return to fulfill unfinished business.

Here, for example, is another childbirth NDE. The details are sketchy, but the spiritual content was profoundly moving:

Silvery Light. When my second child was born I almost bled to death. When the nurse came and told me to stay awake I saw she was a silvery light. As I became more conscious I saw she was a black Army nurse. I was amazed to think/realize that we're all just silvery light and only appear to be black, white, men, women, etc.

Upon returning to the land of the living, people often find it extremely hard to communicate what happened. Typically they have had no extensive spiritual study and may be totally unprepared for a spiritual awakening. They may doubt their sanity and be afraid of rejection and ridicule. And, indeed, when they do try to communicate their experience, they may be rejected by their family and friends. As NDEs become better known, however, this rejection response is becoming less of a problem.

Before her near-death experience at age sixteen, "Evelyn" had had only a single psychic experience— an apparition of her grandfather. She was fortunate in that her mother and aunt were Spiritualist ministers; they encouraged her to explore the transformation resulting from her NDE. I interviewed Evelyn in depth about her near-death experience and its transformative consequences. She told me:

After I had a motorcycle accident when I was sixteen, I had a near-death experience, traveled into spirit, and met certain entities on the other side. In my near-death experience, I was literally hurled out of the physical world. What I saw was a piercing while light way in the distance. It was suction that gradually drew me from the earth. It was a feeling of great joy, great peace, and great surrender. I was just being spiraled gradually up and up. But I got to a point where a great hand drew me from one side of the spiral, and I stopped moving up. I think if I had continued to move up, I wouldn't have been able to get back down.

I was told to come back, a feeling of being pushed back. The next thing I knew I was in a hospital bed.

Then, during the recovery period after I came back, I had a feeling of great peace.

After that, when I came back into my body, the channels were very open. I would retire to bed at night and then all these different things would start up. I would see people in my room and I would be taken places. I had a lot of out-of-body experiences. All this started up after the near-death experience. I didn't have any manifestations like this before my accident, even though I grew up in a family where this was fairly normal. There was a big change. I don't think I was the same person after that. My whole attitude toward life was different after that because of what I saw and what I went through.

The aftermath of Evelyn's NDE was not all positive. She was very glad to have a family willing to work with her and ground her in her newfound state of consciousness.

There were times right after I had my accident that I did have a lot of negative experiences, because I was way open. Everywhere I would go, if I'd walk into a house where something bad had happened, I would take it upon myself. Some of it was crazy, some of it was bizarre, as though I was hallucinating. At first I mainly worked with it myself, by calling to the light and praying. I'd fight with it until it would go away. Then I joined a group, which helped enormously. We were able to channel all the psychic energy into one period of time, during the group meeting.

Evelyn is now a professional psychic and medium, the mother of two young children, and a talented musician. Her gentle counseling inspires all who know her. Yet it took five years for her to integrate the aftermath of her near-death experience into her life, even with a supportive family and friends. The average person who has an NDE typically lacks the words to communicate the experience even to researchers, much less friends and relatives. Integrating the experience with the rest of ordinary life can be the greatest challenge for someone who has a near-death experience.

What Research Has to Say about OBEs and NDEs

The primary question people ask about both OBEs and NDEs is, "Do you *really* travel out of your body?" There are several possible viewpoints, depending both on one's metaphysical assumptions and on the scientific evidence. One, the closest to traditional psychology, is that OBEs and NDEs are simply hallucinations, since consciousness is simply the chemical processes of the brain. Nothing actually travels; the experience is like a dream but with a subjectively different feeling. A second viewpoint, taking into account the experimental evidence of parapsychology, is that the experience itself does not involve travel, but there is sometimes a telepathic/clairvoyant component. That is, the feeling of travel is a hallucination, but psychic perception of a distant place can occur. Finally, if one assumes that the physical body is a *result* of a spiritual form of energy, then there is no reason to assume that consciousness is attached to the physical body, and OBEs and NDEs may be an aspect of a general capability for survival of bodily death.

The evidence from parapsychology experiments suggests that there is some truth in each of these viewpoints. Certainly some OBEs are like dreams, an altered state of consciousness with the illusion of traveling, but there is no correspondence of the destination with what is going on in a real location. In others there may be clear evidence of clairvoyance; the report corresponds to a real happening at a distant location. As we saw in an earlier chapter, however, clairvoyance alone does not prove that a part of the person *actually* travels outside the body. Parapsychologists have had to be very clever to design experiments to show that the OBE is not just an *experience,* but that an aspect of the self actually is capable of extension beyond the physical body and might also be capable of surviving bodily death. Even now, there is not general agreement on whether something actually travels out of body.

Parapsychologists have sought to test two aspects of out-of-body experiences that are very different from ordinary clairvoyance. First, people with OBEs do not just report general "feelings" of a distant location, they say that they have seen things from a specific vantage point (for example, looking down on their body from up near the ceiling). Second, people with OBEs sometimes say that they are able to influence people or animals at the distant location; perhaps a detector of some sort could pick up a "presence" during an OBE.

Some of the earliest experimental work with out-of-body experiences was done with artist and author Ingo Swann. We met Swann earlier, in the chapter on clairvoyance. Swann's amazing talent sparked the remote-viewing work at SRI in California. Yet Swann did not see his perception as simple clairvoyance. He felt that he went out of his body to the distant location, where he was able to "see" things from a specific vantage point. Swann worked with Karlis Osis and his colleagues at the American Society for Psychical Research in New York to explore the nature of this perception. At least subjectively, it appeared to differ from ordinary clairvoyance, in that he needed particular light arrangements in order to see the targets. His success depended on other visual characteristics of the target, which is not the usual case in clairvoyance experiments.

Karlis Osis and Donna McCormick later looked at both the "vantage point" issue and the "presence" detector in a study with Alex Tanous, a well-known psychic with much experience in going out of body. They used a target with a clever optical illusion. Their "optical image device" produces a target that looks very different when viewed from different angles; only one angle yields an image of the correct target. At the same time they had strain gauges in the target area to measure Tanous's physical presence out of body (strain gauges measure very small physical forces). They found that, on the occasions when Tanous correctly described the target, the strain gauge sensors were more active. This suggests that the OBE, at least for Tanous, involves an actual projection of consciousness separate from the body.

Robert Morris and his colleagues at the Psychical Research Foundation used a biological presence detector—the pet kitten of their subject, Keith Harary. Harary, who had had numerous OBEs, was a psychology student at Duke University and is now a parapsychologist himself. In Morris's experiment, Harary lay on a couch in one building, going out of body periodically to visit the cat in another building nearby, with an experimenter keeping track of the trips. At the same time an observer, unaware of when Harary was going out of body, watched the cat. He measured the cat's activity by counting how many squares in a grid in a box the cat crossed. The cat's normal behavior was to prowl around, meowing frequently. But during Harary's OBEs there was a striking reduction in meowing and walking; the cat sat quietly, calmed by his "presence." The results were highly significant statistically. While it is hard to say that this experiment "proves" that a part of the person can actually detach from the physical body and travel to distant locations, it is strong supporting evidence.

Not all OBEs offer as much evidence for actual out-of-body travel as Swann's, Tanous's and Harary's. Like dreams, some OBEs may be genuinely paranormal, while others may be inner visions bearing no relation to an outside reality. But just because a vision is inner, rather than actual travel, does not mean it is less spiritually significant. Even in the 1930s, Edgar Cayce interpreted the following experience as an inner vision that could contribute to a greater understanding.

> *A Trip to California.* In 1934, during my last surgical operation when I was thought dead, I traveled out of the body to California, to realms of light. Where did I go really and what was the meaning and purpose of the experience?
>
> Cayce replied: "This was a coordination of the experiences the body had seen in the experiences of others; correlated with the edges of more than one experience to which the body had been subjected or subjugated in other experiences. As to place—within self. As to conditions, the many experiences of the entity, both mental AND spiritual, in the various realms of consciousness.
>
> "As to its worth within self,—the awareness of the universality of consciousness as may be obtained in the one light, that is ALL light." (Reading 2067-3)

Cayce is explicit, "As to place,—within self." Yet the worth—the awareness of the universality of consciousness—is the transformative aspect of this experience.

Evidence for Survival of Death

Despite the abundant evidence that out-of-body experiences can be more than simple internal hallucinations, it is hard to conclude that they support the concept of life after death. While OBEs suggest that consciousness can *travel* away from the body, they do not really prove that consciousness can exist *indepen-*

dently of the body. Perhaps the brain generates a field of some sort that cannot exist without it, in the same sense that a radio station sends out a signal, and if the radio station went away, so would the signal.

The phenomena of near-death experiences that go beyond the out-of-body component may be more convincing evidence of continuity of life after death. Unfortunately it is hard to do experimental research with NDEs. They can't (at least ethically) be induced at will, and there is always the danger that near-death will simply progress to death, without a return to tell the tale. It is certainly conceivable that some form of experiment could be done in hospital emergency rooms and intensive care wards, but I am not aware of any such work at this time. Instead, NDEs are typically a once-in-a-lifetime event.

Most recent research has focused on the profound transformation that often takes place after a near-death experience has occurred. Kenneth Ring, a psychologist at the University of Connecticut, explored the aftermath of NDEs with extensive psychological questionnaires. Following an NDE, people reported major changes in values such as an appreciation for life, self-acceptance, and compassion for others. For example, about 80 percent had an increase in their concern for planetary welfare—a mission to preserve and protect life on the planet. There was a very marked movement *away* from conventional religious sectarianism and *toward* a more universal spirituality. Importantly, NDEs made people more hopeful concerning the outcome of humanity's spiritual evolution.

Yet Ring does not *assume* that the near-death experience is a journey *beyond death*. Many of its features are similar to the shamanic journey seen in cultures worldwide. The scientific method at present has no way to tell us where someone travels in an NDE or an OBE. But Ring does take very seriously the thesis that near-death experiences "reflect a direct encounter with self-existing properties of an alternative domain of reality. . . . NDEs and shamans, too, are tapping into a realm that in some sense *truly exists* outside time and space."

Like Ring, the other major researchers on NDEs hasten to point out that reports of experiences are not *proof* in the scientific sense. Yet many seem personally convinced that NDEs point to a reality beyond the physical body. Those people who have had the experience often return with an unshakable conviction. Those who have listened to the stories of transformation are often awed by this journey and its promise of a greater reality.

What Can You Do about an Out-of-Body Experience?

First, don't worry, they're normal. Roughly 15 percent of people have had them, and, in themselves, they are not a sign of mental illness. Not all OBEs involve travel to recognizable locations. Some appear to be to other "dimensions" or "planes." Of course, we have no way of knowing if these dimensions or planes are "real." Remember, like any psychic experience, an OBE can be a projection from the unconscious mind. If it does not seem to correspond to an actual location, it is worth interpreting symbolically in the same way as a dream.

Second, many people have learned to have OBEs at will and find them to be an interesting exploration of an altered state of consciousness. One common technique for going out-of-body is to work at becoming conscious while dreaming (known as a "lucid" dream) and launch the OBE from that state. Meditation is also a state that can lead to an OBE. Rather than "how you do it," however, what may be most important is "why you do it." This will determine the quality of your experience. If you enter this state with a lot of psychological baggage, it is likely to express itself in unpleasant ways.

Third, if you have spontaneous OBEs and find them frightening, this can be taken as an opportunity to exercise your will *not* to have them. Attend more to circumstances that trigger an OBE for you (for example, exhaustion or taking drugs). How can you change your life to interrupt that process and focus on something else?

Fourth, and most important, rather than pursuing OBEs as phenomena, you can explore the spiritual path, of which out-of-body experiences are only a byproduct. You can look at them as Cayce did in the above reading (2067-3), as signs of awareness of the universality of consciousness.

What Can You Do about a Near-Death Experience?

Near-death experiences can be more difficult to deal with than out-of-body experiences, but they are an even greater opportunity for growth. Finding sympathetic other people with whom you can discuss your experience can be a great help. These people are easier to find now, since the NDE is becoming better known. Books like Dannion Brinkley's *Saved by the Light* share the struggles of those who seek to understand these experiences. The International Association of Near-Death Studies holds conferences and publishes a journal (see resources in the appendix). Among its members you are likely to find people who can help you work with your unique experience.

What can you do if you have not yet connected with a sympathetic listener? It helps to be aware of some of the conflicts that arise even after very positive experiences. The NDE *can* be an extremely powerful agent of transformation, but you need to overcome your own confusion related to the experience and to deal with the reactions of other people.

If you were not prepared for the experience (and most people aren't), you may have mixed feelings about it. There is a "re-entry" problem, like that an astronaut faces, since you need to fit the insights from the near-death experience into the everyday life situation. It is important to identify the aspects of the NDE that may be causing conflict in your life.

For example, in transcending some part of your ego, you may not have had the opportunity to deal with the sudden loss. That is, in an NDE you may go beyond your conscious self, but in doing so you may feel you have lost a part of that self. Though in one sense you feel enlightened, in another sense you may still have to "grieve" for a part of you that "died."

Another issue, exemplified by the case described earlier of the woman who was told by Saint Peter to return to life and raise her daughter, is the feeling that you were "sent back" to this life against your will to fulfill some mission. You may feel manipulated by a higher power. That woman, for example, said that she was upset with returning because she was ready to leave her body.

Many people, in my surveys and in those of other researchers, report increased psychic experiences after a near-death experience. The danger here is that you may dwell excessively on the psychic aspects of the experience, allowing them to blind you to other aspects that are more important in fostering your spiritual growth.

Sometimes, your family and friends, not understanding the experience, will tend to reject you. Some of this may be only your own fear of being unable to communicate, but there also may be reactions from others that you have come under the influence of a strange force. They may have trouble dealing with the changes in your personality; you may no longer share their priorities. For example, previously you may have primarily wanted to make money, but perhaps now your primary interest is in serving others. Your family might not appreciate this change in priorities.

On the other hand, your family and friends may overreact on the positive side. Having read books about near-death experiences, they may expect unrealistic changes, such as superhuman patience and forgiveness or miraculous healing powers. They may reject you when you are unable to live up to their expectations.

The answer to these issues is that you need to put the near-death experience in the context of normal life and become re-grounded in the present. It can be helpful (and inspiring) to share with others who have had an NDE, but the danger in identifying with NDEers is that, feeling that the physical world is not meaningful or important, you will not deal with the day-to-day functions of living in the physical world. In the next chapter we will look at the potentials and pitfalls of spending time in "another world."

CHAPTER 10

Voices, Spirit Guides, and Channeling

GLENDOWER: I can call spirits from the vasty deep.
HOTSPUR: Why, so can I, or so can any man;
But will they come when you do call for them?
—Shakespeare, *Henry IV, Part 1,* Act 3

Apparitions and near-death experiences come involuntarily, often when we least expect it, opening a door that suggests there is survival of bodily death. Some people, however, as they become aware of the much greater reality that is available, want to initiate contact with that reality themselves. As we saw in the previous chapter, some people can train themselves to have out-of-body experiences. But often people want more. They want to draw on the wisdom that has manifested through psychics like Edgar Cayce.

Contacts with "spirits," "guides," and "entities" are among the most problematic of psychic experiences. Some exciting psychic material has come through apparent contacts with higher beings: the entire Cayce work, Jane Roberts's "Seth material," and "A Course in Miracles." Yet these same phenomena—hearing voices, spirit "possession"—are often considered symptoms of mental illness. Even when the messages are benign, they may fall far short of higher wisdom.

The recent explosion of "channelers" has produced a few with wise things to say but many who offer little. To paraphrase the wisdom of those who have explored spirit contact, from Edgar Cayce to parapsychologist Charles Tart, "Just because you're dead, it doesn't make you smarter."

Not all communications from "the other side" are the same. There is a continuum, from soft inner promptings, to voices from what appear to be spirit guides, to entering a trance and having some apparently discarnate being— a spirit or entity—speak using your voice. There are also the negative aspects of this phenomenon—disruptive splits of personality or apparent possession by a malevolent entity.

These experiences are related to what is known as "dissociation"—a splitting of consciousness. Everyone experiences dissociation at some time. Most of us have had the experience of driving home on "autopilot," when we are thinking of something else and suddenly find ourselves miles down the road, our bodies having done the driving while our conscious focus was elsewhere.

We all share the capacity for dissociation, but some have more capability than others. Some people can allow their conscious personality to "step aside" while something else makes its appearance. That something could be the unconscious mind of that person, a source of wisdom that shouldn't be underrated. Or perhaps it really is a communication from some spirit that no longer has a body. How might we tell the difference between unconscious parts of the self and discarnate entities? Why do some people have positive experiences of personal growth, while others have negative experiences of possession?

How common are contacts with "spirits"? Because of the publicity associated with channeling—from actress Shirley MacLaine's books to channelers with their own television shows—the popular impression is that a few gifted people are able to go into trance while a discarnate being speaks using their voice. But a 1990 Gallup poll revealed that trance channeling is far from a rare phenomenon. In response to the question, Have you "been personally involved in channeling, by participating in a trance during which a 'spirit-being' temporarily assumed control of your body?" 2 percent of the people surveyed by Gallup answered "Yes." While 2 percent may not seem like a lot compared to the 75 percent reporting *any* type of psychic experience, it still translates to *several million* Americans. In a survey of 184 A.R.E. members, I found that 8.2 percent said they had experienced "spontaneous 'trance channeling,' in which some other being speaks using your voice, but you have little awareness afterward of what has been said," and 8.2 percent also said that they had experienced "trance channeling where you controlled entry into the trance state volitionally (through your own intentional efforts)."

A more surprising figure came from my question on inner voices. When I questioned A.R.E. members about the experience of "spontaneous mental contact with higher beings or spirit guides," 58.2 percent had had this happen, and 49.2 percent said that they had experienced "mental contact with higher beings or spirit guides in which you controlled the contact through your own effort, for example, through meditation." So although channeling is relatively rare, inner voices and spirit guides appear to be rather common. In the average American population, I would speculate that about 15 percent occasionally hear helpful voices.

Varieties of Sources beyond the Conscious Personality

The diversity of experiences, some positive and some negative, is great. Let's look at what people have reported of contacts beyond the conscious self, from inner voices to possessing spirits.

Voices and Spirit Guides

"Hearing voices" has become a cliché in our time, a euphemism for "crazy." People are willing to share many types of experiences but often are very reluctant to admit that they have been hearing voices. Yet, as the surveys show, if you ask the questions anonymously, you find that inner voices really aren't so rare.

Most voices communicate only occasionally and offer positive messages and helpful guidance. People often interpret them as coming from a higher source: their own higher selves or a higher guide. A seventy-five-year-old woman sent us this report, one she was probably very hesitant to share when it happened and she might have been thought "crazy."

A Warning Voice and a Compassionate Voice. When I was 15 (about 60 years ago), I had left my coat on a chair in the reading room of the public library and was looking over some books, when I was conscious of a voice saying "Look in your coat pocket, your money's gone." When I checked, of course, the money was gone. I had a similar experience about thirty years later. I had been deeply disturbed and had cried out (silently, in my mind) after I had gone to bed. "Why?" The next morning just as I awakened, I was conscious of a compassionate, loving voice saying, "It's the way you feel about things." I say "conscious" rather than

"heard" because I was aware that it was not a voice
outside but one speaking in my mind's ear.

These occasional voices may come with warnings or
with inspiration. Often they don't identify themselves;
people may interpret them as the voice of their higher
selves or they may interpret them as guardian angels
or spirit guides. It is significant that this woman was
clear about the voice coming from her "mind's ear."
Helpful voices are usually recognized as inner, rather
than as coming from outside.

These voices may mark significant transitions in
people's lives. A fifty-six-year-old woman wrote:

> *Guidance on the Path.* My first psychic experience as
> an adult was a voice in my head giving me direction
> regarding a difficult decision. Immediately after hear-
> ing the voice I felt relieved of a great burden. The
> decision was a good one and I knew within the follow-
> ing week that I was on a "new" path.

Sometimes a person will have a longer or more continuous relationship with voices or guides. The communication not only signals a transition but remains
as guiding force.

Stephen, the Peaceful Warrior

To learn more about such life-transforming voices,
I interviewed "Stephen" at length. At age forty-three,
Stephen has spent most of his adult life in the navy,
working his way up from enlisted man to warrant officer. His current specialty is bomb disposal, one of
the most dangerous jobs in the navy. This demanding
work tends to quickly weed out those who are weak
or unstable. He is not the typical "new-ager," yet his
experiences with spirit guides have been a major
theme of his life.

Like many people capable of dissociation, Stephen

had a difficult childhood, with some unusual experiences. He told me, "My mother was killed violently (in an accident) when I was two and a half years old. I'm sure that has a lot to do with where I am now. I didn't consciously contact my guides when I was a child, but I was able to astral travel. I think a lot of people as kids are able to do that. But it gets stomped on. You're not allowed to get out and fly around the house. It's not cool. . . . I kept it secret from my family and friends."

Stephen's guides claim to be Native American spirits, yet he feels they are also a part of himself. He grew up next to a reservation and developed a deep reverence for Native traditions. He told me that he first remembers contacting his guides when he was going through a difficult divorce in his twenties. "A good friend of mine taught me to meditate, and to reach out and touch base with my higher selves. They were within me, a part of me. I didn't know what they were. In those days I had four or five guides that I could hold long conversations with. I could talk about things that were going on within my world, whether it was codependency, alcohol abuse, lost loved ones, or whatever, and receive answers from them. . . . The guides are a loving and caring energy."

Later in his life, Stephen identified guides he calls the "Circle of Elders." "They are energy forces who have lived and come through this experience many times. They're here to help me move forward on my own medicine path. And they're as real as you and I sitting here looking at each other right now."

Stephen communicates with his guides while fully conscious. I asked him to contact his guides and let me ask them some questions as well. At the time we talked, he had never before tried to relay the answers to questions to another person, but I found no difficulty communicating this way. I asked at what point in his life the guides had first come through, and he relayed this reply, in which his guides initiated a contact before he was consciously aware of them. The guides replied: "The death of Stephen's mother is probably the first time we really had to reach out and protect him. The purpose of the physical state is to learn about emotions, but that can be a very powerful and destructive thing. The emotions can literally destroy the physical. At that time, at the death of his mother, he saw his mother killed, and it would have been too much for him, to take it on all at once. We kind of took over and blocked that for him, blocked it out. We put a darkening on it so it didn't tear him apart from inside out."

Later, during Stephen's divorce, the guides intervened again when he was considering suicide: "When his wife left him . . . he went into what you would call a mental burnout. We put a vision in front of him, for him to see and look at, which was a vision of self-destruction. . . . He was never in any danger, because he recognized the truth as it was placed in front of him. It was death of living a lie. It was a very difficult time for him, but in death is the beginning."

For Stephen, these guides are now a constant presence in his life, advising him and leading him to further spiritual growth. I expressed concern that his colleagues in the navy might feel less than confident if their officer in a bomb-disposal unit consulted spirit guides before giving them orders. He laughed and agreed that he had to keep that aspect of his life quiet: "That's right. So you deal in the physical side, with the rules that are there. In order for my men to stay alive in the physical, there's rules they've got to follow, or they're going to die. . . . Following the spiritual path also takes discipline, and the military taught me discipline."

Stephen is certainly a contrast to the popular image of the person who "hears voices," yet he is probably not all that unusual. He is not especially concerned with whether they are "really" spirits or elements of himself. He follows their guidance because it works in his life.

Troubling Voice Experiences

Unfortunately not all voice experiences are positive. People are often terrified that hearing negative inner voices means that they have a mental disorder. Edgar Cayce was faced with the same question from people who were psychically sensitive. One person asked him, "Am I slightly mentally ill?" Cayce replied, "No, save as to who would be the judge. Every individual is slightly mentally ill to someone else" (Reading 5210-1).

But critical, condemning voices can cause immense emotional pain. In their extreme forms they can be disabling, a sign of a need for serious therapy. Cayce emphasized, however, that what appears to be a curse can become a blessing, if it is taken as a sign of the need to refocus one's life. A negative voice may be a message from a part of yourself that you are failing to exercise your will. It is easy to fall into the habit of avoiding personal responsibility by attributing wisdom to a "higher source," rather than making your own decisions. The shock of hearing a negative voice can be an opportunity for you to consciously examine what the voice says and to assess your life. Many of us are all too willing to abdicate our self-determination to a source of guidance with more "authority."

While voices themselves are not necessarily signs of illness, and can facilitate the growth process, it is important not simply to accept uncritically what the voices say. Is their guidance beneficial, or is it contradictory and distracting?

Edgar Cayce, whose abilities of course went far beyond hearing inner voices, offered the following valuable advice:

As it has been indicated from the first through *this* channel [Cayce himself], there should ever be that ideal, "What does such information as may come through such a channel produce in the experience of individuals, as to not their thoughts, not their relations other than does such make them better parents, better children, better husbands, better wives, better neighbors, better friends, better citizens?" And if and when it does NOT, LEAVE IT ALONE! (Reading 1135-6)

In some cases, however, the voices go beyond the ability of the individual (and his friends and loved ones) to cope. The individual may even have trouble judging whether the voices are helpful or not. Some types of voices do seem to be a symptom of serious mental disturbance. Condemning voices are a common symptom of schizophrenia, a serious disorder that needs professional treatment. Schizophrenia can include a loss of control over most aspects of consciousness—thoughts become disorganized, emotions become chaotic, and the voices are often incoherent, with an intense, persecuting tone. For such symptoms, it is essential to seek medical help.

The current medical viewpoint is that schizophrenia is a disturbance of brain chemistry. It is a physical disease, not a mental weakness. It can be treated with medications that are often effective in stopping the voices. But it seems to be the case, even in the most serious mental disturbances, that there may also be some genuine psychic phenomena and a part of the self that continues to have insight and compassion. A sensitive therapist, aware of the possibility of psychic phenomena, may be helpful here. Edgar Cayce, in agreement with modern psychiatry, traced many such problems to physical causes: glandular and chemical imbalances and physical accidents, especially to the head and spine. David McMillin, a mental health professional and faculty member at Atlantic University, has compiled detailed information on the Cayce recommendations for treating schizophrenia and other serious mental illnesses. His books are available from the Association for Research and Enlightenment (see resource listing in the appendix), and are written to help psychologists and psychiatrists in their treatment of these conditions.

Channeling, Possession, and Multiple Personality

Edgar Cayce may have been the first person to use the word "channel" in conjunction with the ability to set the conscious personality aside to receive guidance. But "channel" has come to have a more specific meaning—channels or channelers, in the popular mind, are people who enter a trance while a 25,000-year-old man, an extraterrestrial, or some other being offers words of wisdom.

A thirty-year-old man sent me this experience, not sure what it meant but convinced that he was tapping a source beyond himself:

> *Maltose Speaks.* I was sitting quietly, then drifted away, powerless to move body or eyes. I heard a sound like a radio frequency—high-pitched—and then an alien-sounding voice, also high-pitched (as one would expect a Martian to sound), spoke: "This is Maltose. I hear you." All the while I felt myself speeding away from my body and struggled to regain control, which I soon did. Felt a certain sense of awe afterward—was very excited yet apprehensive.

Whether the communication is from Maltose, Seth, Ramtha, or any of hundreds of other entities, some people can set aside their conscious personality, enter a trance, and let what appears to be another being speak using their voice. When they return from the trance they often remember little or nothing of what happened during the session. If the entity is benign and offers words of wisdom, the experience can be inspirational, although it does not fit well into our Western views of the material world. But this phenomenon has its frightening side—some people are afraid of possession, fearful that some entity with evil intentions may take over their body against their will. And psychologists have found an alternative explanation for some of these cases—one not involving paranormal phenomena. It is called multiple personality. Two or more personalities, ranging from saintly to violent, coexist in the same body, unpredictably taking over the body and disrupting the person's life. How can we tell if we are dealing with a higher source of wisdom or a mental disorder?

Trance, in which the conscious personality "steps aside," has been a mode of consciousness since ancient times. Shamans, "medicine men" in cultures all over the world, have entered trances to obtain information psychically, contacting whatever "spirits" exist in their belief system. In our modern Western civilization the documented history of trance dates back to the 1700s, to Franz Anton Mesmer, a Viennese doctor who developed the concept of "animal magnetism" or "Mesmerism." This trance state, induced by a variety of means, came to be called "hypnosis," a term coined by Scottish physician James Braid. As I discussed in the chapter on healing, it is a focused state of attention, in which remarkable phenomena of consciousness can manifest, including feats of visualization and memory and control over normally unconscious processes of the body. By the beginning of the twentieth century, hypnosis was recognized as a legitimate means of tapping the unconscious mind, useful in psychotherapy.

In explorations of this state of consciousness, some therapists and researchers found that apparent psychic phenomena occurred—subjects were sometimes able to receive hypnotic suggestions telepathically, for example. Members of the Society for Psychical Research were also interested in it because of its possible relationship to the trances of mediums.

Mediumship, or contacting the spirits of the dead, is known as far back as the Old Testament of the Bible and is probably far older. Its modern history begins in 1848, when mysterious raps were heard in the house of the Fox family in Hydesville, New York. The youngest daughter, Kate, discovered that she could communicate with the raps by snapping her fingers. Soon the family developed a code for yes, no, and the letters of the alphabet, and communication with the "spirit" began in earnest. From coded raps, spirit communication quickly evolved to "mediums" who, while in trance, let spirits use their voices. A new religion appeared, Spiritualism, and the fad spread until thousands of people were communicating with spirits and demonstrating phenomena including raps, table levitation, materializations, and voice communications through the mediums. Although fraud was common, there appears to have been a substantial amount of genuine paranormal communication.

Modern-day channeling is a variant of spirit mediumship. The trance states are similar, but while mediums claim to contact the spirits of dead people on demand (your dead uncle George, for example), channelers typically contact specific discarnate entities with whom they have established a relationship. Channeling is not a new phenomenon. Many mediums not only contacted the dead, they channeled "controls"—discarnate spirits with whom they had a special relationship and who facilitated contact with other spirits.

But with what, or whom, are mediums and channelers communicating? Although the members of the Society for Psychical Research and later investigators published many volumes of transcripts of mediumistic communications, it turned out to be very difficult actually to prove that they had contacted spirits rather than parts of the medium's unconscious mind. Remember that these researchers were in general quite willing to accept the idea that ESP existed, so evidence that the medium could use telepathy or clairvoyance was not proof of the reality of spirits. That is, a medium in trance might come through with a communication from your deceased Aunt Mary, something only you and Mary could have known. But how do we know the medium wasn't telepathically reading your mind and unconsciously creating a personification of Mary? Very rarely do the personalities contacted by mediums seem to be full personalities—instead they often seem to be fragments, with small pieces of information.

In many cases, in addition to contacting spirits, mediums have had what came to be called "controls," entities with whom they had a continuing relationship and who were often more articulate than the typical spirit. They, too, frequently claimed to be deceased individuals, but they identified their purpose as helping the medium work with the other spirits in the trance state. These controls are essentially the same as what are now popularly thought of as channeled entities. In addition to acting as "referees" for all of the other spirits that wished to communicate, they often offered their own wisdom as well.

Evelyn: Generations of Spirits

To learn more about the life of a medium, I interviewed "Evelyn," a thirty-year-old mother of two young children, who was raised with a belief in spirits. In an earlier chapter, I discussed Evelyn's near-death experience. Her parents are both Spiritualists in England, and her mother and aunt are ministers at a Spiritualist healing center. Although spirits were well accepted in her family, surprisingly they were not part of her own early life:

I did not actually have personal experiences of spirits as a child. The first time I really felt that I had contacted the spirit world personally was after I had a motorcycle accident when I was sixteen. I had a near-death experience, traveled into spirit, and met certain entities on the other side.

In one sense I asked for it to happen. I was at the age of thirteen, three years prior to the accident. At that time my grandfather passed away to spirit. His passing was such a grief at the time. I was very, very close to my grandfather. During that time I think I made a pact with myself and the higher power to use me as an instrument, so that I would have a contact with my grandfather."

Despite her Spiritualist upbringing, Evelyn did not have an easy time learning to work with her mediumistic abilities. She was grateful to have a family and a social group who were supportive of her struggles. As she told me:

At the beginning, when I first started developing this ability, it would come in any time day or night and I had no control over it at all. It took a period of seven years of development before I had it under control. . . . After the accident, to develop the ability, I joined a group of about eight people. We would always start with a prayer, so there was a lot of protection. . . . But there were times before the development started, right after I had my accident, that I did have a lot of negative experiences, because I was way open. Some of it was crazy, some of it was bizarre, as though I was hallucinating. The group helped enormously, [and] most of the problems started going away.

Evelyn is now a professional medium, as well as a full-time mother. She described her trance state to me:

When I'm communicating with my guide in trance, it feels like I'm sitting to the side somewhere, lifted up and back. It is as though I am surrendering completely. She's taking over full control. She's taking over my voice box, my thoughts, my physical movements. Everything is just completely taken over. I am aware to a point of what's going on, but it's a fine, fine awareness. It's as though you're looking down from a different frequency. When you come back to the conscious state you can't hold on to it. It's like a dream you've just gone through. You can remember parts of it, certain words or actions, but not quite the whole of it.

I can end the session when I want to, if I feel that the physical body is tired. And if the physical body is very tired, it's hard for the guide to keep the connection for long anyway. It's a two-way thing, a choice on both parts. She will let go and I will come back in. I do have a certain amount of choice, and the guide knows exactly how I feel.

So who are the entities? Are they truly spirits or are they parts of the self? There are no easy answers. Parapsychologists have not been able to demonstrate the reality of spirits—it is hard to see how they could do so. Perhaps it is our limited concept of the self that causes confusion.

Cayce turned the emphasis away from the identities of the sources and focused instead on the purpose of the contact and the application of the information as the appropriate central concerns. He had the following recommendation:

As to how, to whom, or from what sources these emanations or activities may take their action, depends upon first the sincerity of purpose, as to whether it is to be constructive in the experience of such seekers or whether through self there is to be the aggrandizement of power, influence or force upon and in the experience. For, as ye sow, so shall ye reap. (Reading 507-1)

Nevertheless, my own experience is that it is wise not to take entities' claims to specific identities at face value. Channeled "entities" often seem to take on identities claiming some higher authority, for example, a particular biblical figure or famous person. Here are some examples of people who have come to my research project, claiming to channel Edgar Cayce, whereas some consideration of the alternatives might have eased their struggles.

Channeling Edgar Cayce

I have occasionally received letters and phone calls from people whose channeled source claims to be Edgar Cayce, but I have not found the claims very convincing.

One woman was making quite a career of channeling "Edgar Cayce." She arrived in Virginia Beach hoping to be "validated." We arranged a session for her, in which I asked research-related questions, and a relative of Cayce's asked personal questions, to which only Cayce himself would know the answers. At first I was reasonably impressed with the woman. Her answers to my questions were intelligent, although not particularly strong evidence of psychic ability. In response to a set of questions about archaeological sites, she gave answers that were quite interesting. In response to personal questions about Cayce, however, she did not fare as well. Cayce had left specific information known only to his relatives so that he would be recognized if he returned. Not only could she not give any of the personal recognition signs, but she was unable even to identify key people in Cayce's life who would have been known by anyone familiar with the Cayce story. It is possible that this woman had some psychic ability, but her source, whatever its true nature, found it necessary to invest itself with the "authority" of Edgar Cayce.

In another case, a man's source told him that he himself *was* Edgar Cayce—that Cayce had been one of his past lives. In still another life he had been Judas Iscariot, betrayer of Jesus in the Bible. When this man came to see me he was doubly disturbed. Believing that you were Judas in a past life is a heavy burden to bear. To compound the problem, he had read Cayce's own past life readings, and they did not identify Cayce as Judas. Could his source be untrustworthy?

I recommended that he look at the symbolism of the characters Cayce and Judas. Cayce he saw as a benevolent authority figure, Judas as the opposite, as a weak and unprincipled betrayer. I suggested that he consider that these might symbolize parts of his own personality. The part claiming to be Edgar Cayce was in fact his own higher self, taking on the role of Cayce because of the man's conscious trust in Cayce. The Judas personality was a personification of his shadow side.

This new way of looking at these personalities relieved some of his distress. Both appeared to have valuable lessons to teach him, but he didn't have to accept their identities at face value.

Hugh Lynn Cayce, in his book *Venture Inward,* discusses some more difficult cases of channeled entities claiming to be Edgar Cayce. Some of the messages purporting to come from Cayce showed a sense of grandiosity that he never had when he was alive. Others appeared to be messages about the release of suppressed sexual energy, clothed in religious symbolism. Some of the material contained good advice, but much of it was inaccurate and appeared to represent unconscious wishes rather than psychic attunement. In another case, "Edgar Cayce" gave a man advice on compounding a hair tonic that had just enough truth in it to waste a lot of his time with no useful results.

Of course, these people who claim to channel Cayce are just examples. Many channelers have questioned the identities of their sources. Jane Roberts, well known for channeling the "Seth" books, stated this belief: "I do think that Seth represents a kind of psychological extension from my normal state—the self 'ascending' through itself, using itself as a psychological stepping-stone to vaster realities. . . . Seth may be myself at another level of activity, so transformed that even to me the psychological distances between us seem insurmountable."

Another channeler with whom I worked had a source claiming to be a biblical figure. When I asked probing questions, the source admitted that he represented the channeler's higher self and personified himself as an authority figure because that was what people expected.

The Negative Side of Dissociation: Multiple Personality and Possession

Some of the most terrifying and disabling mental problems are also related to hearing voices, episodes of amnesia, and trances in which another personality apparently takes control. Religious beliefs in possession and psychiatric concepts like multiple personality disorder seem to describe similar phenomena, yet prescribe very different treatments.

For most of the twentieth century, multiple personality was considered a very rare condition and possession a superstition. In the 1970s, however, interest in multiple personality reawakened. By the 1980s, multiple personality disorder (MPD) gained a place in the official *Diagnostic and Statistical Manual of Mental Disorders,* and hundreds of cases had been reported. It is now known officially as dissociative identity disorder, but I will use the more common term "multiple personality." It appears that MPD was often misdiagnosed as depression, schizophrenia, and other conditions, since the personalities may not be detected unless the therapist is alert to their possible existence.

Multiple personality has some commonalities with trance channeling, but also some significant differences. In both conditions, the "host" personality usually can't remember what occurred while the other personality had control of the body. In both conditions the identities claimed by the alternate personality or personalities may vary a great deal. Typically they insist that they are a separate person from the host. In MPD, some may identify themselves as ordinary persons, but others may identify themselves as deceased relatives, ascended masters, spirits, or space beings—the same types of entities that claim to communicate thorough channelers.

One of the major differences between multiple personality and channeling is that in MPD one or more of the personalities exhibits pathological behavior. It may appear as a terrified child, as a persecutor, or as a violent defender. In many cases of MPD, there are other personalities filling the role of what psychiatrist Ralph Allison has called the Inner Self Helper. Therapists often report that these helpers have great wisdom and actually assist with the therapy.

Even the most negative entities or personalities— whatever they claim to be—may have a positive role to play. In multiple personality, the persecuting personality is often a defender, seeing his own role as protecting the other personalities by scaring them and by scaring any potential attacker. Such a personality may seem threatening and evil, even claiming to be the devil. Therapists treating MPD have found that these personalities, underneath their "bad attitude," are often frightened children. When approached properly, they are found to contain much of the energy in the system and often can be enlisted to help in the therapy.

There is really no way to distinguish a persecutor in multiple personality from possession by an outside spirit. Much depends on the metaphysical assumptions of the people involved. Possession has a long history in religious tradition and so is assumed by many with religious backgrounds. In contrast, with the advances that have been made in treating even the most disturbed alternate personalities, MPD therapists are unlikely even to consider the possibility of possession.

The belief—multiple personality or possession—dictates the treatment. MPD therapists prefer to try to integrate the personalities into a unitary personality—obviously a mistake if the problem is possession by an external entity. On the other hand, exorcism, violently driving away the possessor, is certain to fail if the entity is a disturbed component of the host personality. The result may be to temporarily transform the symptom, while creating an even more frightened and angry alternate personality.

One alternative to integration or exorcism has come to be called "depossession therapy." Here the assumption is that the problem stems from possession by an outside entity, but instead of fighting it with exorcism, the therapist performs therapy with the entity, exploring its needs and reasons for being there and gently convincing it to leave. This type of therapy may be beneficial, even if we still cannot determine the origin of the problem entity. If it is a part of the host, we may have therapy that helps resolve the problems that caused the split in the first place. If it truly is an external entity, we may have therapy that helps the entity along its own path, which doesn't include harassing the host.

There may be no way to conclusively decide in a given case whether a personality is a part of the self or an external entity. Indeed, if we are all connected at a deeper level, our distinction of self and external may not even be very meaningful. The important issues, however, are the effects on a person's life and the quality of the information that comes through.

Much further research remains to be done, but the important point here is that apparent possession does not require an "exorcist." It may be a symptom of multiple personality and be amenable to treatment. If it is truly possession, depossession therapy offers a gentler alternative to exorcism, with some claims of effectiveness.

How Do Channeling and Multiple Personality Develop?

There are books offering guidance on how to develop a channeling ability, but I am cautious and will take a different approach here. Although certain exercises can awaken this ability, it appears that there are underlying dissociative capacities in both channelers and people with multiple personality. First, there appears to be some degree of natural hypnotic ability, the ability to go into a trance. Second, there is often a traumatic experience or series of experiences in early childhood. For MPD it is most commonly severe, repeated child abuse, including both physical and sexual abuse. To escape the terror, the child walls off parts of the personality to handle the pain, while others carry on the business of daily life. Most channelers, on the other hand, do not report severe abuse, although they often do report lonely and unhappy childhoods. They, too, have typically used trance states as a way to escape from unpleasant situations. Not all channelers report this pattern. Some had ordinary childhoods but experienced trauma as an adult, perhaps an accident or a near-death experience that initiated a psychic opening (for example, Evelyn, discussed above.) Still others were unaware of this ability until they experimented with a ouija board, automatic writing (where the hand writes without conscious control), or a pendulum, all devices for tapping into the unconscious mind. A split in consciousness may spontaneously occur.

Sometimes people fear that simply by playing with a ouija board, they could be possessed by malevolent entities or suddenly develop MPD. The ouija board and the pendulum are just tools for opening access to the unconscious mind. They don't require any training, and so lack the spiritual component. Those people who are already well grounded spiritually may discover an inspiring opening to a new realm. Others may not be so fortunate. Most psychics and channelers who have well-integrated personalities and control over their abilities recommend careful work with the spiritual aspects of these abilities, not random experimentation with techniques. Edgar Cayce, for example, generally did not recommend contacting discarnate entities through such means as ouija boards and automatic writing. Here is a typical comment from his readings:

Question: To further my work in possible radio reception of cosmic messages, should I attempt to train myself in automatic handwriting, or use a medium?
Answer: As has been indicated, rather than [use] automatic writing or a medium, turn to the voice within. If this then finds expression in that which may be given to self in hand, by writing, it is well; but not that the hand be guided by an influence outside of itself. For the universe, God, is within. Thou art his. Thy communion with the cosmic forces of nature, thy communion with thy Creator, is thy birthright! Be satisfied with nothing less than walking with Him! (Reading 1297-1)

The unconscious mind is a repository of much that is good and of much that is denied by the conscious self. For most of us, the dangers of tapping the unconscious are overemphasized. But if you know you were abused as a child, or have amnesia for large parts of your childhood, be *very careful* in your choice of path for personal growth, whether it be meditation or a ouija board. Many psychics have overcome abusive childhoods to exercise their skills for the good of others, but we do not yet understand why some succeed in controlling their ability, while others feel controlled by it. If you have many unresolved issues, experimenting with techniques that facilitate dissociation may open up Pandora's box. If you suspect that this may be the case, exploring your unconscious with the help of an experienced therapist may be the safest route.

PART FOUR

Psychic Experiences and Spiritual Development

CHAPTER 11

Mystical Experiences

A man once asked a farmer how to train a mule. The farmer said, "You train a mule with gentleness." The man spent hours trying to gently coax the mule, all to no avail. He finally asked for help from the farmer, who proceeded to hit the mule over the head with a board. "I thought you said you train a mule with gentleness!" exclaimed the man. "You do," replied the farmer, "but first you have to get his attention."

—Traditional story

Have you ever had an experience that "hit you over the head"? That was so powerful that it made other psychic experiences seem mundane by comparison? That not only got your attention but literally changed your life? For those of us who are stuck in our "mulish" material lives (most of us, I suspect), it is a mystical experience, a brief moment touching a higher realm, that opens the door to a new view of the meaning of life.

Ordinary psychic experiences are glimpses of a world beyond our normal, waking, focused consciousness. It is not always the same world; we have seen some of the diversity of such experiences. A psychic experience may refer to the inner world and may be a potential lesson about our unconscious minds, a window to our inner selves. Or it may refer to the inner world of someone else, an example of connectedness beyond the bounds of the usual senses. It can even refer to an event in the external world, a clairvoyant or precognitive perception of a real event. In all these cases, the process that we are aware of is taking place on what I have referred to as the *personal* level. These psychic experiences are a *different* form of consciousness but not necessarily a *higher* form of consciousness.

We have seen that some of these experiences also appear to point to something higher, to another level of reality. These experiences of a higher reality are termed "mystical." A woman in her sixties wrote:

> *The Doorway to Christ and an Angel of Protection.* In an altered state, achieved spontaneously during a period of intense spiritual growth, I was aware of myself prone and crawling towards a brilliantly lit doorway. I moved with great reluctance towards the doorway and knew that within was the Christ and that he was totally loving and waiting. At another time I woke after a positive dream experience for which I was very grateful, and (still not really awake) looked to see an enormous, snowy angel wing covering my house. The fine convolutions of the feather pattern were very clear. I knew that I and my house were protected.

Such mystical experiences can profoundly affect the lives of those who have had them, yet be rejected or misunderstood by those who have not. There is a saying: "Look where I'm pointing, don't bite the finger." When confronted with something beyond our understanding, our tendency all too often, like a young puppy, is to "bite the finger" rather than to look toward where the experiences are pointing. In our popular culture, "mystical" is often used in opposition to "rational," implying fuzzy thinking. But this is not the real meaning of the term. There are mystical traditions going back thousands of years, in all the religions, traditions of individuals who are able to experience directly a higher, more unitive state of consciousness.

Parapsychologists have not often studied mystical experiences because there is no way to objectively evaluate them. You cannot do an experiment to "prove" the validity of a mystical experience as you can with some psychic phenomena. In fact, a defining characteristic of mystical experiences is that they can't be expressed adequately in words at all—the only way to understand them is to experience them yourself. On the other hand, there is a great deal of agreement across diverse religious traditions that mystical experiences do point to a higher level of consciousness that we all potentially share.

This chapter and the next one explore the possibility of an integrated path of spiritual development, incorporating both psychic and mystical experiences. Here we will look at some of the forms these mystical experiences take and the impacts they have had on people's lives.

The Varieties of Mystical Experience

For some people, the concept of a higher reality is just an idea. If they are religious, they may accept it on faith; if they are not religious, they may reject it based on their own experiences of the world. But for other people, the mystical experience itself is the most compelling feature of their worldview. In his book *The Varieties of Religious Experience*, psychologist William James speaks of the "convincingness" of the experiences; they are as convincing to those who have had them as any ordinary sensory experience can be, and much more convincing than results established by mere logic ever could be. James says, "If you have them . . . the probability is that you cannot help regarding them as genuine perception of truth, as revelations of a new kind of reality which no adverse argument, however unanswerable by you in words, can expel from your belief." James, a Harvard professor in the early twentieth century, was the founder of American psychology. Braver than many of today's psychologists, he sought a science that would address spiritual truths as well as physical facts.

What are the qualities of mystical experiences? James termed the two primary qualities "noetic quality" and "ineffability." Noetic quality refers to the knowledge gained in the experience, states of insight into the heights of truth beyond our rational understanding. Ineffability means that the experience defies expression in words.

James also noted the "transiency" of mystical experiences. They are often short-lived, and the quality of the experience may be difficult to recapture in memory. There may also be a quality of "passivity," the feeling of being in the grasp of a superior power. There is some similarity here to mediumistic trances, but in mystical states some memory of their content always remains, together with a profound sense of their importance.

In looking at the mystical reports I received, I can add other qualities to James's list. Emotions may be intense; often both great joy and great solemnity, evoking a sense of wonder and awe, are reported. There may be religious symbolism and the appearance of religious figures—angels, the Christ—to which profound meaning is attributed.

Some experiences go beyond symbolism. The great mystical traditions universally speak of contacting reality in its "suchness" or "thatness," beyond words, symbols, thoughts, and images. There can be an experience of complete oneness with the universe in a timeless and spaceless act that is beyond description.

Each person's experience of a higher state is unique. Some blend together with psychic experiences or near-death experiences, others involve nature, while still others are apparently direct encounters with religious figures such as Jesus or an angel.

When Psychic Becomes Mystical

Typically, when parapsychologists discuss psychic experiences, they pay little attention to any religious dimension. In the same way, mystical experiences are discussed in religious literature but rarely with any reference to psychic phenomena. These two modes of inquiry—the psychological and the religious—are so often separated that it is surprising to see the amount of overlap between psychic and mystical phenomena when people actually write down their experiences. Many experiences could be labeled either way, depending on the emphasis of the person doing the reporting. Edgar Cayce, for example, read spiritual significance into most psychic experiences that were brought to him for interpretation. Here is an experience described to Cayce by a member of a healing prayer group, and his interpretation:

Colors and a Voice. Question: Please interpret the experience I had on Friday night, May 29th [1936], in which I saw colors and heard a voice speak within me. Answer: Much might be given as to colors, as to voice, as to the experience that came to thee. As has been given, these experiences come as warnings, as strength, as might, as power, that ye may be comforted in those experiences that at times would overwhelm thee and make thee doubt even thine own self. Know then, that the lights, the voice, are as the power of the Christ in thine life, *attuning* thee that thou may be a greater help, a greater blessing to others; at the same time encouraging thee, lifting thee up to a more perfect knowledge of the glories of the Lord as he worketh in and through thee. (Reading 281-27)

In response to a question from another inquirer—"What is the highest possible psychic realization?"—Cayce replied, "That God, the Father, speaks directly to the sons of men—even as He has promised" (Reading 440-4).

Even in modern America, mysticism is on the rise. Based on national surveys, in 1975 sociologist Andrew Greeley found that 35 percent of Americans reported having had mystical experiences at least once or twice. His later surveys confirmed this result, and in 1987 he wrote an article titled, "Mysticism Goes Mainstream." The close relationship between psychic and mystical experiences is confirmed by Greeley's surveys as well as John Palmer's work with the townspeople of Charlottesville, Virginia.

Here, for example, is a mystical experience reported by a sixty-three-year-old woman, which begins with an out-of-body experience.

Washed in the Light. Twenty years ago I was at home alone late on Sunday morning. As I went from my living room into my study, I suddenly "saw" myself kneeling beside a stream of water that crossed a very large sandy beach and entered the ocean a short distance beyond. There were many people on the beach with me. As I looked towards the person nearest me, I saw waves of light being emitted from her body. Then I looked around me and saw that this same kind of light was coming from every person present. Just as I realized this, the "light" from persons close to me reached me and I was engulfed in indescribably loving, blissful feeling—the kind of mystical experience that is beyond words. The experience was completely real

to me. It lasted only moments though it seemed un-
hurried and when I was "back in my room" it was as
if no time at all had passed. The memory of this experience has been sort of a "touch stone" for me. Merely
by remembering it I become centered once more in
that "space"—in that kind of universal love and
good will.

We could look at this event, a woman seeing herself
beside a stream of water, as simply an out-of-body
experience, and ask questions like "Was the stream a
real place?" or "Is there any way to show whether
she actually left her body or just imagined this?" As
we saw in the OBE chapter, these are legitimate questions that can be studied using scientific methods. But
to do so here would completely miss the point of the
experience. For this woman, the experience was one
of universal consciousness, a source of inspiration that
she has carried with her for years.

We should take care not to think of the experiences
in this book as a linear progression, by which first you
have a simple psychic experience, then a more complex one, and finally a mystical experience. These experiences can happen as part of a spiritual path, or
they can happen spontaneously to someone who has
had little previous interest in the spiritual. While for
some a mystical experience can be the culmination of
a series of compelling psychic experiences, for others
the first mystical experience signals a psychic awakening, the beginning of a permanently altered state of
consciousness. Here is an example, from a fifty-two-
year-old woman, of such an awakening experience:

A Psychic Awakening. After a time of turmoil, a
friend and I went to a park where we both had a most
wonderful, profound spiritual experience. Above our
heads formed a rainbow, which then was followed by
three more, making a total of four rainbows, which
was then followed by a vision of an angel arising from

a white waterfall in the midst of the blue sky. There was then a vision of a phoenix, and also a dove. A most fantastic happening for the both of us.

Since that time, I have found myself able to share other people's meditations. I have subsequently become a channel for healing, seeing the organs inside the bodies of people, in color. I continue to receive information from angels and spirit guides teaching divine love, and can sense the multi-leveled layers of people. I can communicate with some who have passed into light. My new level of awareness allows the world to disappear so that I may be in touch with the oneness, and the light.

Her experiences span the range from the sensory splendor of nature to the psychic presence of angels. From an initial experience of an angel, she underwent a psychic opening. But it is obviously far more than psychic in the narrow sense. She has maintained her contact with "the oneness and the light," the hallmark of a mystical state.

Nature and Meditation

What conditions precipitate mystical experiences? In the previous example, the experience began with a walk in the park. When you least expect it, a feeling of peace in nature may escalate to an experience of a higher reality. For those intentionally pursuing spiritual growth, meditation is a specific practice sometimes leading to a mystical experience. Here is an example from a seventy-six-year-old woman who had her first mystical experience while walking in nature.

God in Nature. My most treasured psychic experience occurred when I was in my middle 20's. I was walking to work on a beautiful October day. I was impressed with the intense blueness of the sky, the golden leaves of the trees, feeling myself enfolded in the pleasant atmosphere. I seemed to be all alone; if there were other people around, I was not aware of them. I felt a complete stillness, a feeling of perfect peace and well being. I was not conscious of walking, but when I reached my place of work, the feeling gradually faded. Some 25 years later, I was sitting in the kitchen/den with my sister one night. She was looking at a magazine. I had just put my work aside when I had the same experience I had had that October day described before. The feeling came suddenly, just like the other one had. I have practiced recalling this experience many times, and am successful in attaining a peace and stillness that, however, only approximates the original experience. I think both experiences were of Cosmic consciousness; both were spontaneous.

This was an experience profound enough to be inspirational when she described it to me more than fifty years later. While the first experience may be spontaneous, the effort to recapture that perfect moment can become a lifelong quest. The woman who wrote the above experience added: "I am now a meditator—at least 3 times a day, sometimes more—and more and more I receive enlightenment during meditation—or later, always at the right time."

Meditation can indeed induce such experiences. Although the aim of meditation is a complete transformation of the person (more on this in the next chapter), mystical experiences commonly occur along the way. Here are some experiences that were triggered by meditation, first from a forty-five-year-old woman:

An Awareness of God. While meditating, late evening, alone, I received an awareness that "God is and all is right with the world." This had a profound effect on me, an insight that I don't have to keep pondering the inconsistencies all around me knowing I won't understand them. It reassured and reinforced my positive outlook on life and my optimistic nature.

One of Edgar Cayce's lasting legacies is a study group program known as *A Search for God*. We will see in the next chapter how the study group material is one aid to integrating psychic and mystical experiences into a balanced life. In the original study group that worked with Cayce, many extraordinary experiences were reported during meditation. I surveyed the members of seventy present-day study groups, asking about their mystical experiences. The following experience is from a thirty-one-year-old woman currently in a study group:

> *A Vision of the Christ.* On a Thursday evening, our *Search For God* study group was meeting at the usual time. We had gone through our whole meeting and we were going through the meditation period. We said the Lord's Prayer. I saw the Lord Christ. He was over our heads. He had angels swirling around him. He seemed to be floating on a cloud. He was smiling at me. At the time, I was repenting about how I had been egotistical in my attitudes toward other people. After I realized that Christ appeared, I called out to him in my mind. Then like a lid over my eyes closed. I waited, it opened, I saw him again. I called out again in my mind. The lid closed again. Then the lid opened. He was still there. I said nothing, just watched. I lowered my eyes. I looked up and the angels and Christ had left. No one else had seen them.

This report brings out another characteristic of mystical experiences: They are intensely personal and subjective. Although everyone in the group was meditating, only this woman had this unique experience. The experience can be inspiring, yet the personal quality can be frustrating as well, since it can be difficult to share with others.

Experiencing the Highest Power

Sometimes a mystical experience can be completely overwhelming, so intense as to inspire fear and awe as well as joy. This report, from a twenty-nine-year-old man in the navy, was one of the most eloquent I received. His attempts to compare it with the everyday world heighten the sense of power in the experience, since they refer to some of the most awesome man-made power on earth.

The Christ Lives! Six years ago, in the predawn darkness, I was suddenly awakened and standing (actually floating) next to (and above) my bed was Christ shining in a celestial light. I was startled and my adrenaline was pumping. I learned new meaning of the term "fear of God." I could not face the Master who carried the full power of the Father. I felt unworthy in His presence. In my Navy career, I have stood next to an FA-18 aircraft in a test cell with 100% power and after burners; I have stood on the flag bridge of the USS New Jersey during full salvo: I have stood on the navigation bridge of a Guided Missile Cruiser during all launcher missile firing, but I have yet to experience that degree of power that so cut to the heart and very essence of my being. A few minutes later something prompted me and I rolled over in bed and saw Christ standing beside the bed, close to me. I felt very far from the standards of Christ, I felt shame of my sins and I rolled back over and buried my face in the bed. I then felt a feeling of peace and acceptance and words of the hymn "Just As I Am" came to me. I fell asleep and woke up very rested. I had been baptized a month earlier and was to sing in the church youth group choir at a special outdoor service that morning. One of the hymns of congregational singing was "Just As I Am." It is my testimony HE LIVES! because I have seen Him with my own eyes, and because He lives, so shall you and I.

The Mystical Traditions

Far from being an isolated anomaly of modern consciousness, mystical experiences have a tradition going back thousands—probably tens of thousands—of years. The mystical traditions consist of far more than an occasional mystical experience. Since in our culture we are not well educated in these traditions, someone having a mystical experience may have no point of reference for further development. If you do not look beyond that single peak experience, it is like mistaking a single lecture for an entire college curriculum. The single mystical experience can be looked on as an awakening, but it is only the beginning of the purification and training that the spiritual path comprises in mystical traditions.

Although Eastern religions like Hinduism and Buddhism often first come to mind when we think of mystics, we do not have to begin so far from home. Christianity is rich in mystical tradition. The most significant biblical mystical experience in the New Testament is that of Saul of Tarsus, a persecutor of Christians who was so awed by his experience that he went on to become Saint Paul the Apostle.

> Now as he journeyed he approached Damascus, and suddenly a light from heaven flashed about him. And he fell to the ground and heard a voice saying to him, "Saul, Saul, why do you persecute me?" And he said, "Who are you, Lord?" And he said, "I am Jesus, whom you are persecuting; but rise and enter the city, and you will be told what you are to do." (Acts 9:3–6, RSV)

Temporarily blinded by the light, when he recovered he proclaimed Jesus, saying, "He is the Son of God" (Acts 9:20).

Mystical Christianity does not stop with Paul, of course. Mystics have founded some of the great religious orders. Ignatius of Loyola, founder of the Jesuits, a Catholic order famous for its scholarship, was a mystic of the fifteenth century. He wrote *Spiritual Exercises,* which teach the aspirant contemplation to attain divine love. William James, writing on mystical experiences, said that Loyola perceived "the deep mystery of the holy Trinity [which] flooded his heart with such sweetness, that the mere memory of it in after times made him shed abundant tears."

Saint John of the Cross, a Spanish mystic of the sixteenth century, said, "It is God Himself who is then felt and tasted," and wrote *Dark Night of the Soul.* He recognized that even mystical experiences are not part of a smooth, upward path. The mystic can also experience an extremely painful feeling of separateness from God as part of his developmental process. Many people I have talked to have had a difficult period of separation that contrasts with their mystical insights and pushes them further along the spiritual path.

Of course, women were mystics, too, even in the male-dominated church. Saint Teresa of Avila, a contemporary of Saint John of the Cross, wrote *The Interior Castle.* It describes her own prayer experiences— a series of transformations of consciousness (in the castle of the soul) culminating in a spiritual union with Christ. Saint Teresa, a Carmelite nun, is known as one of the greatest Christian mystics. Evelyn Underhill, in her book *Mysticism,* says of Saint Ignatius, Saint John, and Saint Teresa, "They left behind them in their literary works an abiding influence which has guided the footsteps and explained the discoveries of succeeding generations of adventurers in the transcendental world."

George Fox founded the Society of Friends, or Quakers, in seventeenth-century England. Quakers believe that there is no need for most of the external trappings of religion, since the inner light of Christ shines in the heart of every man and woman. At age twenty-four, Fox had visions of the "hidden unity of the Eternal Being." Fox's *Journal* contains a vivid account of his struggles with messages from God, telling

him to remove his shoes and preach loudly in the
streets of the city, while he perceived the blood of
Christians, martyred a thousand years before, running
down the streets. William James speaks to the authenticity of Fox's spiritual insights: "In a day of shams, it
was a religion of veracity rooted in spiritual in-
wardness, and a return to something more like the
original gospel truth than men had ever known in
England. . . . Everyone who confronted him personally, from Oliver Cromwell down to the county magis-
trates and jailers, seems to have acknowledged his
superior power."

Fox's experiences themselves may appear bizarre to
us, even seeming almost pathological. James cautions
that we must be careful to judge mystical experiences
by their fruits, however, not by appearances. In the
first chapter of his book, "Religion and Neurology,"
he discredits the approach he calls "medical material-
ism" when it is applied to mystical experiences. Thus
one might attempt to dismiss Saint Paul's vision on
the road to Damascus as an epileptic seizure. But is
the spiritual value of an experience undermined if it
can be shown to a have physical correlate? Not at
all—all mental states have correlates in the brain, but
that observation says nothing about their spiritual
value.

James concluded that these states of mind must be
judged on their own merits, not on the basis of their
relationship to some arbitrary standards of physical
health. While it may be difficult to determine the *origin* of a mystical experience (i.e., from inside or from
a higher source), the results can be evaluated. Like
James, Edgar Cayce follows the Bible in speaking of
the "fruits of the spirit." The test of the value of a
mystical experience is that the fruits must be good
for life.

Mystical states, of course, are not known only from

Christianity. Mystical insight is cultivated in branches of virtually all religious traditions.

In the Hindu tradition, training in mystical insight is known as Yoga. Yoga, meaning "yoke," is the experimental union of the individual with the divine. Different systems have different types of exercises, postures, breathing, mental concentration, and moral discipline.

Buddhism, too, has a program of exercises leading to mystical insight. Meditation, both as one-pointed concentration and as equal-pointed attention or mindfulness, leads to enlightenment, a state of seeing things the way they really are, direct knowledge of reality without mediating thoughts.

Islam has the Sufi tradition, brought to popular attention by the works of Idries Shah. Shah's books do not encourage mystical experiences in isolation. Instead, the books tell stories designed to prepare the mind of the student to *begin* study of the Sufi way. Shah cautious against random pursuit of Sufi exercises in the absence of a qualified teacher, since this could lead to experiences that the student is not prepared to interpret and could impede progress. Mysticism is more than a collection of experiences.

In the Native American tradition, Black Elk's mystical vision is famous. This holy man of the Oglala Sioux was nine years old when he "traveled to the clouds," where he met with the "Grandfathers," who showed him the sacred way for his people. It was a profound experience of the unity of all creation.

Even Judaism, a religion not often thought of as mystical, has a tradition known as the Kabbalah, which means "that which has been received." The writings of the Kabbalah are ancient traditions addressing the hidden meaning under the surface of religious customs, laws, and rites, finding a deeper and more profound significance. Rabbi Herbert Weiner, in his book *9½ Mystics,* documents his search for the life secrets of this Jewish mystical tradition. Hebrew tradition is different from Christian or Hindu—union with God is not the object. The goal of Jewish mysticism is the effort to come close to things, a yearning for identification with the innermost aspect of everything. The Jewish scholar Martin Buber explains to Weiner that the goal is not *union* with God but experience of the *unity* of God and the *presence* of God.

How Can I Work with Mystical Experiences?

However they are defined, mystical experiences are the most profound experiences known to humanity. But they are only a step on the spiritual path. A single experience does not make one a mystic; mysticism can be a lifelong vocation.

If you have had a mystical experience, what can you do? Is joining a religious order your only hope of understanding it? Having a mystical experience doesn't automatically make you a better person or solve all your problems. In fact, it may create more problems than it solves. You may feel frustration in being unable to communicate its meaning and importance to others. And if you become obsessed with it and neglect your physical and social environment, it may not even be a positive force for change. Like any psychic experience, it may be difficult to share with friends or loved ones. It may be hard to return to the physical world, yet these experiences are by nature transient—the peak experience is not a lasting state and must be integrated into everyday life.

First, if you have had a mystical experience, it is usually attended with such powerful certainty that only you can be the judge of its value. But it is important to base the judgment not only on the experience itself, for it is transient, but on its fruits in your life. Is it leading you to be a better person—kinder, more helpful, more patient? Integrating such an experience into your life can take a lifetime! The next chapter will look more at paths for balancing the mystical with daily life.

Second, you may have to deal with *someone else's* mystical experience. The very certainty that gives a mystical experience its power can make a person who has had one rather difficult to live with. Trying to convince that person that the experience was not meaningful is unlikely to produce the desired effect. William James concluded, "The mystic is, in short, *invulnerable,* and must be left, whether we relish it or not, in undisturbed enjoyment of his creed."

Yet although the mystical experience is right for the individual, it is not necessarily an insight shared by anyone else. Claims to "the truth" are often made, yet there is little unanimity among mystics as to the application of their insights to the everyday world. If we have not been a party to the mystical experience ourselves, again the only way we can judge it is the same as we would judge any act—rational, psychic, or mystical: by the test of its fruits in the context of living. As James emphasizes, we are under no obligation to acknowledge in those who claim mystical states a superior authority conferred on them simply because they are mystical.

Finally, of what value are these reports if you have not had a mystical experience and do not know anyone who has? Are they merely a psychological curiosity, impossible to verify? James says emphatically, "The existence of mystical states absolutely overthrows the pretension of non-mystical states to be the sole and ultimate dictator of what we may believe. . . . They tell us of the supremacy of the ideal, of vastness, of union, of safety, and of rest. They offer us *hypothe-*

ses, possibilities which we may voluntarily ignore, but which as thinkers we cannot possibly upset. The supernaturalism and optimism to which they would persuade us may, integrated in one way or another, be after all the truest of insights into the meaning of life." Mystical experiences do not necessarily overrule rational thought, but, as James says, "In spite of all the perplexity, [they may] be indispensable stages in our approach to the final fullness of truth."

To integrate these experiences into our lives, we must step back and look at the entire spectrum of development. Mystical experiences are valuable not only in themselves but also for what they point to—the possibility of the complete transformation of the individual. In the next chapter we look at how this transformation can take place.

CHAPTER 12

Pathways to Transformation

> I do not know what I may appear to the world; but to myself I seem to have been only like a boy playing on the sea-shore, and diverting myself in now and then finding a smoother pebble or a prettier shell than ordinary, whilst the great ocean of truth lay all undiscovered before me.
>
> —Sir Isaac Newton, in Brewster,
> *Memoirs of Newton,* Vol. 2, ch. 27

Newton's analogy is apt. The ocean is a perennial symbol for the unconscious, and psychic experiences are the occasional pebbles or shells that appear on the shore—sometimes washed there gently, sometimes thrown up in a storm of chaos. For us to attempt to understand the ocean by studying its pebbles is a presumptuous task indeed.

The great spiritual traditions all say that there is much more to consciousness than psychic experiences. Those experiences can be pointers or distractions along the path, but they are not the final goal. In this chapter we will change our focus from the pointers to the path itself, to bring psychic experiences into the large context of spiritual development and provide some guidance to, as Edgar Cayce put it, "turn stumbling blocks into stepping stones."

What alternatives have we seen for dealing with psychic experiences? The responses range widely:

from dogmatic denial to careful study to uncritical acceptance, yet none of these speaks completely to our search for meaning. For some people the approach to all things psychic has been avoidance—denial that these experiences occur at all, denial that they are anything more than hallucination or delusion, or denial that they have any value in the growth and transformation of the individual. These "deniers," perhaps because of fear, are unwilling to look at a virtually universal component of human experience.

Other people have viewed psychic experiences as worthy of careful study. For the early psychical researchers, these experiences were evidence for survival of bodily death, and for an unconscious mind with astonishing capabilities. Yet the voluminous studies by the members of the Society for Psychical Research still treated such experiences as anomalies, not as part of our normal growth process.

The more recent investigators of these phenomena, identifying themselves as parapsychologists and epitomized by J. B. Rhine, narrowed the scope of study to those phenomena that could be investigated in the laboratory: telepathy, clairvoyance, precognition, and psychokinesis. They have demonstrated the existence of psi using methods as rigorous as any area of psychology, but still have difficulty persuading mainstream science. And in narrowing the scope of investigation, they have often missed the rich experiences that range far beyond the events technically defined as "psychic."

Meanwhile, three-quarters of the people in this country have had psychic experiences, and all sorts of publications, teachers, and groups purport to be able to explain them and aid in their development. We may find uncritical acceptance—anything psychic, metaphysical, or just plain "strange" is seen as good, whether or not it contributes to any lasting transformation. Despite the compelling evidence for a greater reality, all too often "application" of psychic ability is narrowly conceived in terms of "achieving personal power," "intuition for business," or even "winning the lottery." Faced with an array of choices, some people find a sense of spiritual enrichment in these experiences, while others remain confused or frightened.

In this chapter I address the potential for transcending the polarity of dogmatic denial and uncritical acceptance. Mystical experiences point to the possibility of going beyond intellectual study, to direct awareness of higher states of consciousness. I begin by looking at the progression of sensitivity, discernment, and wisdom, and the ever-present Trickster. I explore in depth one example of a spiritual path—the Cayce program called *A Search for God*—and consider some principles for making spiritual choices.

Sensitivity, Discernment, and Wisdom

Early in this book I distinguished sensitivity, discernment, and wisdom as three qualities that work together in the quest to integrate our psychic experiences with our overall path of growth and transformation. To this point we have looked at examples of sensitivity to different forms of psychic experiences, and their potentials and pitfalls. Sensitivity is a talent, a quality like musical ability or athletic ability. It is partly inborn and partly trainable. We all come into this life with a level of sensitivity. For some, psychic experiences are a rarity, something to be wondered at. For others, they are a constant flow. The techniques for enhancing this sensitivity have an ancient history—creating an inward focus through dreams, meditation, and hypnosis can make one more aware of psychic phenomena. Yet sensitivity alone is only the beginning; it is like playing the violin without lessons. Even with great natural talent, it is often a painful experience for all concerned.

I have offered suggestions for improving discernment, for learning to discriminate the activities of the unconscious mind from possible contacts with outer and higher realities. But without wisdom, even discernment won't fulfill the desire for understanding.

In developing discernment and wisdom we are faced with choices. Psychologist Thomas Greening defined these choices or themes, which are the central dilemmas of our existence: life versus death, separateness versus connectedness, free will versus determinism, and meaning versus absurdity. Psychic experiences heighten these contrasts, forcing us to confront polarities that we might often prefer to pass by. For some they elicit avoidance and denial, while for others they present opportunities for growth and transformation. We can succumb to the negative side of these polarities, or we can uncritically accept the apparently positive side. But the great opportunity is to recognize that the essence of each quality requires awareness of the entire range. We can transcend the limiting concept that these are polar opposites.

This realization may be difficult to express in words, but let's look at each of these qualities.

Life and death are central to our existence. We may embrace life and deny death, or dwell on death while missing out on life. Some of the most common and compelling psychic experiences force us to reexamine these apparent opposites. If we are embracing life—the goal of many "human potential" programs—we may be confronted with the reality of death in the form of apparitions or telepathic messages from the dead. Yet these are often messages of hope—evidence that death is not final, that denial is not necessary. If we dwell on death, we may find that our psychic experiences open us up to a wider view of life, that death, "God's other door," as Edgar Cayce put it, is but a transition in a continuing drama. Balancing life and death is a step on the path to wisdom.

As we go through our lives, *separateness and connectedness* are often the most critical issues we face. Look at all the books on relationships. We may at times feel a deep sense of aloneness and isolation, trapped in our bodies and unable to fully join with others. Or we may feel smothered by our relationships, desperate to assert our individuality. Again, psychic experiences may point the way toward transcendence of this polarity. At our most alone times, focused deeply inward, we may have an experience of connectedness so compelling that we, for a while, find the boundary of our skin to be a trivial obstacle. We are telepathically linked with the greater whole. Yet in our own inward focus, we may also find our center. We have the opportunity to learn discernment—to discriminate our own inner processes from those of the others to whom we are connected.

Next, there is probably no more divisive issue in philosophy than the dichotomy of *free will and determinism*. We may insist that we have free will, only to find that there still seem to be forces beyond our control, patterns of which we are unaware, directing our lives. Yet moving to the other pole, a purely determined universe, can lead to apathy and despair. Here again, our psychic experiences provide an opportunity for us to transcend this polarity. When we despair of having control over our own destinies, we discover the power of healing prayer. We find synchronicity calls our attention to the patterns of existence so that we can use our free will to work with them, not against them. On the other side we have precognitive experiences, apparent evidence that the future is indeed fixed. Yet we have seen in our closer study of these experiences that they may speak only of probable futures—free will is always an option.

Finally, we are faced with *meaning and absurdity*. This book is about the search for meaning, yet we are stymied in our search. Countless times in response to letters and phone calls seeking explanation for psychic experiences, I have had to say, "I simply don't know." We need to admit that at our conscious ego level there may be more to these experiences than we *can* know. Attempts to pursue them intellectually lead to absurdity. It is here that the scientific approach fails us. No amount of measurement, analysis, or intellectual synthesis can resolve these questions. Some people are led to declare the entire area as "irrational," off limits to inquiry. Yet there is another path. Spiritual traditions speak of our rational ego selves—the ideal of Western psychology—as only a *stage* on the path of development. Far from demonstrating the height of human potential, those who emphasize rationality may simply be "stuck" at an arrested stage of development. Yet we need to be careful in our pursuit of higher truths. The path of regression to lower stages always beckons.

The Ever-Present Trickster

We simply cannot escape the occasional absurdity in psychic phenomena. Our culture is one of the few that expects that life can always be defined through analysis and reason. Our science is a flight from the fear of delusion and deception. Many other cultures have recognized that an intellectual approach to life's events can be carried too far. They have accorded great respect to the irrational and the humorous.

In earlier chapters we have seen the humorous

Trickster aspects of the psychic. The Trickster is not a "person" or an "entity," it is a category of experience. My own experiences have often been more amusing and strange than enlightening or mystical. Seeing the license plate 1 BIG EGO on a truck right after talking about people with big egos is amusing. And running into people in embarrassing situations can be painful.

Yet the Trickster isn't simply humorous, it is an archetype of transformation. Even the most absurd experiences are opportunities for change. Even the most frightening experiences can stimulate the awakening of the will. The Trickster can lead you down a path of increasing irrationality, forcing an alteration of your worldview.

We first have to realize that, no matter how rational we think we are, we construct reality based on a combination of hopes, desires, fears, and needs. We all have a personal conviction that our perception of the world is the correct one (though we may call it "common sense"). The beginning of transformation is an experience that unsettles you sufficiently to force you to consider alternative worldviews.

The Trickster is "tricky." It enters your rational world and gains some measure of trust and credibility. One's first communications through a ouija board, medium, or channeled entity may appear to be "proof" of the trustworthiness of the source. As events unfold, the Trickster may shift and reframe the context. The acceptable "spirit of dead Uncle George" becomes "'Zork from the planet Zaxxon." Should we continue to trust his advice? Perhaps the point is not either to believe or to disbelieve the information but to stimulate our own creativity.

For someone who always seems to be a victim, being victimized by a *ghost* may be just the jolt needed to stimulate fighting back. Or, for someone who always seems to be fighting one battle or another, conflict with an insubstantial ghost may awaken the realization that sometimes there is a need just to accept that strange things happen.

We must always bear in mind that the Trickster highlights the *limits* of rationality, not the *abandonment* of rationality. We need to apply our intellects as skillfully as possible. Keep an open mind, but not so open that your brain falls out!

A Search for God

Faced with the vastly greater reality to which a sincere exploration of psychic phenomena opens us, and with the unpredictable appearance of the Trickster, many people seek grounding in a formal spiritual tradition—a tested path for transformation. There are an infinite variety of spiritual paths, each with its own claim to legitimacy and authenticity. Some paths ignore psychic phenomena altogether. Others see them as signs of spiritual progress but not the end goal. Here we will look at some research on personal development in *A Search of God,* a program growing out of the desires of Edgar Cayce's associates to become psychic themselves. I chose to look at this program because of my own participation and because I was able to contact a large number of other participants and hear of their experiences.

The original group that developed the lessons for *A Search for God* didn't realize that they were on a spiritual search at first. They were all aware of the possibility of a higher reality; all were close associates of Edgar Cayce and awed by his psychic ability and wisdom. Many had had psychic experiences themselves. Yet despite this awareness, they were confronted with the conditions in the physical world surrounding them.

It was 1931, the early years of the Great Depression. The Cayce hospital, Edgar's lifelong dream, had been lost; Atlantic University had closed for lack of funds; and the Cayce family was barely scraping by. A small group of Cayce's closest associates gathered to request guidance on psychic and spiritual development. They had firsthand experience of the potential of psychic ability, but not an understanding of how it could be used to overcome the reversals suffered by the Cayce work.

They probably expected a few lessons on techniques—visualization, meditation, perhaps trance induction—the same techniques still being taught by psychics today. What they received was far more. They received not only some exercises to increase their sensitivity but a complete course in developing discernment and wisdom.

Cayce began not with instruction in developing telepathy but with the simple concept of *cooperation*. Though it was simple conceptually, it was very difficult for the group to achieve. They not only had to work together physically, they had to come into accord mentally and spiritually. They repeatedly returned to Cayce for further lessons, only to be told they would receive no more until they achieved cooperation. This lesson was to set the tone for the entire series of twenty-four lessons. From the very beginning, Cayce addressed the three basic levels: physical, mental, and spiritual. They are inseparable. Cayce spoke of cooperation on all levels simultaneously—the physical, in working together to accomplish a common purpose; the mental, in achieving alignment of ideals; and the spiritual, in achieving oneness through cooperative meditation.

What had this to do with psychic development? It wasn't clear to the group at first, yet they found that during their meditations they experienced a variety of phenomena, interpreted by Cayce as signs of spiritual progress. And in working to achieve cooperation, they came to realize how separate they had really been, even in their initial common enthusiasm for the Cayce work. Cayce was calling their attention to the connectedness that we have seen is a fundamental characteristic of most psychic functioning.

The lessons continued, with the next one on the topic "Know Thyself." To truly know yourself is the beginning of discernment. The self, of course, is not that simple conscious self that we often think of as "me." It is the complete self—the physical needs and appetites; the unconscious, including the Shadow; and the superconscious or higher self. Each can contribute to those phenomena that we experience as psychic. The goal of the Cayce lessons is the highest spiritual realization, beyond the superconscious to direct knowledge of God. Yet Cayce, in common with all the great spiritual traditions, knew that self-knowledge is a prerequisite to higher knowledge. The denial of unfamiliar parts of the self (the Shadow) in a quest for higher knowledge usually leads to the opposite result—being disturbed by persistent messages from the unacknowledged parts.

Knowing the self is not the final goal. It is only the beginning. Mistaking the beginning for the goal is a common failing of popular human potential groups and seminars. "Know Thyself" is only the second lesson in *A Search for God*. There are twenty-two more. The original group next tackled the question "What Is My Ideal?" Exploring the self without an ideal is like embarking on a voyage on a ship that has no compass or rudder. You could end up anywhere. And that is where the psychic quest can lead—chasing experiences without a vision of the goal. As he did with the earlier lessons, Cayce separated ideals into physical, mental, and spiritual. The physical and mental derive from the spiritual, and Cayce, with his Christian background, encouraged people to set their spiritual ideal as the highest, the Christ. The mental and physical flow from this—what are Christlike thoughts and behavior?

In response to the question "What is the highest possible psychic realization?" Cayce replied, "That God, the Father, speaks directly to the sons of men— even as He has promised" (Reading 440-4).

Cayce was not willing to relieve the group of the need to think for themselves. Instead he made them experiment with the concepts until they achieved understanding and arrived at answers based on personal experience. They adopted the practice of choosing weekly "disciplines," exercises in application of the truths they were discovering in their intellectual, meditative, and psychic insights. Thus if the weekly discipline was to study your dreams for insights, it would not stop at simple study. True growth comes in application of the insight. Some of the dreams might be psychic, most will probably represent inner issues. But the test is not identifying the *source* of the dream— that can lead to endless speculation. It is the *application* of the dream to create a better life for yourself or someone else. This is good advice against being led astray by the Trickster.

The *Search for God* material contains twenty more lessons. Some, such as "Love," "Glory," and "Wisdom," focus on attaining the highest level of spiritual enlightenment, while always returning to practical exercises in application in the physical world. Other lessons, such as "Day and Night," address the conflicts that arise on the spiritual path. It is not always a smooth path. In all the spiritual traditions we find accounts of crises along the way. "Day and Night" contrasts our experience of the spiritual light with what Christian mystics have called the "dark night of the soul." Yet Cayce emphasizes that it is only with this contrast that we begin to realize the true nature of spiritual growth.

What claim to authenticity does the *A Search for God* program have, aside from Cayce's recommendation? Cayce himself constantly emphasized that his work should not become an "ism or schism," but rather that it should be an adjunct to a productive life within each person's spiritual tradition and that nothing should be accepted without first being tested in experience.

As a researcher, I decided to pursue the question beyond individual experiences to look at the collective experience of a large number of participants in *A Search for God,* to answer the question "Where does this path lead?" My answers are not complete—such research is limited to questions and answers that can be expressed in words. Yet they affirm that the spiritual path is complex and rewarding, with psychic experiences as an integral part, but never confused with the goal, which is, as a reading for Cayce himself stated, "a universal consciousness, guided or guarded by the Lord of the Way or the WAY itself" (Reading 294-140).

The Study Group Research Project

To look at whether the principles expressed by Cayce and the original group are reflected in the experience of contemporary members, I asked questions about a variety of elements of spiritual development, including psychic experiences. Important factors in group work included meditation, prayer, dream interpretation, and most important, following the weekly discipline chosen by the group. Consistency in application was the significant commonality among these factors. People who worked with these practices consistently reported major changes in their conscious awareness.

But what of psychic development? Do the groups fulfill the desires of people to develop psychic ability?

The results were quite interesting. The groups appear to develop an understanding of the true nature of psychic ability, but they certainly do not turn everyone into a psychic like Edgar Cayce. Virtually everyone enters a group having had some kind of psychic experience—this is often what attracts them in the first place. Through meditation, dreams, and practical application they are likely to have more psychic experiences as they continue in the group process. Here are some typical comments I received:

"Sharing opens the doors to freedom by looking at oneself in relation to the group and reflecting on it. Psychic abilities, for me, have increased as universal ego replaces me, myself, and I. That becomes the key that unlocks all doors for me."

"I have found increased awareness of what is psychic and what is wishful thinking."

"As a result of my participation in a study group, I have consciously become more aware of psychic phenomena in my life. I have discovered that I must analyze myself—my actions and reactions to situations—but I have also come to be aware of promptings from some superconsciousness."

"As we think less of our satisfactions, we are free to focus on the needs of others and in doing so free up our innate psychic ability, which is always subordinate to our will and higher self."

On the other hand, for most people in the group, the group process was *not* seen *primarily* as one of psychic development. I even received some comments indicating that group participation had led to *fewer* psychic experiences. Yet the participants did not consider this a problem. It went along with the expectation that the group was primarily for spiritual development, not for simply increasing psychic sensitivity to no purpose. Recall that for some of the experiences reported in the earlier chapters of this book, people wanted to know how to *reduce* their psychic sensitivity. This can apparently be done by focusing on application of spiritual principles, not on the psychic phenomena themselves. Here are some relevant comments I received:

> "I feel that being overly sensitive psychically often made me wish to wall myself away from others. The study group has helped me deal with the emotional upheaval that came earlier with a painful and disorienting psychic opening."

> "I am much more aware of synchronicity and try to pay attention to my intuitions. Otherwise there have been few psychic experiences, perhaps because they are not my primary concern. I am trying to live the life God would have me live as best I can."

> "Our psychic abilities have progressed little over the past ten years. However, I believe our discernment has increased '10' fold. We all recognize love and compassion as keys to progress."

> "It seems as though it is a growth in sensitivity toward and with others—no great 'flashes,' but total knowing and understanding."

> "Psychic experiences would be the icing on the cake. I'd be happy just to make a fine cake!"

To some, these results may be unsatisfying. *A Search for God* is not a training program to produce Edgar Cayce clones. I had the following encounter with a reporter from a major national magazine who was doing a story on Edgar Cayce. Having interviewed several other people before he reached me, he said, "The main problem I see with the Edgar Cayce work is that it offers no programs to develop your psychic powers." I replied that the entire basis of the work was spiritual development, including psychic development. I explained about the study groups and how the materials had been created over eleven years by a group who sought lessons from Cayce in psychic development. He interrupted me and said, "That's fine, but what about the people who are already spiritually enlightened and want to develop their psychic powers?" I replied that the essence of spiritual growth was the awareness that one's needs for psychic powers were already being answered. People that far along the spiritual path aren't interested in simply developing their "psychic powers."

Does *A Search for God* appeal to you? If so, there are groups throughout the country, and you can receive further information by contacting the Study Group Department at the A.R.E., at the address given in this book (appendix). If you are not sure, there are many other options you can explore for spiritual growth. Cayce developed *A* search for god, not *The* search for God. There are a bewildering array of choices. Some are tested paths with established teaching lineages going back thousands of years, while others are bizarre cults, newly formed and untested for spiritual value. How are you to thread your course through this maze of paths?

Spiritual Choices

For some guidelines I will draw on the insights offered by transpersonal philosopher Ken Wilber, in his book *Eye to Eye*. Wilber lists some of the characteristics that distinguish problematic spiritual groups from ones leading to authentic transformation.

The problematic groups, those that could lead to regression rather than transformation, are distinguished by engaging primarily in the prepersonal realms—what Cayce called the "carnal forces"—rather than in the transpersonal realms. That is, these paths focus on physical power, material wealth, sexual concerns, and raw impulsiveness—the basic desires of a child or adolescent. In contrast, a positive, authentically spiritual group promotes transformation to higher levels first by resting on a solid moral foundation and then encourages development through sustained practice and use of the will. It is necessary to work through some of the prepersonal issues, not denying them but also not dwelling on them or being trapped by them.

A second quality of problematic paths is that they focus on the *personality* of a specific authority—the leader—rather than on the teachings of that leader. The leader may claim to be unique, requiring rejection of all other teachers and teachings. A better alternative is to anchor legitimacy in a tradition—Christian, Buddhist, and so on—rather than simply in a person. One can then extend that tradition with new insights, while remaining rooted in a tested set of principles.

A related problem occurs when the authority declares itself to be *permanent,* a teacher who is the ultimate authority that no student can equal. In contrast, in most authentic spiritual traditions, the purpose of the teacher is to facilitate the students' growth. The ultimate authority is above the teacher or the student, and the student eventually reaches a point where he or she becomes equal to the teacher in his search.

Finally, the problematic groups may encourage or even demand rejection of other paths and of individuals who are not members of the group. They may be convinced that they have *the* answer. But psychic and mystical insights are characterized by their diversity. Groups more likely to offer positive guidance do not set out to impose their insights on others but offer them as choices. The spiritual path should not be seen as an opportunity to relinquish your own responsibility to exercise your will.

This is a very general set of principles for choosing a path or group for spiritual growth. Some groups have a strong sense of mission in the physical world; others focus on inner experience. Some groups clearly define a particular *goal*; others emphasize the *process* of transformation. Specific groups may vary along any of these dimensions, and you may have to balance several factors in making your choice.

The spiritual path is a lifelong process, not something that can be learned in a few lessons. Yet even a small amount of inward attention can lead to major changes in consciousness. It took the original Search for God group eleven years to write two thin volumes, because they had to put into practice everything they wrote. Even at the end, the lesson "Spirit," they were not finished. Cayce delivered the outline for four more lessons just before he died. They were, to people's surprise, not about evolution to higher realms. Awareness of spirit did not entail abandoning the physical. Just the opposite. The new lessons had titles like "Man's Relationship to Man," and "Righteousness vs. Sin." Enlightenment is a process of closing the circle, not of escape into the spiritual but of bringing the spiritual to earth. Psychic experiences are no longer paranormal but are part of the fabric of life.

You can understand your psychic experiences on many levels. You can ignore or deny them, yet often these experiences resist being ignored and hit you over the head. The denial in our culture has had tragic consequences. Thousands, even millions, of people who have had what are truly common experiences are afraid to share them because of the perception that they are weird or "crazy." People who do have serious mental illnesses yet may also be having psychic experiences mistakenly confuse the two (as do their doctors). They are treated for the wrong problem—a "problem" that may actually be a solution to the real problem. Even the most pathological cases of multiple personality have Inner Self Helpers that can provide guidance and wisdom.

As an alternative, you can try to study these experiences objectively, follow the lead of early psychical researchers and modern parapsychologists, and go beyond your own inner experiences to explore the rich diversity of the experiences of others. That has been one of the goals of this book—to expand your awareness beyond your own glimpses of a greater reality and to illuminate the shared reality that is all too often denied in our culture. In pursuing this path, you will find that some experiences are *not* what they appear to be. Developing a capacity for critical thinking through scientific research is a form of discernment. It allows you to select that which has value and discard the rest.

For many people, though, the purely objective approach still leaves a feeling of emptiness. It doesn't touch the heart of the matter—the experiential source that initiated the psychic quest. You can choose to work with your own development, yet you are confronted with a bewildering array of choices—books, groups, self-improvement programs. All may offer insight into experiences; none come with guarantees.

In this final chapter I have provided some guidelines for choosing an authentic path for spiritual growth. *A Search for God* is an example, not a recommendation for everyone. Only you can choose the lessons that will facilitate your growth. We all come into this life with different abilities and challenges. For some, a simple psychic experience will remain a source of wonder, to be pondered throughout life. For others, the constant stream of psychic experiences forces attention to the process of transformation.

This quote from the Cayce readings may say it best:

These are, then, as experiences. Learn ye to use them, for they will give expressions in many ways and manners. Seek experiences not as experiences alone but as purposefulness. For what be the profit to thyself, to thy neighbor, if experiences alone of such natures rack thy body . . . owing to its high vibration . . . without being able to make thee a kinder mother, a more loving wife, a better neighbor, a better individual in every manner? *These* be the fruits, that it makes thee kinder, gentler, stronger in body, in mind, in purpose, to *be* a channel through which the love of *God*, through Jesus Christ, may be manifested in the world. (Reading 281-27)

I wish you wonderment, joy, peace, and wisdom on your quest.

APPENDIX

Resources in Parapsychology and Transpersonal Studies

The following is a list of organizations, schools, and resource centers that you can contact for further information about psychic and transpersonal phenomena. Most have publications and programs for the general public; some offer courses and degree programs.

American Society for Psychical Research
5 West 73rd Street
New York, NY 10023
(212) 799-5050
This is a membership organization that publishes a journal and a newsletter and has an extensive library. The ASPR publishes a list of courses in parapsychology offered at colleges and universities around the world.

Association for Research and Enlightenment (A.R.E.)
P.O. Box 595
Virginia Beach, VA 23451
(757) 428-3588 or (800) 333-4499
This is a membership organization with the mission of promoting the study, application, and dissemination of the information in the psychic readings of Edgar Cayce. The A.R.E. publishes books and a magazine and holds conferences. It has a library of more than

60,000 volumes on parapsychology, spirituality, and related topics. It sponsors the *A Search for God* study groups.

Association for the Study of Dreams
P.O. Box 1600
Vienna, VA 22183
(703) 242-0062
This membership organization publishes a newsletter, *Dream Time,* and holds conferences.

Association for Transpersonal Psychology
P.O. Box 3049
Stanford, CA 94305
(415) 327-2066
This membership organization publishes the *Journal of Transpersonal Psychology,* publishes a list of transpersonal schools and programs, and holds conferences.

Atlantic University
P.O. Box 988
Virginia Beach, VA 23451
(800) 428-1512
Atlantic University was founded by the A.R.E. and offers a master's degree program in transpersonal studies. Courses can be taken by correspondence as well as in residence.

Common Boundary
5272 River Road, Suite 650
Bethesda, MD 20816
(301) 652-9495
This organization publishes a magazine, *Common Boundary* (referring to the common boundary of psychotherapy, creativity, and spirituality), and hosts annual conferences. It publishes a directory of

transpersonal educational programs throughout the country.

Exceptional Human Experience Network
414 Rockledge Road
New Bern, NC 28562
(919) 636-8734
This organization publishes a journal of people's stories of their "exceptional" experiences, e.g., psychic and mystical experiences.

IANDS: The International Association of Near Death Studies
P.O. Box U-20
University of Connecticut
Storrs, CT 06268
This organization conducts research on near-death experiences and publishes a journal, *Anabiosis*.

Institute for Parapsychology (Rhine Research Center)
402 North Buchanan Boulevard
Durham, NC 27701–1728
(919) 688-8241
This is the organization founded by J. B. and Louisa Rhine. It conducts laboratory and field research, hosts programs, and publishes the *Journal of Parapsychology*. Of special interest is its annual Summer Study Program in parapsychology.

Institute of Noetic Sciences
475 Gate Five Road, Suite 300
Sausalito, CA 94965
(415) 331-5650
This is a membership organization that sponsors research, conferences, and publications on psychic and transpersonal themes.

Parapsychology Foundation
228 East 71st Street
New York, NY 10021
(212) 628-1550
This organization, founded by Eileen Garrett, offers grants for research and study in parapsychology and has an excellent library.

Society for Psychical Research
46 Marloes Road
London W8 6LA
England
0171-937-8984
This is the original organization of psychical researchers, founded in 1882. It holds conferences, conducts research, and publishes the *Journal of the Society for Psychical Research*.

Bibliography

Below is a list, arranged by chapter, of books and articles referred to in the text. Some books are discussed in several chapters, but are only listed for the first chapter in which they appear. An especially good overview of parapsychology, by the director of one of the world's major parapsychology laboratories, is:

Broughton, R. S. (1991). *Parapsychology: The Controversial Science.* New York: Ballantine.

Introduction

Cayce, C. T. (n.d.) *Working with Children Who May Have Psychic Ability.* Virginia Beach: A.R.E. Child Development Series, no. 15.

Gallup, G. H., Jr., & Newport, F. (1991, Winter). Belief in paranormal phenomena among adult Americans. *Skeptical Inquirer,* 15(2), 137–146.

Palmer, J. (1979). A community mail survey of psychic experiences. *Journal of the American Society for Psychical Research,* 73, 221–251.

Chapter 1. Telepathy

Dean, D., Mihalsky, J., Ostrander, S., & Schroeder, L. (1974). *Executive ESP.* Englewood Cliffs, NJ: Prentice-Hall.

Gurney, E., Myers, F. W. H., & Podmore, F. (1886). *Phantasms of the Living.* London: Trubner.

Miller, A. (1990 Nov./Dec.). Tapping into the force. *Venture Inward, 6*(6), 36–39.

Myers, F. W. H. (1961). *Human Personality and Its Survival of Bodily Death.* New Hyde Park, NY: University Books.

Sinclair, U. (1930). *Mental Radio.* New York: Collier.

Stanford, R. (1974). An experimentally testable model for spontaneous psi events. I. Extrasensory events. *Journal of the American Society for Psychical Research, 68,* 34–57.

Stevenson, I. (1978). *Telepathic Impressions.* Charlottesville: University Press of Virginia.

Chapter 2. Clairvoyance

Bem, D. J., & Honorton, C. (1994) Does psi exist? Replicable evidence for an anomalous process of information transfer. *Psychological Bulletin, 115,* 4–18.

Cayce, H. L., & Cayce, E. E. (1971). *The Outer Limits of Edgar Cayce's Power.* Virginia Beach: A.R.E. Press.

Honorton, C., Berger, R. E., Varvoglis, M. P., Quant, M., Derr, P., Schechter, E. I., & Ferrari, D. C. (1990). Psi communication in the ganzfeld: Experiments with an automated testing system and a comparison with a meta-analysis of earlier studies. *Journal of Parapsychology, 54,* 99–139.

Jahn, R. G., & Dunne, B. J. (1987). *Margins of Reality: The Role of Consciousness in the Physical World.* San Diego: Harcourt Brace Jovanovich.

Morris, R. L., Roll, W. G., Klein, J., & Wheeler, J. (1972). EEG patterns and ESP results in forced-choice experiments with Lalsingh Harribance. *Journal of the American Society for Psychical Research, 66,* 253–268.

Pratt, J. G., Rhine, J. B., Smith, B. M., Stuart, C. E., & Greenwood, J. A. (1940). *Extra-Sensory Perception after Sixty Years.* New York: Henry Holt.

Puthoff, H. E., & Targ, R. (1976). A perceptual channel for information transfer over kilometer distances: Historical perspective and recent research. *Proceedings of the IEEE, 64,* 329–354.

Schlitz, M., & Gruber, E. (1980). Transcontinental remote viewing. *Journal of Parapsychology, 44,* 305–317.

Schwartz, S. A., & DeMattei, R. (1989). The discovery of an American brig: Field work involving applied archeological remote viewing. In Henkel, L. A., & Berger, R. E. (Eds.). *Research in Parapsychology 1988,* pp. 73–78. Metuchen, NJ: Scarecrow Press.

Sugrue, T. (1942). *There Is a River: The Story of Edgar Cayce.* Virginia Beach: A.R.E. Press.

Targ, R., & Puthoff, H. E. (1978). *Mind Reach: Scientists Look at Psychic Ability.* New York: Delacorte.

Chapter 3. Precognition

Bro, H. (1970). *Edgar Cayce on Religion and Psychic Experience.* New York: Warner Books.

Honorton, C., & Ferrari, D. C. (1989). "Future telling": A meta-analysis of forced-choice precognition experiments. *Journal of Parapsychology, 53,* 281–308.

James, W. (1968). *The Writings of William James.* New York: Modern Library.

Radin, D. I. (1988). Precognition of probable vs. actual futures: Exploring futures that will never be. In Weiner, D. H., & Morris, R. L. (Eds.). *Research in Parapsychology 1987,* pp. 1–5. Metuchen, NJ: Scarecrow Press.

Thurston, M. (1987). *The Paradox of Power.* Virginia Beach: A.R.E. Press.

Chapter 4. Psychic Dreams

Child, I. (1985). Psychology and anomalous observations: The question of ESP in dreams. *American Psychologist, 40,* 1219–1230.

Jung, C. (1964). *Man and His Symbols.* New York: Dell.

Michaels, S. (1995). *The Bedside Guide to Dreams.* New York: Fawcett Crest.

Mintz, E. (1983). *The Psychic Thread: Paranormal and Transpersonal Aspects of Psychotherapy.* New York: Human Science Press.

Perls, F., Hefferline, R. F., & Goodman, P. (1977). *Gestalt Therapy*. New York: Bantam.

Reed, H., & Van De Castle, R. (1991). The dream helper ceremony: A small-group paradigm for transcendent psi. *Theta, 16*(1), 12–20.

Sechrist, E. (1995). *Dreams: Your Magic Mirror*. Virginia Beach: A.R.E. Press.

Ullman, M., Krippner, S., with Vaughan, A. (1973). *Dream Telepathy: Experiments in Nocturnal ESP*. New York: Macmillan.

Van De Castle, R. (1994). *Our Dreaming Mind*. New York: Ballantine.

Chapter 5. Synchronicity

Combs, A., & Holland, M. (1990). *Synchronicity: Science, Myth, and the Trickster*. New York: Paragon House.

Jung, C. (1973). *Synchronicity*. Princeton: Princeton University Press.

Chapter 6. Psychokinesis

Batcheldor, K. J. (1984). Contributions to the theory of PK induction from sitter-group work. *Journal of the American Society for Psychical Research, 78*, 105–122.

Green, E., & Green, A. (1977). *Beyond Biofeedback*. New York: Delacorte Press.

Haraldsson. E. (1987). *Modern Miracles: An Investigative Report on Psychic Phenomena Associated with Sathya Sai Baba.* New York: Fawcett Columbine.

Haraldsson, E., & Osis, K. (1977). The appearance and disappearance of objects in the presence of Sathya Sai Baba. *Journal of the American Society for Psychical Research, 71,* 33–43.

Houck, J. (1985). PK parties: An overview. In White, R. A., & Solfvin, J. (Eds.). *Research in Parapsychology 1984,* p. 107. Metuchen, NJ: Scarecrow Press.

Owen, I., with Sparrow, M. (1976). *Conjuring Up Philip.* New York: Harper & Row.

Rhine, L. (1972). *Mind over Matter.* New York: Collier Macmillan.

Roll, W. G. (1976). *The Poltergeist.* Metuchen, NJ: Scarecrow Press.

Schmeidler, G. R. (1984). Further analysis of PK with continuous temperature readings. *Journal of the American Society for Psychical Research, 78,* 355–362.

Schmidt, H. (1970). A PK test with electronic equipment. *Journal of Parapsychology, 34,* 175–181.

Schmidt, H. (1970). PK experiments with animals as subjects. *Journal of Parapsychology, 34,* 255–261.

Siegel, C. (1985). PK party survey. In White, R. A., & Solfvin, J. (Eds.). *Research in Parapsychology 1984,* pp. 8–11. Metuchen, NJ: Scarecrow Press.

Chapter 7. Psychic Healing

Braud, W., & Schlitz, M. (1983). Psychokinetic influence on electrodermal activity. *Journal of Parapsychology, 47,* 95–119.

Brennan, B. A. (1987). *Hands of Light: A Guide to Healing through the Human Energy Field.* New York: Bantam.

Brennan, B. A. (1993). *Light Emerging: The Journal of Personal Healing.* New York: Bantam.

Byrd, R. C. (1988). Positive therapeutic effects of intercessory prayer in a coronary care unit population. *Southern Medical Journal, 81,* 826–829.

Callan, J. P. (1979). Editorial. *Journal of the American Medical Association, 241,* 1156.

Chopra, D. (1993). *Ageless Body, Timeless Mind: The Quantum Alternative to Growing Old.* New York: Harmony Books.

Dean, D. (1983). Infrared measurements of healer-treated water. In Roll, W. G., Beloff, J., & White, R. A. (Eds.). *Research in Parapsychology 1982.* Metuchen, NJ: Scarecrow Press.

Dossey, L. (1993). *Healing Words: The Power of Prayer and the Practice of Medicine.* San Francisco: HarperSanFrancisco.

Grad, B. (1965). Some biological effects of the 'Laying on of Hands': A review of experiments with animals and plants. *Journal of the American Society for Psychical Research, 59,* 95–127.

Krieger, D. (1979). *The Therapeutic Touch: How to Use Your Hands to Help or Heal.* Englewood Cliffs, NJ: Prentice-Hall.

Myss, C. (1996). *Anatomy of the Spirit: The Seven Stages of Power and Healing.* New York: Harmony Books.

Puryear, M. (1978). *Healing through Meditation and Prayer.* Virginia Beach: A.R.E. Press.

Schwartz, S. A., DeMattei, R. J., Brame, E. G., Jr., & Spottiswoode, S. J. P. (1990). Infrared spectra alteration in water proximate to the palms of therapeutic practitioners. *Subtle Energies, 1,* 43–72.

Shealy, C. N., & Myss, C. M. (1993). *The Creation of Health.* Walpole, NH: Stillpoint Publishing.

Wickramaskera, I. E. (1988). *Clinical Behavioral Medicine.* New York: Plenum Press.

Wirth, D. P. (1990). The effect of non-contact therapeutic touch on the healing rate of full thickness dermal wounds. *Subtle Energies, 1,* 1–20.

Chapter 8. Apparitions and Hauntings

Auerbach, L. (1986). *ESP, Hauntings, and Poltergeists: A Parapsychologists's Handbook.* New York: Warner Books.

Guggenheim, B., & Guggenheim, J. (1995). *Hello from Heaven.* New York: Bantam.

Jaffé, A. (1963). *Apparitions and Precognition.* New Hyde Park, NY: University Books.

Maher, M. C., & Hansen, G. P. (1992). Quantitative investigation of a reported haunting using several detection techniques. *Journal of the American Society for Psychical Research, 86,* 347–374.

Moody, R. (1993). *Reunions: Visionary Encounters with Departed Loved Ones.* New York: Villard Books.

Moss, T., & Schmeidler, G. R. (1968). Quantitative investigation of a "haunted house" with sensitives and a control group. *Journal of the American Society for Psychical Research, 62,* 399–410.

Solfvin, S. (1986). Clinical issues and parapsychology. In Weiner, D. H., & Radin, D. I. (Eds.). *Research in Parapsychology 1985,* pp. 174–175. Metuchen, NJ: Scarecrow Press.

Tyrrell, G.N.M. (1942). *Apparitions.* London: Duckworth.

Chapter 9. Out-of-Body Experiences and Near-Death Experiences

Brinkley, D., with Perry, P. (1994). *Saved by the Light.* New York: HarperCollins.

Gabbard, G.D., & Twemlow, S. W. (1994). *With the Eyes of the Mind: An Empirical Analysis of Out-of-Body States.* New York: Praeger.

Moody, R. (1975). *Life after Life.* Atlanta: Mockingbird Books.

Morris, R. L., Harary, S. B., Janis, J., Hartwell, J., & Roll, W. G. (1978). Studies of communication during out-of-body experiences. *Journal of the American Society for Psychical Research, 72,* 1–21

Osis, K., & McCormick, D. (1980). Kinetic effects at the ostensible location of an out-of-body projection during perceptual testing. *Journal of the American Society for Psychical Research, 74,* 319–329.

Ring, K. (1992). *The Omega Project.* New York: William Morrow.

Chapter 10. Voices, Spirit Guides, and Channeling

Allison, R., with Schwartz, T. (1980). *Minds in Many Pieces.* New York: Rawson, Wade.

Cayce, H. L. (1964). *Venture Inward.* Virginia Beach: A.R.E. Press.

A Course in Miracles. (1995). Tiburon, CA: Foundation for Inner Peace.

McMillin, D. (1991). *The Treatment of Schizophrenia: A Holistic Approach.* Virginia Beach: Lifeline Press.

Roberts, J. (1981). *The God of Jane: A Psychic Manifesto.* Englewood Cliffs, NJ: Prentice-Hall.

Chapter 11. Mystical Experiences

Greeley, A. (1975). *The Sociology of the Paranormal: A Reconnaissance.* Beverly Hills: Sage Publications.

Greeley, A. (1987). Mysticism goes mainstream. *American Health, 6*(1), 47–49.

James, W. (1961). *The Varieties of Religious Experience.* New York: Macmillan.

Neihardt, J. (1932). *Black Elk Speaks*. Lincoln: University of Nebraska Press.

Shah, I. (1964). *The Sufis*. Garden City, NY: Doubleday.

Weiner, H. (1969). *9½ Mystics*. New York: Collier.

Welch, J. (1982). *Spiritual Pilgrims: Carl Jung and Teresa of Avila*. New York: Paulist Press..

Underhill, E. (1961). *Mysticism*. New York: Dutton.

Chapter 12. Pathways to Transformation

A Search for God. (1942). Virginia Beach: A.R.E. Press.

Wilber, K. (1990). *Eye to Eye: The Quest for the New Paradigm*. Boston: Shambhala.

ENLIGHTENING READING

☐ **THE UPANISHADS:** *Breath of the Eternal* **translated by Swami Prab-havananda and Frederick Manchester.** Concerned with the knowledge of God and the highest aspects of religious truth, these ancient Hindu scriptures are presented in a readable translation.

(626079—$5.99)

☐ **THE WAY OF LIFE: TAO TE CHANG.** Eighty-one brief poems embodying the beliefs of Taoism, in a fresh translation by R. B. Blakney.

(626745—$4.99)

☐ **THE SONG OF GOD: BHAGAVAD-GITA with an Introduction by Aldous Huxley.** The timeless epic of Hindu faith vividly translated for Western readers by Swami Prabhavananda and Christopher Isherwood.

(627571—$5.99)

Prices slightly higher in Canada.
